Hello Darkness, My Old Friend

Hello Darkness, My Old Friend

Embracing ANGER to Heal Your Life

Isaac Steven Herschkopf, M.D.
Department of Psychiatry
New York University School of Medicine
Bellevue Hospital

To my healers,
Marta, Jayme, Davida, and Becky.

All profits from this book are being donated to charity.

ACKNOWLEDGEMENTS

The author is sincerely grateful to Ira Berkow, Sandee Brawarsky, Professor Richard Brown, Bruce Jay Friedman, Lewis Burke Frumkes, Ari Goldman, David B. Larson, M.D., of blessed memory, Rabbi Haskel Lookstein, Courtney Love, Aryeh Maidenbaum, Ph.D., Gwyneth Paltrow, Gay Talese, Rabbi Joseph Telushkin, Dr. Ruth Westheimer and Professor Elie Wiesel, each of whom was kind enough to read all or part of the manuscript during its prolonged development.

CONTENTS

INTRODUCTION

Not Another Self-Help Book

I'm embarrassed.

For years, people have asked my opinion of the latest self-help book. My practiced deflection is: "I haven't had the opportunity to read it." Unfortunately, they usually persevere.

I retreat to my fail-safe position. My mouth says: "You can't argue with success. If *you* find it helpful, then *I* think the book is great." Yet simultaneously, my mind is thinking: "Are you kidding? These books are nothing but a catchy title with a single provocative thought."

If pressed by someone I trust, I'll come clean with my reservations. How can anything designed for the masses be as helpful as a personalized one-on-one experience? Yes, the cost of an entire book is a fraction of one therapy session, but you get what you pay for.

At worst, these books are psychobabble, analytic jargon out of touch with real life. They remind me of a colleague who always says: "Let's attempt closure," when he means: "I've got to go." He thinks he sounds id—ego astute. I think he sounds idiotic.

At best, self-help books are like horoscope columns. Invariably you find something familiar under your sign, but if you read further, you recognize yourself under *all* the signs. How do you know what's valid and what isn't? You might assume that if one recommendation applies to you, then they all do. Because of that, some argue that self-help books are dangerous.

Knowing this, imagine my embarrassment as I introduce what can only be described as a self-help book. And it has a catchy title to boot.

My justification consists of three metaphors: #1—a tape recorder, #2—a mechanical massage chair, and, #3—a diary.

#1—A Tape Recorder

A surprising number of people, (most of whom are not paranoid), enter a psychiatrist's office concerned that they will be recorded by a hidden tape recorder. They're wrong, of course. (Who has the time to listen to the tape?) Ironically however, there are times I wish I *did* have that tape. *Not* to listen to my patients, but to record myself. How often have I found myself explaining the identical issue yet again?

The problem is the same for any physician. A cardiovascular surgeon is going to have to explain the intricacies of cardiac bypass surgery, its advantages, disadvantages, anatomy and risks again and again. Invariably he, like I, will sometimes do it better and sometimes do it worse. Sometimes, he'll be indulgent; other times, he'll be impatient. Sometimes, he'll be particularly eloquent. The words will flow cohesively, persuasively, like he's never done before, and perhaps, like he'll never do again. Other times, he'll have a headache.

A good safeguard against our natural inconsistency is something in writing. Accordingly, the surgeon will have literature on the procedure. It will include all the relevant details which can be read and re-read at leisure. In some cases he will have written it himself. In most cases it's a standardized booklet, since the surgery itself is fairly standardized. It's not a substitute for personal attention. It's not meant to be. It might answer most questions, but not all. That's what the surgeon is for.

This book is a more complicated version of that booklet. That's only fair, since the mind is frankly, a hell of a lot more complicated than the heart.

The idea of a tape recorder has become increasingly popular. A recent phenomenon is patients bringing their *own* tape recorders to record their sessions. They want to be able to review the material again at their leisure. Similarly, in group therapy, members will point out how certain subjects, (like anger), come up repeatedly. Some suggest, semi-facetiously, that new group members should be issued tapes of our previous discussions.

Hopefully, a book like this serves that purpose for patients and non-patients alike.

#2—A Massage Chair

This technological innovation is fundamentally a chair which has hidden in its back a mechanical roller. Turn the electricity on and the roller moves slowly up and down your spine mimicking the action of a massage. Your own weight leaning back provides the pressure. More elaborate versions provide a remote control to adjust the length and width of the roller. Other frills can include heat, vibration and music, but the fundamental mechanism remains the same.

The massage chair is the single best metaphor I can think of for a self-help book. The chair, like the book, is designed to replicate for the masses the benefits of a classic, therapeutic one on one experience. Both are designed for use in the privacy of your home, whenever and as often as you'd like, at no cost beyond the original investment. The chair, like the book, is a relatively recent innovation compared to the centuries that both massage therapy and psychotherapy have been practiced in various forms.

Most importantly, with both chair and book, the benefit you derive will be directly proportional to the pressure that you apply. Unlike the real thing, there's no trained professional present to lean on you.

Perhaps a final similarity should be, "Caveat Emptor!"— "Let the buyer beware!" All these chairs come with manufacturers' warnings advising the purchasers to use discretion. Don't apply too much friction. Don't push, if it doesn't seem to fit. Above all, if it hurts, stop. The same warnings should apply to all self-help books, including this one.

Do I like massage chairs? No.

How can any machine compare to a sensitive, empathetic, experienced human being? It can't. A machine can't feel your body. A machine can't listen to you. A machine doesn't know you. A machine can't sense your pain.

I've experienced wonderful massages. I've also tried out various massage chairs. They don't begin to compare. Beyond all the obvious differences is the fact that no machine can replicate, or even approximate, the human touch. For me personally, the human touch is the best part of a massage. (And of psychotherapy.)

Yet, I own a massage chair.

My wife has a chronic back condition. Over the years it has necessitated orthopedists, osteopaths, chiropractors, physical therapists, and masseurs. They've all helped, albeit temporarily.

Does *she* prefer the massage chair to the real thing? Usually, not. On occasion however, she gets a knot or spasm sharply localized in one isolated spot on her back.

What if it's at 3 A.M.? What if a massage isn't available? If available, a masseur with tireless fingers of steel and the patience of a saint, can, after a seemingly interminable period, knead it out. But how many human beings have both qualities, massage after massage after massage?

Furthermore, even if the masseur isn't feeling any resentment for the pain and boredom that he's experiencing, (after all, he *is* getting paid), my wife is lying there feeling guilty. She knows that this trained professional would prefer a full massage, rather than some numbing, mindless, repetitive motion that an automaton could do better, which is precisely why in that scenario she prefers the automaton. The massage chair does in fact have tireless fingers of steel and the patience of a saint. The best part of all, according to my wife, is that she doesn't feel self-conscious. She doesn't feel the need to apologize to the chair.

Does this sound familiar to you? It does to me. All too often a patient embarrassedly, apologetically, asks to discuss their anger again. There should be no reason for them to be embarrassed. They certainly shouldn't have to apologize.

Hopefully, this book can help everyone unravel that knot.

#3—A Diary

Diaries are usually associated with adolescent girls. The particular diary that affected me most however, was far from the usual.

I only had one uncle. He passed away in 1988, but he had an extraordinary life. Our youngest daughter is named after him, a promise my wife and I made to him, and to ourselves, on his death-bed.

He, like all of my family, was a victim of the Holocaust. Unlike the other victims however, because he was a brilliant physician, he was able to achieve some control over his inhuman environment. Like all Jews, he was sent to an extermination camp. He became the chief Jewish physician of the camp. Through his position he was able to save the lives of countless prisoners, including my mother and my sister.

The details of all that he went through are harrowing, and for me personally, incredibly painful. Many times, when I was a young man, he would start to tell me some of them, but I would beg off. I would claim to be too busy, but the truth was, unbeknownst to me, I wasn't ready to hear it. Eventually, he decided to write a diary of his years in the death camp. Ultimately, he took this poignant diary and published it.[1]

In his introduction he wrote that he had originally intended his diary to be for his children. It was intended for the next generation. His generation knew his remarkable story. They had either heard it from him or, in many cases, they had witnessed it first hand. The next generation hadn't.

His concern was, that by the time we were able to hear it, he wouldn't be able to tell it.

His dilemma is familiar if you ever felt that you had something original to contribute. Is your priority the generation, or the generations? You want to be able to effect the people you come into contact with, on the one hand, but you don't want your effect to be thus limited on the other.

I can't pretend that my life has been nearly as extraordinary, or as valuable, as my uncle's. I like to think however, that some of what I do in my office is unique. The primary reason I chose psychiatry was because it was the only specialty that was still more of an art than a science. Most cardiac bypass operations will be virtually identical. Not only could any competent cardiac surgeon perform them, but for the most part, their results would be indistinguishable. That's far from the case with psychiatry. Surgeons use identical scalpels. In psychiatry, *we* are the scalpels. As different as we are as human beings, that's how different our brands of therapy are.

This book then, is *my* diary. It preserves part of what I've been doing within the confidential four walls of my office for over a quarter century. The book, unlike me, will still be here when someone is ready to read it.

It's also my tape recorder, and my massage chair. Hopefully, it's not just another self-help book.

I.S.H.
December 2002
New York City

Notes

---

[1] *From Death Row To Freedom* (1984) Dr. David Wainapel, Block Publishing.

PART I

THE DARK SIDE

Anger Makes The World Go Round

CHAPTER ONE

A Looney Tunes World

Where Anger Lives

"God gets angry every single day.
But it only lasts a moment."[1]

Barry was a freckle-faced, flaxen-haired, short, slight twelve-year-old with an angelic countenance and a devilish problem.

He wanted to have his Bar Mitzvah in Disneyland.

His parents offered to have it in Israel. They offered to fly his two best friends. They offered the kind of lavish affair that Philip Roth[2] had made infamous. They offered to rent a hotel for an entire weekend. They offered to hire the sports celebrity of his choice. They offered everything and anything.

He wanted Disneyland.

At first, they were amused. Then, they were annoyed. In the end, they were confused. I was intrigued.

Was this a manifestation of a boy not wanting to become a man? After all, Disneyland *is* home to Peter Pan. If so, why not "Sesame Place" or "Great Adventure," child-oriented theme parks closer to home?

Maybe, it's precisely because Disneyland is farther away. The other coast's grass is always greener. Using that hypothesis, Israel is even farther.

His answer was predictable, when I asked him why he wanted Disneyland: "I don't know! I just want to!" Obviously, I wasn't the first person to ask him the question.

I was however, the first person being paid to do so. I persisted. I took the back door instead. I asked him his associations to Disneyland, his feelings about it, what made the place different. The last question hit pay dirt. His answer startled me.

"Nobody's angry in Disneyland."

He was right of course, on the surface anyway. I thought back to my children. Even before they could speak, they knew their preferences in cartoons. They liked Mickey Mouse. They hated Bugs Bunny. They liked Disney. They hated "Looney Tunes."

Why? For the same reason that as they got older their tastes reversed. Disney cartoons are sugar-sweet. "Looney Tunes" are madcap, with the emphasis on mad.

Bugs Bunny has a lifetime adversary, Elmer Fudd, constantly trying to kill that "wascally wabbit." He's usually holding a shotgun and is always angry at Bugs. Just as Bugs has Elmer, Tweety has Sylvester and Road Runner has Wile E. Coyote. Daffy Duck and Yosemite Sam go even further. They're angry at everybody.

Mickey Mouse, on the other hand, has no archenemy. Neither does Goofy, nor Pluto. (Come on. How could *anyone* not like Pluto?) True, Donald Duck is irritable, but his comical short fuse is directed towards his mischievous nephews, Huey, Dewey and Louie. There's no enmity involved. He isn't shooting six-guns, like Yosemite Sam. No one is attempting murder, as in "Looney Tunes." There are no Devils, Tasmanian or otherwise, in Disneyland.

Disney represents the *Ozzie and Harriet, Father Knows Best, Cosby* type idyllic family. Mickey and Donald aren't legally married (that would be *too* adult), but they have life-long companions in Minnie and Daisy, respectively. Bugs and Daffy, on the other hand, clearly don't have the temperament for that. If Mickey Mouse is the cartoon equivalent of the reassuring, paternal, married Bill Cosby, then Bugs' parallel would be *M.A.S.H.*'s cynical, wisecracking, bachelor, Hawkeye Pierce.

It's not coincidental that *Cosby* was a family show broadcast at the earliest possible hour, and *M.A.S.H.* was an adult show televised at a later hour. When both shows were syndicated and shown in repeats, their respective broadcast times became even earlier and later. *Cosby* could be seen after school, while *M.A.S.H.* was meant for bed. Neither is it coincidental that when "Looney Tunes" characters are used for children's books, they introduce lifetime companions, e.g. Porky and Petunia Pig, and the story lines are homogenized and sweetened to resemble Disney.

Furthermore, as my young friend instinctively realized, Disneyland, and its Florida twin, Disney World, are indeed oases in a "Looney Tunes" world. The parks are every bit as conflict-free as the cartoons. They are not only the cleanest places on our planet, but also, every employee is smiling, cooperative, and seems genuinely happy to see you. (They don't even get paid by commission.) They go to extremes. The parks are the only place, (outside of boot camp), that male employees are prohibited from beards or mustaches or wearing their hair long.

Why? Because Walt Disney understood that some people are subconsciously offended or even subliminally threatened by them. (The one exception was his own mustache, of course.) A Disney park is deliberately designed to be a clean, pure, unadulterated, unspoiled, innocent, virginal, conflict-free Shangri-La. (Walt had originally preferred to exclude minorities for that reason, as well.)

It works. Despite exorbitant prices and interminable lines, the parks, open 365 days a year, never have a slow day. Revealingly, they appeal to adults as much as to children. Disney World is the single most popular destination for honeymooners in the world. The parks host innumerable business conventions and professional seminars. To the many who have been there, and even the rare few who haven't, they represent an escape, a safe harbor in our stormy world.

Is the world really so angry? Maybe our twelve-year-old's perspective is an aberration. After all, *he's* the one seeing a psychiatrist.

Consider the following. In medical school, in the early 70's, I was startled to learn that more prescriptions were written for Valium and Librium than every other type of medicine *combined*. What an amazing statistic.[3]

Add up all the antibiotics, pain-killers, children's cold preparations, anti-depressants, cancer drugs, gastro-intestinal pills, neuroleptics (psychiatric drugs), all the eye, ear, nose and throat medications, and all the prescriptions for every other organ in the body (e.g. gall bladder, liver, prostate, uterus, kidney, etc.), and they still didn't equal one medicine.

What are Valium and Librium? Two almost identical drugs produced by the same company, which is why I refer to them as one medicine. The medicine is a tranquilizer. It makes people more tranquil, more calm, less angry. Its phenomenal usage was a quantifiable criterion of anger's ubiquity.

By the 80's prescribing practices had evolved: "It is a sorry sign of the times that the three best-selling drugs in the country are an ulcer medication (Tagamet), a hypertension drug (Inderal) and a tranquilizer (Valium) . . . No one really knows if there is more stress now than in the past, but many experts believe it has become more pervasive."—*TIME*, June 6, 1983.

Two decades later nothing had changed. In its cover story on stress, *TIME* (June 10, 2002) again stated: " . . . we live in a particularly anxious age." The cover headline read: "Now more than ever we are worrying ourselves sick." From the 60's, to the 80's, to the 2000's, we are overwhelmed by stress.

One could argue that stress is not anger. What is stress?

Physiologically we would define it as any stimulus, external or internal, which precipitates a fight or flight response. (Our body automatically secretes cortisol and adrenaline to prepare us for either eventuality.) Flight implies fear, but fight clearly indicates anger.

Unfortunately, our world doesn't commonly allow for flight. If we feel stressed in our job, we might want to quit, but we don't have that luxury. It would be irresponsible. We have to fight it out. Similarly, if we're tired of fighting traffic in our daily commute, we have no choice either. Notice how ubiquitously we use the metaphor of "fighting."

A loud parameter of our anger is our use of the car horn. Station yourself near any bottleneck, at any rush hour, in any city in the world. What do you hear? (I live this experiment every day. My office is immediately adjacent to Manhattan's Midtown Tunnel.)

Does the horn serve a purpose? It does, when a child or pet runs into the street in front of your car. It does when someone pulling out of a driveway doesn't see you coming. What purpose does it serve when fifty cars are combining into one lane? Does blowing your horn get you there one car sooner?

No. All it accomplishes is provoking the car next to you to blow his horn. You blow your horn instead of blowing your stack. It allows you to express your anger and frustration.

Are anger and frustration synonymous? Yes. Whether you're frustrated by traffic inexplicably stopping dead, or angry at a slowpoke, your reaction is the same.

Two additional vehicular phenomena deserve mention. The first is innocuous. The second is not.

Years ago a popular gift was another technological advance, (albeit significantly cheaper than the massage chair.) It was marketed under different names, but it was basically an improvement over the car horn. It offered exotic acoustic possibilities. If you're angry at the car in front of you, you're not limited to leaning on your horn and flashing your brights. Now you could mimic the sound of machine gun fire, or a laser attack, or artillery.

This gift proved more popular than the visual equivalents that preceded it. Electric signs in the back window that said "You idiot!," or worse, were limited not only by the fact that you had to be in front of your adversary, but more importantly, by not receiving the catharsis of hearing your anger expressed yourself.

This might seem perversely amusing, but the second phenomenon isn't. It's the real-life version of the gunfire. What's being transmitted is more deadly than noise. It's "road rage."

The phenomenon of total strangers engaging in violence, frequently fatal, over traffic slights, both real and imagined, transcends all geographical boundaries. A notorious epidemic occurred in Southern California. Ironically, the freeways had been designed as multi-laned thoroughfares to deliberately avoid the traffic congestion associated with the East. The congestion had been lessened. The anger had not.

With "air rage" frustrated airline passengers assault each other, as well as airline personnel, in some cases critically. People literally die to get somewhere. One passenger deliberately defecated onto a food cart when denied another drink. Another murdered an attendant who tried to prevent him from boarding.

Court ordered anger management courses have become so common, for celebrities and commoners alike, that *Anger Management* became a movie starring Adam Sandler and, ironically enough, Jack Nicholson[4]. Celebrities, besides Nicholson, who have anger issues include the late Lisa "Left Eye" Lopes[5], Sean Young[6], Naomi Campbell[7], Tawny Kitaen[8], Tonya Harding[9], innumerable rock stars and, of course, O. J. Simpson[10].

Witness yet another technologically innovative gift sensation. It looks like a beeper. You wear it on your belt like a beeper. It even has the red button on top like a beeper. Press the button however, and you don't hear a beep. Instead what spews forth is an endless, angry tirade of the vilest imaginable obscenities. It's commonly used as a gag at parties or at the office to express anger in a business confrontation.

What *is* an obscenity? What is its purpose? Is "Fuck you!" an expression of sexual desire, the literal meaning of the words?

Of course not. "Fuck you!" is transparently interchangeable with "Asshole!", or "Shithead!", or "Bitch!", or "Bastard!", or innumerable other imprecations. They all express the same thought: "I am very angry at you!" The actual words themselves mean nothing. Change their context and tone of voice and they can become a compliment, e.g. "Holy shit! *You* are fucking amazing!" What gives curses their power is the anger behind them.

Whenever and wherever they are used they are meant as a warning. I am very angry right now. If you don't back down, beware the consequences! In the office you risk being demoted, or fired. On the street you risk a fight, or worse. As Ashley Montagu wrote: "Swearing . . . replaces physical violence."[11]

Obscenities *are* anger. Mark Twain wrote: "When angry, count four; when very angry, swear."[12]

Managers use obscenities and anger as a motivational tool. "(Anger) is a management vehicle."—Alexander Haig[13]. They provoke their employees to excel. Executives use it to threaten. Colleagues use it to gain advantage in competition.

As a business consultant, I often hear it argued that an office without anger is complacent. Walter B. Cannon wrote: "Anger is the emotion preeminently serviceable for the display of power."[14] You'll never get to be number one if you're at peace. Jeremy Irons has said that peaceful sets never produce great movies. In the legendary, possibly apocryphal, words of the late Leo Durocher:[15] "Nice guys finish last!"

Apparently work is a no holds barred, dog eat dog, swimming with the sharks rat race, and every other metaphor of animal aggression. Is play any different from work? Do cars leaving the city on a weekend blow their horns less than on a weeknight? Is the competition on your local basketball court less aggressive than at work?

Watch basketball, football, baseball, golf, hockey, rugby, or any other athletic competition. Yes, there's camaraderie among teammates, even occasionally among opponents. There's good cheer, there's joking, but there's also anger.

Anger and frustration are as much a part of the game as losing is. We get angry at our opponents. We get angry at our teammates. We get angry at our children, if they're the players. We get angry at ourselves.

Chuck Knoblauch, a Gold Glove second basemen, after an angry divorce could no longer make the simple throw to first base. Pete Sampras, seeded first, was eliminated in the opening round after he learned that his two closest relatives had been diagnosed with the same unfair fearsome disease. Mike Tyson, the heavyweight champion, repeatedly bit his opponent's ear and was disqualified, after he was frustrated.

We call it choking. We call it unprofessional. We boo. Yet the fact remains, in every sport, there are innumerable professionals whose anger destroys them: Steve Blass, Von McDaniel, Mark Wohlers, Rick Ankiel, pitchers no longer able to throw a strike; Mackey Sasser, the catcher no longer able to lob the ball back to the pitcher (though he could accurately rifle the ball to second base, twice as far); Jana Novotna, points away from winning 1993 Wimbledon, double faulting and losing five games in a row; Greg "The White Shark" Norman missing a three-foot putt and dropping ten strokes in the last nine holes of the 1996 Masters.

Every coach, on every level, knows the best way to motivate their team is to incite them. Post some insulting quote from the opposition. Let your team know how everyone has already counted them out. Let them prove themselves by disproving everyone else. Let them believe that the only way that they can protect their school's reputation, their manhood, their womanhood, their pride, is by "killing" the opposing team.

In 2002, the U.S. faced Europe in the Ryder Cup to determine world supremacy in golf, the civilized game of millionaires, where any sound beyond a muted whisper is inexcusable. Revealingly the headline describing the match stated simply: "Gentlemen, start your anger."[16] In a less refined sport, baseball, pitching superstar Randy Johnson explained similarly: "I've learned to use my anger as an advantage on the mound. Not that I ever needed anger management, although that's been brought up."[17]

Are teams named the "Doves," or the "Falcons"? The reason that most teams, on all levels of competition, are named after predators[18], or other aggressive metaphors[19], is because "competitive games provide an . . . outlet for the instinctive aggressive drive."—Karl Menninger[20].

What do basketball crowds yell when opponents are taking foul shots? Anything they can think of to infuriate and thus distract them. What do football crowds do when opposing quarterbacks are calling signals? They make as much noise as they can to interfere. What do infielders yell to encourage their pitcher? "No batter! No batter!," insulting the person waiting at the plate.

A spirited rivalry requires that two adversaries genuinely hate each other. The Dodgers and the Giants despised each other when they were both in New York. One should have been delighted to see the other leave. Instead, they left together and transposed their bad blood to California. Ebbetts Field and the Polo Grounds had seen more than their share of brawls, beanballs and blood. Now California had the privilege of seeing the Giants' Juan Marichal strike the Dodgers' John Roseboro over the head with a baseball bat.

Back in New York the Yankees and Mets picked up where

the Giants and Dodgers had left off. Yankees' star Roger Clemens not only badly beaned Mets' star Mike Piazza but subsequently threw a bat at him for good measure. In turn, Met Glendon Rusch hit Yankee Tino Martinez who had been previously hit by Armando Benitez. Clemens himself was thrown at by Shawn Estes.

The New York Times[21] concluded: " . . . baseball New York needed a psychiatrist to explore the complexities of its anger and id." The Mets' psychiatrist[22] responded: "It's comparable to the function of sports in childhood—how far do you take the conflict?" The most amazing fact of all is that, unlike the Dodgers and Giants, the Yankees and Mets aren't even in the same league[23].

A despised opponent is simply a bigger draw. The popular play and movie was called *Damn Yankees.* In every sport it's harder to repeat as champions because now everyone hates you.

The box office is even bigger if we're matching individuals rather than teams. Boxing matches are promoted by creating a publicized animosity, more apparent than real, between the two pugilists. Every promoter's dream is an inter-racial fight. A "great white hope" attracts pre-existing racial anger.

The anger isn't hidden. Watch the "Dawg Pound" in the Cleveland end zone during a Browns football game. Listen to the chants and look at the placards at a Duke University basketball game[24]. Sit in the blue seats during a New York Rangers hockey game. Wear a Yankees cap in the Boston Red Sox's Fenway Park and you might get a battery dropped on you. A cup of beer is guaranteed. (Children and aesthetes are strongly advised to avoid all four.) "Trash talk" used to be a hidden, ugly part of the game. Now it is publicized, even glorified.

Once the most commercially desirable athletes were the ones most successful at pretending to be gentlemen. Now, all pretense is gone. The best-known athletes and coaches are the surliest, most obnoxious, most temperamental people in the game. Dennis Rodman, John Rocker, Ilie Nastase, and Mike Ditka were of different sports, but of the same mind-set. Angry John McEnroe, retired, got more endorsement deals than nice world champion Pete Sampras.

When, after 30 seasons, Hall of Fame coach Bob Knight was finally fired by Indiana University, the reason wasn't for losing. Knight was arguably the most successful basketball coach in the history of college basketball, winning three national championships in three different eras.

The reason was unarguably his temper. Though he had previously claimed that he "didn't really have a problem with anger," he had physically and verbally confronted students, colleagues, opponents and referees his entire career. He had thrown a chair, choked a player, kicked his son and gotten arrested. In his final press conference he defended himself saying he would have to be "an absolute moron" to lose his temper yet again and jeopardize his job.

No. Just very angry[25].

Anger is an inherent part of all competition, avocational as well as vocational. Furthermore, since the playing field, unlike the office, is a venue for physical action, when anger supervenes, there is a greater likelihood that it will be expressed physically as in Latrell Sprewell repeatedly choking his coach who had angered him.

While a fight can happen anywhere, including the most prestigious office, the odds are that it won't. That's not true in a Junior High School playground, or a professional hockey rink. It's not even true in amateur hockey. Witness the hockey Dad who, displeased with his son's practice, sat on his son's coach and pounded him to death in front of all the kids, including the coach's and his own.

Violence is the ultimate expression of anger. As such, it simultaneously attracts us and repels us. It attracts us as a forbidden fruit that we would all like to taste, but repels us because we all know the consequences of tasting it.

Walking to the hospital I chanced upon two burly taxi drivers engaged in a fistfight in the middle of the street. More interesting than their confrontation was the reaction of the crowd. Most literally stopped to watch. Cars even pulled over, like rubber-neckers at a traffic accident. On the other hand, there were those who crossed the street to avoid it. Even there, they kept their eyes resolutely fixed forward, as if they would suffer the punishment of Lot's wife if they looked back.

Of the hundreds of people, how many interceded? Not a single one.

There were many reasons. Both men were big, so it was a fair fight. Furthermore, potential peacemakers ran the risk of injury themselves. In addition, most city dwellers have little sympathy for cabbies, generally perceived to be aggressive road hogs. (Some cheer when they come across two cabs in a fender bender.)

Another reason was that no one was invested in these strangers. When fighting breaks out at our local gym, we all immediately grab the pugilists. We care about our friends and don't want them to get hurt.

The major reason for the lack of intervention however, was the aforementioned dichotomy between those attracted and those repulsed. The former didn't want the fight to end. The latter didn't want to acknowledge its existence. Consequently, there were no peacemakers until the professional ones, the police, eventually arrived. Even then, several onlookers loudly expressed their disappointment that the fight had been stopped.

When similar, albeit non-violent, confrontations occur at the office, the same dichotomy ensues. There will be those who leave their offices and stand there fascinated until it's finally over. There will be others who uncharacteristically close their office doors.

Yet, even the rapt observers are in some ways frightened by what they're seeing, and the hermits often inquire later about what they chose to miss. Both the attraction *and* the repulsion occur to some degree in all of us.

Some argue that *all* competition is unhealthy. It should be avoided on all levels. We should endeavor to be allies, rather than adversaries. We should work together for a common cause, rather than in opposition.

It's idealistic, yet it doesn't eliminate anger. In fact, it doesn't even reduce it. It just changes the labels.

I live across from the United Nations, the ultimate alliance. Consequently I constantly see and hear the pickets who parade there, (whether I want to or not). They come in all colors and creeds. They speak and display all imaginable languages. In many cases I have no idea who they are, or what they're protesting. In all cases, they're angry.

There doesn't have to be a visible counter-protest to make them angry, (although it certainly exacerbates matters). In the five decades that I've lived in New York City, (arguably the protest Mecca of the world), I have yet to see a picket with a smile. After all, what does the very word "protest" imply, if not anger?

It doesn't matter if you're for or against abortion, prayer in schools, the environment, banning of fur, gay rights, women's liberation, animal experimentation, AIDS funding, indeed, any cause. There are two things of which you can be certain.

Number one, there exists a sizable group of people who strongly oppose your point of view. Someone is protesting what you support, and vice-versa. Number two, both your side and their side feel justifiably angry. Given the opportunity, both of you will be screaming at each other. Or worse.

The cause need not be esoteric. Take the most universal, primary cause of all. God.

Have divergent religious populations *ever* peacefully coexisted *anywhere?* The rare examples are in countries (like our own) where one religion predominates and thus can afford to be magnanimous. Examples to the contrary however, are the rule: The Catholics and Protestants of Northern Ireland, The Hindus and Moslems of India, The Hutus and Tutsis of Africa, The Jews and Moslems of the Mideast.

This is hardly a recent phenomenon. What were the Crusades, the Inquisition and the countless wars of the old world? "Ethnic cleansing" wasn't invented in our decade, or even in our century.

Nor would warfare decrease if the entire world were one religion. Instead of Moslems fighting Jews we would have Shiite Moslems fighting Sunni Moslems, or Satmar Jews fighting Lubavitch Jews, both of which we already see. We even see Satmar Jews fighting Satmar Jews, or Pentecostals fighting Pentecostals.

How ironic. A godly cause which should be used to better us is instead used to further justify our anger towards each other. Is there any greater oxymoron than a "Holy War"?

War is the ultimate expression of anger. Has any country ever gone to war without being angry? It isn't possible. In war, as in work, as in play, if we don't have a reason to be angry at our adversary, we'll find one. The "Krauts" had Hitler, the "Japs" Pearl Harbor, so we had reason for anger in World War II. What about Korea and Viet Nam? Why were we angry at those "Gooks"? Even our brave veterans don't remember any more.

If we're not divided by religion or country, we keep looking. We focus on shade of skin color, or clothing, or language. Where there's a will to anger, there's always a way to justify it.

Isn't it remarkable that certain people are always angry at their government? It doesn't matter what the government did, or didn't do. The same people who were outraged at a Republican President for being the world's policeman and militarily intervening in the Persian Gulf, or Vietnam, are outraged at a Democratic President for *not* being the world's policeman and *not* militarily intervening in Bosnia, or the Mideast.

This implacable anger isn't limited to either end of the political spectrum. There are those who consider any criticism of the government to be treason, and any critic to be a traitor. As but one example, the *Weekly World News,* a satirical post World War II tabloid, had a "fictional, foaming at the mouth, super-patriot columnist."[26] His name? Ed Anger.

Which comes first, the issue or the anger?

There are many to whom hatred is not an occasional avocation, but a full-time obsession. There are skinheads, Ku Klux Klansman, and other White supremacists, who think, eat and breathe anger towards Blacks and Jews 24/7. Similarly, there are Black supremacists who celebrate the violent death of any Caucasian. A large Black audience cheered when Louis Farrakhan invoked the Black gunman who murdered seven White commuters on the Long Island Railroad.

There are misogynists who consider all women inferior, differing only in if they're "cunts" or "JAPS." (For those not fluent in vulgarity, "cunts" are sluts, and "JAPS" are snobs. The delineating variable is whether or not the said female ever agreed to have sex with you.)

There are misandrysts, to whom all men "just don't get it." Men are all selfish and insensitive at best, rapists and batterers at worst. In the ostensibly facetious words of one, "Give every woman a trust fund, a sperm bank, and a dildo, exterminate the men, and the world would be a better place."

There are homobigots[27] who believe that all our problems are attributable to homosexuals. "Goddammit . . . You know what happened to the Greeks? Homosexuality destroyed them. Sure, Aristotle was a homo, we all know that. So was Socrates . . . The last six Roman emperors were fags." [White House transcript of President Richard Nixon.] By the same token, there are homosexuals who resent and dismiss all heterosexuals as "breeders", a lower form of life.

There are Christians who still believe that Jews are Christ-killers, and the world would be better without them. Some religious Christians, including televangelists and professional basketball players, believe that all who deny Christ go to hell. There are Jews who believe that all non-Jews are "Goyim," and constitute an inferior species. Some religious Jews consider it morally permissible to cheat non-Jews, including the government. There are Muslims who believe that any non-Muslim is an infidel, and therefore worthy of slaughter. Some religious Muslims planned, committed and supported the flagitious attacks of *September 11, 2001.*

Ironically, our sanctuaries, our homes are often the angriest places of all. Our twelve-year-old's home was exceptional only in the degree of anger, not in its presence. Moreover, anger doesn't enter as an intruder, but as an invited guest.

Pick three newspapers, a local, city, and national edition. Open each to a page at random. The respective headlines read: "Town Fuming Over Building On Saved Land.," "Democrats In Turmoil.," "A Bitter Split For Albania." Can you read three successive stories without either sensing someone else's anger, or your own?

Turn to the magazines. *TIME* has on its cover: "Violence goes mainstream." *People* focuses on an ugly celebrity divorce. *Sports Illustrated* details an irresolvable contract dispute. *TV Guide* leads with this week's "Battle for Broadcast Viewers." *Entertainment Weekly* invites you to "meet the 101 most influential, tough makers and breakers."

This is precisely the reason that Dr. Andrew Weil and other health gurus advocate taking periodic "vacations" from reading or listening to the news. You're not on vacation if you're still being aggravated.

Turn on the tube. "That's entertainment!"

Start with an informative news-oriented show. Which

network's confrontation would you prefer? *60 Minutes* on CBS, *Meet The Press* on NBC, *Nightline* on ABC, *Crossfire* on CNN, *Hardball* on CNBC, or *Firing Line* on PBS? There will be anger on all.

Switch to real people interviews. You will find the very same anger, albeit from less educated sources. No one ever turned on *Jerry Springer, Montel Williams, Ricki Lake, Jenny Jones, Sally Jessy Raphael* or *Maury Povich* to listen to an interview with Henry Kissinger. They came to see Henry kiss Ginger, or Jill slap Trixie. They won't be disappointed. Before the hour is over they hear yelling and cursing and see fisticuffs and the ever-popular (albeit censored) exposed breasts and derrieres. In all likelihood there will have been cross-dressing, marital betrayal and sexual experimentation as well.

Turn on *Judge Judy, Judge Joe Brown, Judge Hatchett, The People's Court* and innumerable others and you get more of the same, but with a judicial presence to reprimand everyone at the conclusion.

Move the reality show out of the studio and you add production costs, but you don't change the dynamics. Whether it's surviving, fearing, racing, enduring or other contrived activity, the angry competition remains, but now with an additional layer of sadism.

Watch enough action shows and they all seem identical. In the first few minutes some villain commits a heinous misdeed. It infuriates you, compelling you to watch the remainder of the episode to see the hero avenge the crime, and, more importantly, the villain get his due. Only then is your anger abated.

Depending on the hour of broadcast, there are added elements of humor, suspense, sex or violence, but fundamentally, though the personalities and talent may differ, the plot stays the same. Most importantly, your remaining involved in the show requires your anger.

There's only one thing left. Thank God for comedy.

When Steve Allen[28] lectured on comedy, he pointed

out that all comedy is fundamentally the expression of anger. Woody Allen would agree. So would any other comedian. (Freud even said the same thing. He called it sublimation. He wasn't funny.)

A joke is always at another's expense. Will Rogers said famously: "Everything is funny as long as it's happening to somebody else." Mel Brooks said funnily: "If I slip and fall, it's tragedy; if you slip and fall, it's comedy."

As you surf the channels, you realize they're right. Every laugh is at someone's expense. In action shows, anger is between enemies and expressed physically. In comedy shows, it's between friends and expressed verbally.

On *Cheers*, Carla insults Cliff. On *Mary Tyler Moore*, Murray insults Ted. On *Dick Van Dyke*, Buddy insults Mel. On *The Honeymooners*, Alice insults Ralph. On *Frasier*, brother insults brother, and father insults both. On *Everybody Loves Raymond*, everybody insults his brother. On *Seinfeld*, everyone insults everyone. On radio, Jack Benny and Fred Allen were insulting each other.

From Fred Allen, to Steve Allen, to Woody Allen, comedy *is* angry. The diminutive British comic Dudley Moore said: "If I'd been able to hit someone in the nose, I wouldn't have been a comic."

Larry Gelbart[29], the prolific comedy writer, was asked if he could still be funny in his 70's. He replied: "I may have lost some of my hearing and vision, but I don't think I've lost much of my rage."

Is angry humor indigenously American? In 1933 Christopher Morely, a Brit, wrote: "There has always been something sui generis in the American comic spirit . . . A touch of brutality perhaps? Anger rather than humor?" Of course this was before the British *Monty Python and The Holy Grail* in which a knight has his arms and legs comedically hacked off, or *Monty Python's the Meaning of Life* in which a massively obese restaurant patron humorously bursts apart.

Subsequently Malcolm Muggeridge, editor of the British

humor magazine *Punch*, acknowledged the universality of angry humor when he wrote: "By its nature humor is anarchistic, and implies, when it does not state, criticism of existing institutions, beliefs and functionaries. All great humor is in bad taste." Mark Twain put it simpler: "Against the assault of laughter nothing can stand."

A group studying comedy ambitiously endeavored to determine the world's funniest joke. Their ultimate pick was the following:

> Sherlock Holmes and his faithful companion, Dr. Watson, are camping out. In the middle of the night Holmes wakes Watson.
>
> "Watson, open your eyes, and tell me what you deduce."
>
> Watson rubs his eyes, stares thoughtfully for a minute, and finally responds.
>
> "From the positioning of the stars, I deduce that we are north of the equator, and in the Western hemisphere. From the foliage on the trees, I deduce we are in late autumn, probably October. From the light on the horizon, I deduce that it is shortly before dawn, probably 6 A.M. From the clouds in the distance, I deduce that is going to rain shortly."
>
> Holmes says nothing. Watson chortles.
>
> "Admit it, Holmes. The student has finally outdone the master."
>
> "Watson, you idiot! Someone has stolen our tent!"

At what point do we laugh? At the punch line, of course. What makes the punch line funny however, is two seemingly superfluous words: "You idiot!" Absent Holmes' expression of anger, the joke is clever, but not funny.

This version of the joke utilizes the personages of Holmes and Watson because the audience implicitly understands that the latter is less intelligent. As such, this is essentially a sophisticated version of the classic "stupid" joke[30]. The punch line translates into: "He's so stupid he didn't realize their tent was gone."

"Stupid" jokes traditionally, albeit politically incorrectly, have as their prey the Polish, or the New Foundlanders, if in Canada, or any nationality or religion the joker wishes to ridicule. The world's funniest joke is angry, like all the others.

Arguably television and radio are more common forms of entertainment. Perhaps a play would be better, or a movie, or a book. Presciently, the first word of the first book ever written[31], Homer's *Iliad*, is "rage."

Neil Simon, our most successful playwright, points out, as have many others, that all plays, both comedic and dramatic, essentially involve the creation and resolution of a conflict. The same is true regarding literature, both fiction and non-fiction.

We are moved by a play or book when the conflict and the characters speak to us. We recognize them, or we want to. Yet, without the conflict, there is no theater and there is no literature. Without conflict there would be no Daumier, no Ibsen, no Melville, no Hemingway, no Tolstoy, nothing. In Shakespeare's *Titus Andronicus* the eponymous hero tortures and murders his daughter's rapists and feeds their cut-up, cooked cadavers to their mother. Shakespeare understood anger.

The movies? A movie is nothing more than aggrandized theater or television. The luxury of time and money allows for better production values, special effects and (hopefully) talent, but the fundamental structure stays the same. If a movie is successful, it entertains us. It releases our anger so that we feel satisfied, identical to an orgasm, a release of sexual energy. Not coincidentally the rush we feel at both experiences are commonly described in similarly euphoric terms.

If a movie is unsuccessful however, we say it bores us. If it bores us enough, we'll even walk out despite having paid significant money for the experience. We'll subsequently describe the movie as boring to everyone including ourselves, but the truth is, we're wrong. "Boring" literally means unstimulating and monotonous. If a movie is truly boring, we wouldn't walk out. We'd fall asleep. At its conclusion we'd wake up pleasantly refreshed after an unexpected, albeit expensive, nap.

When we walk out of a movie, it's because the film is irritating. On a subliminal level it bothered us for reasons that we are neither aware of, nor understand. Consequently we prematurely terminated the experience, the same way we would turn off a massage chair that was hurting us. The successful movie is a catharsis of our anger. The unsuccessful one is a precipitant of it.

Our ultimate retreat is our family. Unfortunately our potential for anger is directly proportional to our degree of closeness. There's no one we're closer to, than our own flesh and blood.

Every parent is aware of the phenomenon of sibling rivalry. All of us seek the ideal of the happy family and consequently are continuously frustrated by the kids' competition, animosity and acrimony. Furthermore, every child has to learn to express their anger toward their parent. Mark David Chapman murdered John Lennon because he was angry at his father. In my years teaching on Bellevue's psychiatric prison ward, I have seen innumerable similar examples.

We have each other, but even that isn't conflict-free. Every friendship, every love, every marriage inevitably includes both competition and resentment. Consequently, there will be disagreement, and anger. Whether we advertise it or not, whether we're married or not, whether we love each other or not, all couples fight.

Ironically, yet appropriately, the harder we try to escape anger, the more frustrated and angry we become, because it can't be done.

Anger makes the world go round. It's as much a part of our life as breathing and eating.

A better metaphor is another healthy human activity, defecating. Both anger and feces build up and eventually need to come out. Both are unpleasant and not fit for company, or polite conversation. Both stink. Nevertheless, both are inevitable and undeniable. "Shit happens." So does anger.

Both need to be expelled from within us or we'll be poisoned by their toxicity. If we're healthy, we encourage these expulsions and privately discharge them on a regular basis. We remove any residue and flush the by-products away.

We all instinctively understand anger from as soon as we can intuit. "Mommy/Daddy angry" is one of the earliest phrases in every child's lexicon. Our instincts are healthy. Anger, like fire, is something to be avoided. We've been burnt by both, so we know they hurt. The next time we encounter them, we keep away. The problem is, unlike fire, anger is everywhere. It can't be avoided. Eventually it must be confronted. Ultimately it must be embraced. Our success in life, and more importantly, our happiness, is in large part determined by our ability to do so.

None of this is new. As we see in the biblical quotations that begin each chapter and the historical quotes that conclude them, references to anger are as ancient as recorded time. Even the ancient Greeks were familiar with "the yellow, choleric, bile type of personality."

In the coming chapters we will be exploring in clinical detail the examples that we have here superficially reviewed. More importantly, we will try to better understand the phenomenon, and why it makes us so uncomfortable. Most importantly, we will learn better strategies in how to cope with others' anger, and our own.

When, in *Star Wars*, Darth Vader implores his son Luke Skywalker to embrace "the dark side," he was referring to Luke's anger. Anger *is* our dark side, but it's still a part of us.

By recognizing it, understanding it, embracing it and resolving it, we can turn it from our adversary to our friend.

At times the world certainly seems looney. Nevertheless, the tunes that we choose to hum when confronting it can make all the difference.

"Consider how much more you suffer from your own anger, than from those very things for which you are angered."
—Marcus Aurelius, (121-180 A.D.)

Notes

---

[1] *Talmud* Blessings: 7A.

[2] *Goodbye, Columbus* (1959), Philip Roth, Random House.

[3] The promiscuous use of Valium and Librium took place in the 60's. It bothered not only me, but the medical establishment and government as well. Accordingly, changes in prescribing protocol and state regulations (e.g. triplicate forms) have sharply reduced the usage of Valium and Librium. In addition, there's more competition. A newer tranquilizer, Xanax, which is shorter-acting and therefore less addicting, today exceeds both Valium and Librium in sales.

[4] Multi Oscar winner Jack Nicholson in a fit of "road rage" attacked a car with a golf club.

[5] In 1994 singer Lisa "Left Eye" Lopes burned down the home of her boyfriend, Atlanta Falcon football player Andre Rison.

[6] Actress Sean Young has been accused by many colleagues of having a volatile temper, most famously when boyfriend James Woods claimed she super-glued his penis to his thigh.

[7] Model Naomi Campbell was ordered by a court to take anger management classes after she struck an assistant with a cellphone in 1998.

[8] Actress Tawny Kitaen was charged in a "road rage" incident in a parking lot and was subsequently arrested and imprisoned for

assaulting her husband, Cleveland Indian baseball player Chuck Finley.

[9] Ice skater Tonya Harding was convicted of conspiring in the assault of her competitor Nancy Kerrigan and was subsequently accused of throwing a hubcap at her boyfriend.

[10] Although controversially acquitted in criminal court, football player O. J. Simpson was in civil court found responsible for the murder of his ex-wife and a male friend. He was subsequently accused of "road rage" in following and assaulting a motorist.

[11] *The Anatomy of Swearing* (1967) Ashley Montagu, Collier.

[12] Mark Twain's advice on anger was intended as a humorous counterpoint to Thomas Jefferson's famous aphorism: "When angry, count ten before you speak; if very angry, an hundred."

[13] General Alexander Haig served in many of the highest offices of the U.S. government including, controversially, being "in charge" after Ronald Reagan was shot.

[14] *Bodily Changes in Pain Hunger Fear and Anger* (1915) Walter B. Cannon, Appleton.

[15] A successful baseball manager, Leo Durocher was a fierce competitor who was never accused of being a "nice guy." Perhaps not coincidentally, Durocher was also known for once being beaten within an inch of his life by his roommate, Babe Ruth.

[16] *The New York Post*, September 27, 2002.

[17] *The New York Times Magazine*, September 29, 2002.

[18] Popular athletic team names include lions, tigers, bears, grizzlies, cougars, sharks, barracuda, eagles, falcons, hawks, even prehistoric raptors, and mythical dragons.

[19] Aggressive team names can derive from humans: pirates, raiders, cowboys, Indians, braves, chiefs, or even from nature: hurricane, cyclone, storm.

[20] Karl Menninger is a patriarch of the first family of American psychiatry, founders of the Menninger Clinic.

[21] Harvey Araton, June 16, 2002.

[22] Dr. Allan Lans, *The New York Times*, June 16, 2002.

[23] The Yankees and Mets only face each other in the occasional interleague game and in one famous "subway" world series.

Despite their not being rivals in the literal sense, their competition is so spirited that their games are invariably the most popular.

[24] Not only have Duke "fans" hurled panties, bras, and condoms on the court, but when an opponent suffered a collapsed lung they chanted: "Inhale! Exhale!" Even Duke fans' tastelessness pales in comparison to that of Arizona State fans. In February 1988, rival star Steve Kerr, whose father had been murdered by Arab terrorists, was serenaded by chants of "PLO!"

[25] In an example of art imitating life, both Bob Knight and John McEnroe had cameos in the movie *Anger Management.*

[26] James Wolcott, *VANITY FAIR,* June 2002.

[27] Homophobia is a clever insult, but is totally inaccurate, and hurtful to those who actually suffer from phobias. Homobigots are *not* phobic of gays, just as racists are not phobic of Blacks, or Jew haters phobic of Jews. Phobias are defined by avoidance. Snake phobics do not beat up snakes, drunk or sober. Gay bashers are, in fact, the antipodes of so-called homophobes.

Anti-Semitism is an equally nonsensical term. It was created in 1879 by Wilhelm Marr, the German author of *The Victory of Judaism Over Germanism,* to confer a pseudo-Darwinian respectability to his movement which had previously been referred to, more accurately and simply, as "Judenfeindschaft" or "Jew-hatred." The fact is most Jews are not Semites and most Semites are not Jews. Jew haters however, remain Jew haters.

It is fascinating to note that the two human activities that demand euphemisms the most are sex and hatred, the two attributes of which we are the most ashamed.

[28] Steve Allen once confided that his biggest laugh was in response to his angry ad-lib. He had followed an interminably boring mind-reader to the stage and remarked to the audience: "He reads minds and he couldn't tell what we were all thinking? When the hell will he finally finish?"

[29] Larry Gelbart wrote for Bob Hope, Sid Caesar, Danny Kaye, and created *M.A.S.H., Oh, God!, Tootsie* and *A Funny Thing Happened on the Way to the Forum.*

[30] Professor Avital Ronell, of N.Y.U., explains at length what offends

us about stupidity in her eponymous book on the subject. We resent stupidity, unlike inability or ignorance, because it stubbornly denies itself. Like Watson in the joke, the stupid person is absolutely confident. Their arrogance justifies our anger and precipitates the joke. *Stupidity* (2002) Avital Ronell, University of Illinois Press.

[31] Of course, it is impossible to ascertain what exactly was the first book ever written. People of faith would insist on the *Bible*, though Biblical scholars claim it was an aggregation of many authors. Historians might vote for some anonymous cave drawing, or hieroglyphics on papyrus. Nonetheless, Homer's *Iliad*, from approximately 1000 B.C., would probably be the general consensus.

PART I

CHAPTER TWO

A Bitter Price to Pay

What Anger Costs

"My punishment (for my anger) is greater than I can bear."[1]

B o[2] knew baseball and football, Pancho[3] knew tennis, but Eduardo knew microbiology. Eduardo (Eddie to his friends) was the most proficient student in my microbiology section. This fact in combination with my visceral distaste for the subject, (I must have had a traumatic experience with a microbe during my infancy), led me to frequently seek his counsel. In the process, we became friends.

Eddie, the child of immigrant parents, (like myself), was studious and soft-spoken, (unlike myself). As you got to know him however, you quickly discovered his keen insight and sharp wit. As you got to know him better, you discovered how disturbed his upbringing had been. His parents divorced, and he had been raised by his punitive mother, who had been frankly psychotic. To make matters worse, she favored Eddie's younger half brother. No matter what went wrong, no matter what Geraldo did, Eddie got blamed for it.

Eddie seemed to have good perspective, *most* of the time. When she frequently called to yell at him or, worse, made one of her infrequent, embarrassing pilgrimages from the South Bronx, he would laugh her off as his "crazy mother." Unfortunately, there were also times that he couldn't. On occasion I would walk into his room, (dorm protocol was that, unless we were "entertaining," we kept our rooms unlocked and entered without knocking), and find him in tears. Once, while under the influence, he loudly cursed God, (in both Spanish and English), complaining about life's inequities.

In our third year he began to exhibit an obsessive inability to forgive and forget. During our strenuous clerkships we all occasionally got stuck with sadistic supervisors. All of us, including Eddie, gritted our teeth and got through it.

Eddie took it personally. He wasn't paranoid. He didn't think they were out to get him. He just couldn't accept the fact of the injustice. Long after the clerkship was over, long after he had received honors, he would still be ruminating about his supervisor. None of us liked them or what they did to us, but we accepted it as a rite of passage. Eddie couldn't.

Our fourth, final year was dedicated to electives. The pressures of demanding days and sleepless nights were behind us. This would be the last such extended vacation for the rest of our lives. Yet, Eddie wouldn't rest. He took one grueling subinternship after another. When most of us were working on our jump shots or our tans, Eddie was working his ass off.

He simultaneously became merciless. We had classmates who were universally despised because they were too competitive, aggressive, narcissistic or arrogant, or, in some cases, all four. Eddie however, couldn't stop at disdain. He complained about them interminably. It bothered him if they achieved any triumph, no matter how insignificant. Shortly before graduation someone posted a list of sarcastic "awards" that they should each receive. The "awards" were very funny, but very cruel. The perpetrator was never identified. I had my suspicions.

By graduation, we were ready to celebrate. We had ample opportunity. There was the medical school ceremony, the university convocation, the parties, the dinner dance. We had ample reason to as well, Eddie moreso than most.

He had not only received many awards, but he had also been selected to a top residency.

Nevertheless, he was bitter. *We* were occupied by the euphoria of the present, and our dreams of the future. He was consumed by recriminations of the past. At a time when the most cynical of us couldn't help but feel nostalgic, he couldn't let go of his vendettas. Throughout the festivities there were classmates sitting next to him, but he sat alone.

His residency took him out of New York. We lost touch. He decided that he had erred in his choice of specialty. He returned home and started over in a new field. We started to see each other a great deal.

Around that time I fell in love and, with the zeal of the newly converted, I set him up with the cream of my black book. The story was always the same. They would hit it off. For several weeks both would be on cloud nine. The woman, invariably more exuberant, would thank me for this "catch." Then, something would happen.

At first it would seem like nothing, a trivial mistake on her part. She wouldn't notice it. When he would point it out to her, she would take it lightly. When she saw how much it bothered him, she would apologize, albeit not understanding why it was such a tempest in a teapot. Before long, the relationship would be over. Sometimes he would make the final break; sometimes she would, but it was always his sullen anger that was the precipitant. He would readily acknowledge, both to her and to me, that it was his fault.

His professional life recapitulated his social life. He had no trouble getting jobs. His employers, like his dates, marveled at their luck in obtaining someone with his ability and credentials. In the end, it never worked out. As a candid employer put it: "You don't play well with other campers." Once again, Eddie acknowledged it was his bad.

His personal life was no better. He bought himself a breathtaking penthouse apartment, but derived no pleasure from it. He was proud that he had separated himself from his destructive family, but he was still alone. His intolerance of imperfection had alienated him from all.

As revealingly as Dorian Gray's portrait[4], his body was a mess. He developed high blood pressure, constant headaches and a bleeding ulcer. He didn't need me to tell him that all three were psychogenic in origin. Neither did he need me to suggest seeing a psychiatrist, although I facilitated the process.

The story was again the same. Both psychiatrist and patient thanked me for what seemed to be, at first, a good match. Eventually the psychiatrist, and the one after him, and the one after her, made a mistake. In every case that was the end of therapy. As Eddie put it: "It's hard to listen to someone when you know you're smarter than they are."

I didn't argue. I did, however, respond: "It's impossible to listen to someone when you're too busy listening to your own anger." He didn't argue, either.

Eddie was very private. He didn't like anyone talking about him. I respected his wishes. The sole exception occurred at our medical school reunion when I asked my classmates to rise for a moment of silence in Eddie's memory.

Eddie died by his own hand. That hand had been set in motion decades earlier by his mother's anger. It had been kept in motion however, by his own. His anger blazed until it consumed the most promising physician I had ever known.

The price of anger in our lives cannot be over-estimated. Decades of research have documented that children of angry parents, like Eduardo, are as disfigured by their parents' actions as children of DES parents[5]. These children are more likely, as adults, to abuse alcohol and drugs, to commit crimes and be incarcerated, to develop chronic health problems, and to experience profound psychiatric illness and commit suicide.

Sadly, though they painfully remember their suffering, these children do not learn from their parents' mistakes. As much as they hated getting beaten themselves as children, they grow up to prove George Bernard Shaw's observation that the child is the father of the man. The only skill these children acquire is to recognize anger sooner than their healthier peers[6]. Perhaps this is what the Bible is referring to when God says in the Ten Commandments that He will punish children, grandchildren, and great grandchildren for the sins of their parents[7].

The price of anger is as obvious in an internist's office as it is in a psychiatrist's. Clinical practitioners readily acknowledge that many of the problems they encounter are caused by anger. "People who are (angry) have more illnesses of all sorts."[8] A textbook on the subject, *A History of Psychosomatic Illness in the Modern Era,*[9] claims that most illness is, in fact, psychosomatic. "Psychogenesis—the conversion of stress or psychological problems into physical symptoms—is one of nature's basic mechanisms in mobilizing the body to cope with medical distress."

What does "psychogenesis" mean? It means that the "genesis," or creation of the illness, came from the "psyche," the mind. It doesn't mean that the patient is imagining or feigning the symptom. It does mean that their mind, often in the form of anger, has caused this problem.

The New York Times wrote[10] in 2002 of a "new medical model in which the mind and body are seen as parts of a single system." The same article suggested that it might be as common to "somaticize" our negative emotions as to "psychologize" them. Cardiologists calling for emergency psychiatric intervention to prevent a heart attack are merely acknowledging what we implicitly understand when we speak of being "heartbroken."

"Then how come my belly hurts, *not* my head?"

Whether we're aware of it or not, whether we like it or not, whether we accept it or not, the fact remains that our brain controls every activity in every part of our body. Including our belly. The hole in our stomach wall is as big, if not bigger, when it's caused by a flood of hydrochloric acid, released untimely by our brain, in response to unceasing anger, than if it was caused by a knife. The only difference is, since a blade can be more readily removed, the latter wound has a better prognosis.

An ulcer is an easy example, not only because of Eddie, but also because ulcers are commonly acknowledged to be psychogenic in origin[11]. The euphemisms that are used to describe the etiology are words like "stress" and "pressure." "Stress" and "pressure" are more societally acceptable because they're external in origin. *We* played no part in this disease. We're innocent bystanders. Anyone in our situation would have gotten an ulcer.

That sounds nice. It relieves us of blame or guilt. Unfortunately, it isn't true. In reality, different people respond to identical stresses in different ways. Different employees react differently to the same, difficult boss. Different students handle the same demanding teacher differently. It's *not* the external stress that causes the ulcer. It's our internal reaction to that stress. As Plutarch said in *Moralia*: " . . . he who gives no fuel to fire puts it out, . . . likewise he who does not . . . nurse his wrath . . . destroys it." Ironically Shakespeare wrote: "Hi-stomach'd are they both, and full of ire, In rage deaf as the sea, hasty as fire."[12]

Similarly, it's not external tension that causes the ubiquitous "tension headache." It's the internal tension expressed by the unconscious contraction of the musculature of the head. If it's our neck or back that's our weak link, the result is a neckache or backache. When we speak of someone being "a pain in the neck" or a "pain in the ass" we are unconsciously acknowledging the angry etiology of our somatic pain.

"I don't get mere tension headaches. I get migraines!"

Not only can a tension headache hurt worse than a migraine; not only are they infinitely more common, but also, as any headache specialist will attest, many self-diagnosed migraines are in fact tension headaches. Moreover, migraines have a significant psychogenic component as well, which is why Botox[13] significantly prevents both migraine and tension headaches by paralyzing the muscles. Calling it a migraine however, not only elicits more sympathy, but more importantly, it avoids the question of the source of the tension. (A good-natured, albeit not good-featured, friend used to refer to himself as "Migraine Max," since that malady coincidentally befell all his blind dates.)

A headache sounds innocuous. (It only sounds that way *before* it happens to you.) The physiologic process that causes it however, has dire long-term consequences. Constricting our arterioles is helpful in an emergency. On a long-term basis, it can be fatal. The resultant hypertension, (increased blood pressure) is a leading cause of both cerebral vascular accidents (strokes), and myocardial infarctions (heart attacks). Not coincidentally, the two are the leading cause of mortality and morbidity.

Studies[14] have shown that anger is a greater risk factor for dying of a heart attack than even elevated cholesterol levels[15]. "This is a life or death matter. We now know that treating anger reduces the risk of Myocardial Infarction (heart attack) and death."[16] "People who are chronically angry are more than twice as likely to have a heart attack than laid-back folks."[17]

By now it is universally accepted that certain behavioral characteristics, commonly referred to as "Type A," significantly increase our cardiac risk. What is "Type A"? Someone who is impatient, aggressive, intolerant, consumed, can't relax, can't let go. Apparently "Type A" stands for angry. In an article on "Type A" *The New York Times*[18] explained that "People who are quick to anger . . . evoke the fight or flight response to their detriment."

Over countless centuries of evolution our bodies have become incredibly sensitized to danger. Our thalamus analyzes all incoming visual, auditory, olfactory and tactile data and screens it for emergency information. Our cortex, the site of analytic thinking, has the ability to overrule our thalamus. Our thalamus, for example, might be frightened by what we see and hear on screen, but our cortex reassures us that "it's only a movie." Our amygdala, however is a wild card. If it instinctively senses danger it bypasses everyone and sends out a "code red." If you ever jumped at a spider on your arm that turned out to be a feather, blame your amygdala.

Whether the emergency was called in by the amygdala, thalamus, or cortex, whether it's a real threat or not, the result is the same: sweaty palms, rapid heartbeat, increased blood pressure, increased sweat, sensitized nerve endings on the skin commonly referred to as "goose bumps," massive bursts of cortisol and adrenaline. All blood is diverted from non-essential functions like digestion. Your body has been primed to fight or run for your life.

If it happens once, it can save your life. If it happens repeatedly, in response to a hyper-vigilant cortex, it will cost you your life.

The power of the mind is as indisputable, as it is infinite. It can kill suddenly, as well as slowly. "The Baskerville Effect,"[19] named after the Sherlock Holmes novel *The Hound of the Baskervilles*[20], in which Charles Baskerville is deliberately frightened to death, refers to someone dying of fright. It was demonstrated on a global scale in a retrospective analysis[21] of the deaths of a quarter million Americans from China or Japan. They were 13% more likely to die on the fourth day of any month than controls. Why? Because in their language[22] the number 4 sounds like the word "death," producing a fear[23] far greater than the Western triskaidekaphobic 13.

Anger doesn't cause every medical problem. There are diseases like diabetes and cancer. There are external threats like injuries and infections. There are self-destructive habits like alcohol, drugs and cigarettes. Yet, even in all of the above, anger plays a crucial role.

Murray was a 39-year-old diabetic looking for group therapy. He was large, loud and exuberantly funny. As he left our first session, I sensed how infectious his enthusiasm was, and how helpful that would be in the group. I looked forward to our next meeting.

I started it by delving into his family history. Murray's father had died at 44 of a heart attack. His heart disease had been secondary to his diabetes. I followed up with the obvious questions. No, Murray was not restricting his sugar intake. No, he didn't check his urine. No, he wasn't concerned about his obesity. No, he hadn't seen his endocrinologist in three years.

There was a protracted silence. I sat there bewildered. How could such an intelligent man be acting so stupidly self-destructive? It didn't take long to discover the answer. With a smile on his face Murray started to express his many resentments. For a few seconds, his smile fooled me. I thought he was mocking himself. Surely he realized that his words made no sense. He couldn't mean them seriously. Quickly however, the intensity of his comments dispelled my illusion. He was furious with his father not only for abandoning him by dying, but also for leaving him with this genetic inheritance. He hated God for this ungodly injustice. He was angry with his doctor for telling him that if he didn't modify his diet, he would be dead within five years. He was angry with his wife and kids for wincing when he indulged.

"Fuck them all!" He wasn't going to give anyone the satisfaction of spoiling his life. He would sooner die than give up La Cote Basque, or Ben and Jerry's.

By the end of the session the tenor of our relationship had dramatically changed. His exuberance was gone. Apparently he was also angry at me for asking uncomfortable questions. He left my office without asking when he could start group. He knew the answer.

Murray's mourners will lament that his diabetes led to his untimely death. They will be unaware that studies show that "high hostility levels . . . boost risk for . . . diabetes."[24] They will be blaming the wrong culprit.

Cancer, like diabetes, has an environmental as well as a genetic component. Many authors, prominently including Norman Cousins and Dr. David Spiegel, point out how important a constructive, positive outlook is in confronting these illnesses. Studies show that angry patients, those who curse the darkness, can have a significantly worse outcome. "Hostile folks have less effective natural-killer cells—the cells that wipe out tumor cells—than their more mellow counterparts."[25]

Similarly, external threats like injury and infection can come without rhyme or reason. At times, frustratingly, they come without justice. In the words of the best-selling rabbi[26], bad things happen to good people. Yet, any experienced observer will tell you that accidents are less random than they seem. Haven't you ever seen someone speed by and thought to yourself: "There goes an accident waiting to happen."?

Actuaries accurately predict that young males have an astronomically higher incidence of auto accidents. Why? They're impulsive. They're indiscreet. They think they're immortal. They're also angry.

They resent having had to bow to authority for their first two decades. Now that they're finally the masters of their own fate, (on the highway anyway), they're going to make their angry mark. Unfortunately it's often on some roadside tree. It's a sad commentary when high school and college yearbooks have obituary pages for traffic fatalities.

Ultimately, the angry young man is like a flaming comet in a dimly lit sky. It makes a vivid impression, but then quickly disappears. The James Deans of our world never last as long as the James Stewarts. An "accident waiting to happen" is only compelling until it happens. Then it's over, and quickly forgotten.

Most accidents however, don't occur on our highways.

They occur in our homes, our jobs, our backyards, our workrooms, our driveways, etc. No matter their location, they are exacerbated by anger. Your chances of the hammer hitting your thumbnail, instead of the metal nail, rise in direct proportion to your temper.

The psychiatric literature contains many articles on the accident-prone individual. These are not theories, but actual people who repeatedly get into accidents. You've probably known some yourself. What are the articles' conclusions? No surprise. These patients repress their anger and never express their feelings verbally.

After getting off the phone with his mother, unable to argue with her when she insisted on his returning home for Christmas, Mike decided to slice a cucumber. The operation on his finger kept him in the hospital over Christmas. He lost his fingertip but got his way. Years earlier, while unsuccessfully trying to break up with his girlfriend, he had managed to severely impale his thigh skiing with her. He joked that his future children were lucky that he had missed his target. She missed the humor.

Even infections can be angry in origin. Xavier discovered he had the AIDS virus. He wasn't particularly surprised, since his sexual practices had been as unsafe as his many assorted partners would allow him. He went directly from his doctor's office to his parents' home. With a smile on his face, he bluntly informed them. As he had expected, they were devastated. If they couldn't appreciate it themselves, he spelled out the delicious irony for them.

His father was a fire and brimstone preacher of a Black fundamentalist church. His mother was a respected and feared community leader. Now the first family's only son had contacted the disease that his father had previously sermonized to be "God's Revenge." In tears, Xavier's mother spat at him: "You're enjoying this, aren't you?" Still smiling he replied: "Telling you I was gay, was the only other moment in my life that I enjoyed as much!"

Examples like this are obviously the exception. Most infections in general, AIDS in particular, are inadvertent. That's not the case with self-destructive drug habits. Whether legal or illegal; whether powder, liquid or smoke; whether alone or socially; chronic drug usage always has an anger component.

Any policeman or emergency room physician can tell you, the incidence of fights and accidents on Saturday nights increases dramatically. The reason isn't based on astrology, but on alcohol. An E.R. colleague will not allow any member of his family in a car after 10 P.M. on Saturday nights or New Year's Eve. Statistically, he's justified.

It's not limited to fights and accidents. What percentage of rapes and murders are committed under the influence? Many think a majority. Recently it has become fashionable to say that rape isn't an act of sex; it's an act of violence. I think it's both, but above and beyond both, rape is an act of anger.

Similarly, while the emotionless contract murder might be common in reel life, in real life, the vast majority of murders are impulsive expressions of anger. The anger escalates into a fight because of the absence of self-control, or the presence of alcohol. The fight escalates into murder because of the presence of a deadly weapon, or the absence of the grace of God.

Self-control and alcohol are often mutually exclusive. Revealingly, many people only smoke when they're drinking. Though smoking doesn't increase incidents of violence, (with the exception of non-smokers who feel provoked to such when subjected to second-hand smoke), smoking clearly has an anger component as well.

How could it not? How can any rational human being engage in a practice that unequivocally destroys their body and not be engaged in an angry act? When children are angry, they destroy whatever they've built. Adults are no different. At best, by smoking, smokers are expressing anger at themselves. At worst, they are expressing it at their loved ones as well.

Sloan-Kettering Memorial Hospital in New York City is dedicated exclusively to cancer. Understandably it is a smoke-free facility. Walk by its entrance, in any weather, and you'll find cancer patients standing outside, holding on to their IV poles, smoking. If, as in some cases, their smoking has destroyed their naso-pharynx, they hold the cigarette to the breathing hole in their trachea, to suck in the carcinogenic smoke. How do you imagine their visiting relatives feel, watching this?

If *you* have a priceless, irreplaceable favorite possession, and *I* endanger it, isn't that an act of anger on my part? Wouldn't you be furious with me? Endangering yourself is no different. Neither is the reaction. In the words of a ten-year-old: "If you loved me Mommy, you wouldn't smoke. I hate you for smoking."

Destroying our possessions isn't limited to our bodies. The name partner of a prominent Manhattan law firm often muses that his hundred plus lawyer group couldn't exist if not for the anger of his clients. How many billions of dollars are spent on never-ending suits, on "unfriendly" corporate assaults, on "pissing matches" that serve only to express the anger of the initiator? How many employee hours are wasted on these personal vendettas? Can we ever fully calculate the cost of anger in business? Legal costs are but the tip of the iceberg.

Yet we've made progress. In a previous age tens of thousands would have fought, and thousands would have perished, to assuage the anger of the high and mighty. Today our knights no longer wear armor, but pin stripes, though they still call each other "Sir." They still try to overwhelm their opposition, whether in a frontal assault, or more commonly, in a battle of attrition. Now, like then, the battles are still fought by hired mercenaries, far from the physical presence of the warring rulers who hired them. Now, like then, the majority of these battles could be avoided if not for the pride and anger that precipitated them. Now, like then, successful combatants are very handsomely paid. At least now, the unsuccessful ones live to battle again.

Now, like then, most battles are actually fought on a much smaller scale. The epic conflicts that history records are far outnumbered by the transient, petty, intra-mural disputes that no one notices.

Lawyers provide the appearance of anger, without the actual emotion. From 10 to 4, in front of their clients, they scream at each other and pound the table[27]. After their clients leave however, they're going out for drinks together. In this respect they are no different from boxers, professional athletes in general, or politicians. Psychiatrists call it affect without emotion.

The converse of this apparent, yet faux anger, is anger without affect. The best examples are parapraxes, better known as Freudian slips. A psychologist, who secretly despises his patient, neglects to inform him that he's away on vacation the following week. A passive-aggressive suitor completely forgets a date. A bitter accountant accidentally omits a major deduction. Though on the surface these people appear devoid of anger, at times as obsequious as Uriah Heep or Eddie Haskell[28], their actions belie their appearance.

Verbal Freudian slips are more undeniable. Stan was taking his last law school exam. The course was required, tedious and despised. Professor Blank, popularly known as "Blinky" because of his eye twitch, was patronizing, turgid and equally despised. His saving grace was that he never failed anyone.

As Stan handed in his paper, Blank extended his hand and offered his traditional benediction: "Lad, may fortune smile on your legal career." Stan shook his hand and replied: "Thank you, Professor Blinky." Stan failed.

While all Freudian slips are libidinal, not all primal

instincts are based on anger. Some are based on lust. Years earlier, in college, Stan had fantasized about a buxom classmate, but was too shy to ask her for a date. It wasn't until his senior year, when he noticed her struggling with change for a 15 cent candy bar, that he finally spoke to her: "Would you like two nipples for a dime?"

Stan's parapraxes were both embarrassing and costly in the short run, but meaningless in the long run, and fortunately, witnessed by no one. Jimmy's was witnessed by millions.

In 1948, at the Democratic National Convention, Hubert Horatio Humphrey, then Mayor of Minneapolis, gave the "greatest speech ever heard."[29] Humphrey's speech single-handedly persuaded[30] the convention to reject the Platform Committee's majority position avoiding the issue of Civil Rights. To the consternation of the White House[31], and the eternal fury of Southern Democrats, Humphrey goaded the convention into adopting an uncompromising advocacy of full civil rights for all Black Americans[32]. Southern Democrats blamed Humphrey for destroying their lock on Southern elections and publicly ridiculed him as "a pip-squeak[33]," "the demagogue[34]," "that damned fool[35]," "goddamned ass[36]," and humiliatingly, on the floor of the Senate, "a lying . . . misinformed . . . publicity expert[37]." They never forgave him.

In 1980, President Jimmy Carter, the first Southern Democrat to be elected to the White House since 1948[38], eulogized Hubert Humphrey at the Democratic National Convention. In the 30 years between the 1948 Convention and his death in 1978, Humphrey had become Senator, Vice-President, Presidential candidate four separate times and Democratic icon. Nevertheless, Southern Democrats had neither forgotten nor forgiven. As the thousands in the convention hall, and millions watching on television, gasped in shock, Jimmy Carter slowly, deliberately, named him: "Hubert Horatio Hornblower." Carter subsequently lost the election[39].

Twenty years later an even uglier political parapraxis occurred in the United States House of Representatives. In a contentious argument, Barney Frank, the openly homosexual Democrat from Massachusetts, was referred to by his opponent as "Barney Fag." It is not entirely clear if this comment was truly a Freudian slip, or worse, a sophomoric slur, akin to the televangelist referring to openly homosexual comedienne Ellen DeGeneres as "Ellen Degenerate."

In every age political, professional, athletic[40], teammates, colleagues and neighbors have their personal conflicts. Even if the immediate confrontation is controlled, the residual acrimony remains. The inevitable result weakens and threatens the collective unit, be it the team, company, army, country or even planet. Paraphrasing Longfellow: in union there is strength, is discord there is danger.

It is paradoxical that while anger strengthens us immediately, it weakens us in the long run. The adrenaline that super-charges us to extra-ordinary strength in a crisis will, if repeatedly called upon, destroy us. Our bodies and our minds were not designed for continual crises. Our anger destroys not only the physical vehicle of our existence but also, more importantly, its emotional pleasures.

Dean, a very successful C.P.A., had been looking forward to his only daughter's wedding since before she was born, twenty-five years earlier. No expense was spared. No detail was overlooked, from the elaborate flowers to the oriental rugs purchased for the occasion. The million dollars that he was spending was designed to make this day one that no one would ever forget. He was on top of the world as he drove up to the catering hall. He greeted one and all effusively. The photographer didn't have to remind him to smile as he posed with his daughter.

Then came the family pictures. Dean couldn't believe his eyes. His brother in law wasn't wearing a tuxedo. The invitation had specified "Black Tie." Dean knew that he owned a tuxedo. He hadn't bothered to wear it. Dean was incandescent with rage. He refused to greet anyone. No matter how often the photographer asked, he refused to smile. Dean, the accountant, had lost sight of the bottom line.

Dean's wife begged him to forget about it. He couldn't. His brother in law's action had poisoned his perfect day. It was inexcusable. His teeth were clenched as he walked his daughter down the aisle. The moment that he had been delightedly imagining for years was irretrievably lost. Dean had spent his life savings on a wedding that he, and his family, wanted to forget. It didn't add up.

Like Eduardo's graduation, Dean's wedding had been completely destroyed, *not* by his brother in law, but by himself. Two angry men, one young, one old, denied themselves a once in a lifetime pleasure that each had deserved, and that each had spent many years and many dollars to earn.

Dean understood accounting, Eduardo understood medicine, Pancho understood tennis, but none of them understood themselves, or their anger.

Pancho Gonzalez, "the best tennis player of all time,"[41] had it all. He was tall, dark and handsome, photogenic, charismatic, a national hero in two countries. He could have anything, or anyone, and he knew it.

In the end, he had nothing. His unceasing rage alienated him from all seven of his grown children, cost him his six marriages, all of his friends, all of his tennis relationships, all of his jobs and all of his endorsements. He died from cancer, in pain, at age 66, broke and alone. His estranged brother Ralph forgave him yet again and came to care for him. They got into a fistfight on his deathbed.

Whether we measure the cost of our anger in years, in dollars, in love matches, in health or in happiness, we all eventually find that it is a price that none of us can afford.

"When anger arises, think of the consequences"
-Confucius, (551-479 B.C.E.)

Notes

---

[1] *Genesis* IV: 13.

[2] Bo Jackson, until a career ending injury, was a professional athlete starring simultaneously in baseball and football. His popular ad at the time exclaimed: "Bo knows baseball! Bo knows football!"

[3] "Pancho Gonzalez may have been the best tennis player of all time."— *Sports Illustrated,* June 24, 2002.

[4] *The Picture of Dorian Gray* (1890) Oscar Wilde, Viking Press.

[5] Diethylstilbestrol (DES) was a ubiquitous drug prescribed in the 1950's by obstetricians to reduce the risk of miscarriage. Only decades later did they discover that it caused malformations and cancer in the children.

[6] Dr. Seth Pollak, et al from the University of Wisconsin, published on June 18, 2002 in the National Academy of Sciences, that children exposed to rage perceived anger in others earlier. Unfortunately they consequently also saw non-existent anger and spent so much time scanning for anger that they missed other social cues that interfered with their interpersonal relationships.

[7] *Exodus* XX:5.

[8] Dr. Redford Williams, Director of Behavioral Medicine Research at Duke University Medical Center. *Reader's Digest,* July 2002.

[9] *From Paralysis to Fatigue: A History of Psychosomatic Illness in the Modern Era* (1992) Dr. Edward Shorter, *The Free Press.*

[10] Anna Fels, M.D. *The New York Times,* May 21, 2002.

[11] Recent research by Dr. Martin Blaser of N.Y.U. School of Medicine, et. al. ironically has revealed a bacterial etiology to ulcers as well.

[12] *King Richard II,* I, i, William Shakespeare.

[13] Botox, a botulinum toxin, is a lethal paralytic drug. In trace amounts it is used cosmetically to temporarily eliminate facial wrinkles. Serendipitously these patients noticed that their headaches had disappeared together with their frown lines. The American Headache Society reported in June 2002 that 13 studies confirmed Botox's efficacy in preventing migraine as well as tension headaches.

[14] Research on anger and heart attacks has been conducted at the Henry Ford Hospital in Detroit.

[15] *Clinical Psychiatry News*, May 2002.

[16] Dr. Mark Ketterer at 2002 meeting of the Academy of Psychosomatic Medicine.

[17] *Reader's Digest*, July 2002 reporting on a 2001 study in the American Journal of Epidemiology.

[18] Jane E. Brody, *The New York Times*, May 21, 2002.

[19] The term, "The Baskerville Effect," was coined by Dr. David Phillips of U.C.—San Diego.

[20] The author of *The Hound of the Baskervilles*, and all of Sherlock Holmes, was Sir Arthur Conan Doyle, a physician. In reference to "The Baskerville Effect," Conan Doyle was described in the December 22, 2001 edition of the *British Medical Journal* as "not only a great writer but a remarkably intuitive physician as well."

[21] This study was conducted by the Sociology department at the University of California at San Diego.

[22] The homophonic similarity between "4" and "death" occurs in Mandarin, Cantonese and Japanese.

[23] Because of the fear of the number "4," throughout China and Japan frequently there are no fourth floors in hotels and hospitals. Furthermore, many will not travel on the fourth day of any month because they are considered "unlucky days."

[24] *Clinical Psychiatry News*, June 2002, reporting studies by Dr. Richard Surwit at Duke University and Dr. Peter Vitaliano at the University of Washington in Seattle.

[25] *Reader's Digest*, July 2002, reporting on research from the University of Colorado.

[26] Rabbi Harold Kushner, *When Bad Things Happen to Good People* (1981), Schocken Books.

[27] A well known law school adage states: "When the facts are on your side, you pound the facts; when the law is on your side, you pound the law; when neither is, you pound the table."

[28] Uriah Heep and Eddie Haskell are memorable minor characters, from respectively *David Copperfield* and *Leave It To Beaver*, whose

unctuous manner deceived their counterparts, but not the audience.

29 This was the assessment of Senator Paul H. Douglas, of Illinois, who had been both present and powerful at the convention.

30 The impact of Humphrey's convention speech can only be compared to that of the legendary *Cross of Gold* oration by William Jennings Bryan.

31 Incumbent President Harry S. Truman thought Humphrey a "crackpot" who would cause the South to abandon the Democrats, and cost Truman the election. Truman won, not despite Humphrey, but precisely because of him. (David McCullough)

32 Readers interested in this neglected, fascinating episode in American history should consult: *In the Fullness of Time: The Memoirs of Paul H. Douglas* (1972), Paul H. Douglas, Harcourt Brace Janovich, *Truman* (1992), David G. McCullough, Simon and Schuster, and *Master of the Senate* (2002), Robert A. Caro, Alfred A. Knopf.

33 Senate Majority Leader Scott Lucas.

34 An editorial in the Dothan, Alabama *Register.*

35 Senator Richard Russell of Georgia.

36 Vice-President Alben Barkley.

37 Senator Harry Byrd of Virginia.

38 The only other Southern Democratic president, Lyndon B. Johnson, had been elected *in* the White House with all the attendant advantages of incumbency.

39 Jimmy Carter lost decisively to Ronald Reagan in 1980 for many reasons: his "general malaise" speech, double digit inflation, Reagan's "Now there you go again" debate victory, the energy crisis and the Iranian Hostage rescue debacle.

40 In the same week in June 2002 physical fights coincidentally erupted, in dugouts, between teammates on several baseball teams. Roberto Alomar and Roger Cedeno of the Mets, and Barry Bonds and Jeff Kent of the Giants were the most famous of the combatants.

41 *Sports Illustrated,* June 24, 2002

The Fear of God

Why Anger Frightens

"Oh, let not the Lord be angry." [1]

In your entire life, when were you the most scared?
Can you think of the second scariest moment?
How about a third?

Take as much time as necessary, and, please, don't limit yourself to recent events.

I have been asking this question for many years. It fascinates me. It isn't confrontational. It seems, on the surface, innocently curious, even innocuous.

In reality, it's not. A candid answer is not only incredibly private, but also invariably revealing. Even remembering the incident renders the respondent uncomfortable.

If you took the time to answer the three questions, (you'll get much more out of this chapter if you do), then you discovered that at least one of your three answers involved anger.

The typical answer involves someone you're legitimately afraid of, being very mad at you. That someone is always either bigger, older, stronger or more powerful than you, and commonly, all of the above. It might be a boss, a teacher, an older sibling, a supervisor, an enemy, an unknown stranger or even a dog. (Can a dog be angry? More on that later.)

An unusual exercise, you might say, but what's the point? The presence of anger is coincidental, and predictable, since threats are commonly accompanied by anger. The threat is the issue, *not* the anger. That's what being frightened means, being threatened.

To prove the point, you cite examples that don't involve anger: The time you were lost in the woods alone after dark. The time the doctor told you that he found a growth that looked cancerous. The time you were overwhelmed by a wave and almost drowned.

The examples are all valid, but they lose the focus of the question. The question wasn't about being threatened. It wasn't even about being frightened. It was about being scared.

You remember being scared. When you're scared, you cry, you scream, you make in your pants[2]. You don't cry or scream or make in your pants when your physician gives you a threatening diagnosis. You do when your grade school principal is hovering over you, yelling at the top of his lungs, angrier than you've ever seen him before in your life.

Is being scared then a phenomenon of childhood? Clearly it has its roots there. We never completely outgrow it. No matter how old we mature, with the right stimulus, we can be made to feel like the scared child again. It is most apparent in situations with anger in the absence of threat.

Years ago *Macbeth*[3] was being performed in New York City's Lincoln Center theater in the round. The actors were intensely convincing. The entire audience was caught up in the play. At one particularly tense moment I rubbed my knuckle against my lip and shifted my focus from the stage to the audience to relieve the anxiety I was feeling.

I was stunned by what I saw. Virtually every member of the audience had some part of their hand (or playbill, or ticket, or gloves) touching their lips, same as me. It was an amazing sight. I wished I could have captured it in a photo.

Was it coincidental? Of course not. Look for it yourself. This oral reassurance[4], a vestige of infancy, the security of our mother's nipple, is a salient manifestation of the anxiety the audience was feeling. It wasn't the only one. An astute observer could have noticed increased heartbeat, breathing, sweating, blinking, and licking of lips[5].

Why were we all so uncomfortable? There was no threat here. There wasn't even a fear of the unknown. Most of us were familiar with the play. We knew what was going to happen and when. Yet, we were all still scared because people were screaming at each other. They seemed angry. Their anger made us uncomfortable.

If you expose a child of any age to a movie that they're not old enough to handle, at what point do they get upset? At the precise moment that someone on the screen gets angry. If the child is pre-verbal, then it doesn't matter who is angry or why. The actor in question might be the hero screaming good-naturedly. The baby cries nevertheless.

In a similar scenario, our twin girls, toddlers at the time, were fast asleep in the back seat of our car. My wife turned on Howard Stern, a popular radio host who is funny in a sarcastic, biting manner. Immediately both girls woke up crying. "I don't like that man!," they both cried. "He's very angry."

The girls were right. Howard Stern and other comedians in his mode, (Imus, Don Rickles, Sam Kinnison, Roseanne Barr, Jack E. Leonard, Richard Pryor, Joan Rivers, Bobcat Goldthwait, Sandra Bernhart, Phyllis Diller, Judy Tenuto, Jack Carter, Chris Tucker, Richard Belzer, Dennis Miller, Chris Rock, to pick diverse examples), radiate anger. As adults, we ignore the anger and focus on the humor. As children, we can't.

With an older child, the content and context of the anger is more critical in determining their threshold of fear. An older child is less likely to cry. Instead they'll leave the theater, put their fingers in their ears, or bury their heads in their parent's laps. Don't they know they are in no way threatened? Of course they do. Does it help when a parent says: "It's only a movie."? Of course not.

I remember my own children scared by the angry villainess in *The Little Mermaid*. They had seen the movie before. They knew it was a cartoon. They knew that she died in the end. They had drawn her likeness themselves. They had seen the actress dubbing her voice. Nevertheless, the anger remained.

> "Take a bone from a dog: what remains?" (said the Red Queen).
> Alice considered. "The bone wouldn't remain . . . the dog wouldn't remain: it would come to bite me—and I'm sure I wouldn't remain!"
> "Then you think nothing would remain?" said the Red Queen . . .
> "Wrong, as usual, the dog's temper would remain . . .
> The dog would lose its temper . . . Then if the dog went away, **its temper would remain!**"[6]

In college I had a neighbor with a large German Shepherd. The dog was penned in the back yard. The chain link fence was eight feet high. It was apparent to everyone, except the dog, that he couldn't get over it. The dog was effectively harmless. Nevertheless the dog attacked every passing pedestrian, following every step, snarling and barking as loudly as caninely possible.

While I understand German, I don't understand German Shepherd, so I don't know for a fact what the dog was saying. I don't understand Portuguese either, but I know when a Portuguese is angry. This dog was angry. Though I was in no way practically threatened, I always felt that way. So did everyone else.

Most people walked on the very periphery of the sidewalk, not that it made the least bit of difference to the dog. Many people learned to cross the street. (The dog's sphere of influence in his mind extended only to the curb.)

All people disliked walking past that yard. Anger phobia commonly occurs in our own back yard.

Rochelle couldn't sleep if ever a member of her church gave her a frosty reception. It didn't matter who. It didn't matter why. It didn't even matter if the snub was intended. She couldn't abide the thought that someone was angry at her.

She was hardly in a position to be threatened by their anger. She was smarter and wealthier than anyone. She knew it, and so did they. Nor was she so enamored of them that their rejection threatened her self-esteem. On the contrary, she thought very little of them. Truth be told, *she* was usually angry at them. *That* she could tolerate. The reverse she couldn't.

Rochelle is an excellent example of why anger is so frightening. It seems paradoxical that Rochelle was simultaneously so disconcerted by others' anger and yet so angry herself. To Rochelle's neighbors, it would seem unbelievable to describe Rochelle as angry.

On the surface, Rochelle was polite and considerate, to excess. When someone moved into the community, she was the first to greet them, invariably with enough provisions for several meals. When someone lost a loved one, she was the first one over to help out. When she and her husband were invited out, her gift was invariably the nicest. It wasn't just the most expensive. It was also selected with the most thought for the hostess' taste. Subsequently, Rochelle's thank you note was prompt and faultless.

When Rochelle had others over, she reviewed the menu with each guest, in case there was an aversion of which she was unaware. She always served three different cakes for dessert, even if she was only having one other family over. One was chocolate, the most popular. The second was fruit, in case someone didn't like chocolate. The third was dietetic. (Rochelle's family invariably wound up eating the latter two in the following days.)

The day guests came, Rochelle's family was forbidden from using any of the entertaining rooms for fear of getting them dirty. The paradox wasn't lost on her children: "Mom, you don't even like these people! What difference does it make if I leave a smudge?"

The paradox was precisely the point. It is always the angriest who are the most frightened of others' anger. It is the result of the cycle of fear and anger. The cycle starts with my anger.

I am angry at you. Why I am angry at you is irrelevant. Perhaps I'm jealous of you. You have something that I don't, but feel that I deserve. Perhaps I like you more than you like me. Perhaps you don't treat me as well as I think you should. Perhaps I consider myself better than you and I resent your being on my level, the case with Rochelle. "A nobleman is angry if he be insulted by a peasant. If a peasant is insulted by a nobleman, anger does not ensue, but only sorrow."—St. Thomas Aquinas.

Though I keep it to myself, my anger is always with me. I might share my reasons with people I trust, my family and close friends. Yet, my wishes and fantasies, i.e. your pain, loss, humiliation and death, I share with no one, at times not even myself. It's just too ugly, too sadistic. I can't tell anyone because I know it would reflect poorly on me.

Even when my psychiatrist asks me how I would feel if something terrible happened to you, I say all the right things. I say I don't want anything bad to happen to you, or anyone else. But when my psychiatrist persists and describes detailed, catastrophic scenarios befalling you, I can't help but smile. I explain that I smile *not* because I want them to happen, but only because they're so preposterous that they're funny.

What happens when I'm with you? I couldn't be nicer, more polite or more solicitous. If someone who knows my true feelings questions my seeming hypocrisy, my answer is: "Because that's the way I was brought up," or "That's the Christian thing to do," or "I'm above that."

The unattractive reality is, my angry feelings toward you are *not* an aberration. We all have competitive feelings towards our neighbors, acquaintances, friends, even total strangers. We derive pleasure from their misfortune. The Germans even had a name for it, schadenfreude. (No relation to Sigmund.) At times we derive more pleasure from our competitor's loss than our own gain. Innumerable Boston fans savor a Yankee loss even more than a Red Sox win.[7] "I can endure my own despair, but not another's hope."[8]

Schadenfreude increases in direct proportion to the perceived status of the victim of the misfortune. The wealthier, more celebrated, more powerful they are, the more we enjoy their downfall. When Martha Stewart, Leona Helmsley or Ivan Boesky go to jail, it is far more audience pleasing than when Tom, Dick or Harry do. As Thomas Fuller wrote: "Anger makes a rich man hated . . . a poor man scorned."

Schadenfreude even empowers gossip. Whether it turns out to be true or not, we get a thrill when we hear rumors of a dalliance or a divorce. As Dorothy Parker said: "If you have nothing good to say about anyone, come sit next to me." The inevitable price of success is the creation of an audience eagerly anticipating your downfall. Standing on a pedestal precipitates the same onlooker reaction as standing on a ledge: "Jump! Jump!"

Like our Disneyphilic Barry, Rochelle's anger was unusual, and consequently symptomatic, only because of its degree. My anger towards you is not something to be proud of, but it's not something that can be denied either.

What happens if you get angry at me? It could be because in one foolish, unguarded, possibly intoxicated, moment I revealed my true feelings; it could be because one of my confidantes betrayed by trust; it could be because you saw through my saccharine facade; or it could be because you really are no good scum, as I've known all along.

Why you're angry at me is also largely irrelevant. As Ben

Franklin[9] said: "Anger is never without a reason, but seldom with a good one." The fact is, you are. If you're angry at me, I can only assume that you're going to want to do to me all those devastating things that I've been wanting to do to you. I have to assume that your anger and aggressive wishes are commensurate with mine. What a frightening thought.

A cabbie on a narrow country road had to brake because of a bicyclist hogging the road. The driver muttered: "I should hit him. Putting him in the hospital would teach him a lesson." After the cyclist pulled over, the cabbie let him know what she thought of his road etiquette. He seemed startled, but said nothing in reply. Two hundred yards later she came to a red light. As she watched in her rear view mirror the cyclist come closer, she grew increasingly nervous. As he was about to reach her, she tore through the intersection, though the light hadn't yet changed. She explained: "Who knows what a stupid son of a bitch like that might do?" The cyclist had never given any indication of what was on his mind. The driver only knew what was on hers.

Since we are intimately familiar with the depth of our own anger, we project an identical ferocity onto our perceived adversary. Indeed we can be so panic-stricken that we will do absolutely anything to avoid that catastrophic alternative, at times leading to "panic attacks."

The Freudian version of this cycle goes back to childhood. We adore our mother. We wish her to ourselves. We resent having to share her with our fathers. (Reverse the genders if you're female.) We unconsciously wish our father dead or impotent. (The word has more than one meaning.) The very thought frightens us so, we go out of our way to be respectful to him.

Invariably however, at some point we misbehave and our father gets angry at us. (In unfortunate cases, we don't have to.) What happens when our father gets angry at us? We're overwhelmed with fear. We can only assume that our father will want to kill us (or castrate us, if we're really into Freud) identical to our Oedipal wishes towards him.

Freud in fact postulated[10] that all human emotions could be neatly divided into three parts, Id, Ego and Superego. Our Id contains all our instinctual drives including sex, greed, hunger and anger. Both our desire for our mother and our hatred of our father are driven by our Id.

Our Superego is continually struggling against our Id. It contains our conscience and our many fears, both rational and neurotic. It prevents us from sinning, but also, at times, from enjoying ourselves.

Our Ego is our conscious self, constantly striving to balance between the libidinal Id and the puritanical Superego. Freud compared it to a rider reining in the superior strength of the Id-driven horse[11], similar to Plato comparing the mind to a charioteer trying to control a horse called "appetite which is ugly, hot-blooded, deaf and hard to control."[12] "Anger is like a full-hot horse."[13]—William Shakespeare. Freud, Plato and Shakespeare all understood how dangerous that horse could be.

A famous family therapist named Evander was ironically obsessed with a member of his own family, his brother, Alexander. Evander couldn't sleep, or enjoy his success. A decade earlier he had been the executor of their father's estate. Their father had left the family home to Alexander, and the family business to Evander. At the time of death the business had been worth considerably more than the home. Alex claimed the split was unfair, that the father had intended an even division of his assets.

Though Alex's claim was questionable, and legally baseless, Van chose to mollify his younger brother by voluntarily giving him a generous lump sum of money. At the time Alex was pleased, but since then, because of his declining fortunes, Alex insisted that he had been cheated out of his inheritance. Every chance he got, he complained to Van. Sometimes he was sarcastic; sometimes he was serious; he was always bitter. Inevitably the brothers grew estranged.

On the one hand, Alex's absence was no loss to Van. He'd always considered Alex selfish and mean. Truth be told, he had hated his brother as long as he could remember. On the other hand he was irreversibly convinced that Alex would succeed in destroying him. He tortured himself with scenarios of Alex starting an ugly lawsuit. As he tried to fall asleep, he would be preparing for a merciless cross-examination. He could visualize the humiliating headlines in the tabloids at his expense. He would literally wince at the imagined pain and embarrassment that his wife and children would suffer.

How realistic was Van's obsession? Like most obsessions, it had but a kernel of truth, and ten tons of doomsday fantasies overlaid. It's true that anyone can sue anyone. It was also true however that Alex had signed a general release when Van originally paid him, and, at this point, no money with which to pursue such a suit. The likelihood of his even starting it was infinitesimal. The likelihood of the imagined catastrophic consequences was zero. It didn't matter. In his mind, Van understood the reality of the situation. In his heart he continued to anticipate Armageddon. Why?

Because everything that Van feared *from* his brother, he had previously wished *on* his brother. The pain, embarrassment and humiliation were all very familiar. Before, they had been in his daydreams. Now, they were in his nightmares.

Why had he wished such suffering on his only sibling? His negative feelings about his brother were only part of the story. There was also the fact that he identified his brother with his father. Everyone agreed that while Van was the spitting image of his industrious mother, Alex was a virtual clone of his father, lazy, mean and selfish. Revealingly, and not coincidentally, Van had had a less intense version of this obsession years earlier. He had developed an obsessive fear of his supervising analyst during his training. Not surprisingly, Van had despised the man, considering him lazy, mean and selfish.

Yet, it was only in discussing Alex, that Van was able to candidly evaluate his father. When asked about his father previously, Van had described him in unremarkable terms. Before his father's death, Van had been too scared to acknowledge his hatred. After his death, he had been too guilty. Instead he had displaced his Oedipal anger and fear onto the most appropriate candidate.

One need not be aware of Freud to realize that the fear of anger indeed has its roots in childhood. A child need not be aware of Oedipus to realize how dependent he is on his parents. Their power comes not merely from their dominating size, but also from their absolute necessity. To a child, a parent's anger implies the threat of abandonment, and *that* is a truly terrifying thought.

My medical school roommate, Mark[14], the youngest of four brothers, was, by all accounts, a spoiled brat. When he was nine, his family drove across the country. He complained every mile of the way. He wanted his television. He wanted his air conditioner. He wanted his own room. He was a human version of the impossible comic strip character, Calvin[15]. As they drove through a Iowa cornfield, his father was trying to explain the concept of farming. Mark wouldn't let up. "I'm bored!" he continually shouted. "Why can't we get the Dodgers on the radio?!"

Finally his father abruptly braked, stopping the car in the middle of a desolate highway. Without a word he went to the back, picked out Mark's suitcase and heaved it twenty yards into the rows of corn. He then picked Mark up and threw him on the side of the road. He got back in the car, and sped away. Ten minutes later he returned. Mark got into the car without a peep. For the rest of that trip, Mark was the best-behaved boy in the family.

Similarly Bjorn Borg[16] wrote[17]: "Once I was like John

McEnroe . . . swearing and throwing rackets. Real bad temper . . . Then, when I was 13, . . . My parents locked my racket in a cupboard for six months . . . It was terrible. But it was a very good lesson. I never opened my mouth on the court again. I still get really mad but I keep my emotions inside."

The parents' anger need not be focused on the child to be threatening. Children are petrified by the sound of their parents arguing because their parents' relationship is the foundation of their existence. When parents fight, that foundation is threatened. The child naturally assumes that if the parents' relationship ends, the family ends, and there's no one to take care of the child. It's no wonder then, that every child is scared of their parents' anger. It's also no wonder that precise fear should remain with us, to some degree, all of our lives.

That fear can be recapitulated in adults. For example, if a partnership breaks up, and consequently a company folds, there's no one to provide for the loyal, lifetime employee. This fear can understandably turn to panic in a recession, or with an older employee. On a mammoth scale, this was experienced by hundreds of thousands of employees threatened by the scandals of Enron, Arthur Anderson, WorldCom, Tyco, ImClone and Adelphia. They had been betrayed by their parents.

If you think back to your original three answers, and to your scariest moment, you'll likely discover that one of your answers involved your parent. Furthermore, another answer probably focused on a parent surrogate (a boss, a teacher, a supervisor, a spouse).

Interestingly, it wasn't Freud the psychiatrist who first described the reciprocal nature of anger and fear. In 1872 Charles Darwin[18] argued that "rage," as he called it, is the normal healthy defensive response to any threat. He felt that this was the case in the entire animal kingdom, particularly including man.

Our fascination with, and fear of, anger of course predates even Darwin. The Bible is full of anger and it's not limited to mere mortals. The father we fear is often spelled with a capital "F". Biblical scholars are extremely familiar with the concept of the wrath of God. "And when God is angry at you, He will close the heaven, so there will be no rain, so the earth will bear no food, and you will quickly perish from the good land that God gave you."[19] Divine anger bears repercussions. If you anger God, you not only get expelled from Paradise, but you also risk having the entire world destroyed in a flood, or other natural disaster.

God's punishment can be sharply localized as well. Superstitions can be culture-specific, but still delusional. "Zar" is commonly seen in the Middle East and North Africa where you're convinced that you're possessed by an evil spirit, similar to the Dybbuks[20] or exorcisms[21] of literary and cinematic fame. "Mal de Ojo," literally the "evil eye," found in Latin America, is a delusion wherein you're doomed by a curse. God can destroy you in so many different ways.

From the dawn of civilization until today, the need to appease God's anger is central to many societies. The appeasement need not be as destructive as the legendary sacrifice of the virgin to quell the volcano. It can be as healthy as charity and prayer. It can operate on an individual basis, rather than on a societal basis. Many feel they have their own personal relationship with God, often in the form of an angel, one reason why *Highway to Heaven*, *7ᵗʰ Heaven* and *Touched By An Angel* were television successes.

Unfortunately that relationship can include the aforementioned anger-fear cycle. In some adults the reciprocal anger that had previously been present with their parents, has now been projected upon their God. Satan, the embodiment of evil to all, and anger to some, was originally an angel.

The relationship between fear, anger and God has occupied philosophers forever. In ancient Rome, Statius stated: "Primus in orbe deos fecit timor." ("It was fear that first made gods in the world.") Karl Marx similarly called religion "the opiate of the masses," implying that a belief in God relieved not only our fear, but also our anger. Freud famously claimed that all religious practices were nothing more than neurotic superstitions,[22] designed to falsely reassure us that God wouldn't let anything bad happen to us. Statius, Marx and Freud, skeptics all, would still acknowledge the curative power of the belief. God, the omniscient solution, must be commensurately omnipotent to the omnipresent fear.

A common, clinical example of the God-anger-fear relationship occurs in Hypochondriasis. Consciously, or not, many hypochondriacs fear God's retribution.

An oncologist is convinced that every time he feels something peculiar in his belly, it indicates stomach cancer. Countless clean endoscopies have been unsuccessful in alleviating his fears. Not coincidentally, his hypochondriacal obsessions invariably follow his eating lobster. He was raised in an orthodox Jewish family and never even tasted lobster until he was 30. Although he is now no longer remotely kosher, (his wife and children aren't Jewish), his appetite for lobster is still accompanied by his childhood revulsion. Nevertheless, on occasion he orders it. Why? "To teach God a lesson." Sometimes he finds himself so angry at a God-given injustice, (as a cancer specialist, he inevitably witnesses many), he feels he has to get even. Eating lobster is his revenge.

All this he understood himself. I suggested that his obsession with stomach cancer was his fear of God striking back. He dismissed it as "the usual psychiatric bullshit." (I sometimes hate treating physicians.)

How was the problem resolved? He eventually came to the conclusion that he was "allergic" to lobster. That explained the uncomfortable sensations that he was feeling. Sure enough, he informed me, as soon as he started avoiding lobster, the sensations disappeared. Yet, I had witnessed an occasion when he had unknowingly eaten a lobster-laden dish, and not felt anything. How did his allergy theory account for that? I didn't ask. He had "solved" his problem. Unfortunately, most anger-fear problems are not so easily resolved.

It is hardly coincidental that our pain is always directly proportional to our fear. We wake up with a pain in our chest. As soon as we notice it, we pray to God that it's not a heart attack, or, perish the thought, cancer. That fear exacerbates the pain, which in turn worsens the fear, creating a pain-fear cycle, a proximate root of hypochondriasis. Until we can see our physician, we are obsessed with the pain, and often incapacitated by its severity. Yet, the instant we are examined and reassured that it's only a muscle strain, the pain disappears. Even innocuous diagnostic procedures[23] will be painful if the diagnosis is feared.

A dramatic example of the cycle occurred with Tamara, a celebrated model-actress. At the age of 17 Tamara had been raped. Three years later she developed an obsession and phobia of AIDS. She was unshakably convinced that the rapist had infected her. Negative HIV tests succeeded only in temporarily alleviating her anxiety. A psychiatrist diagnosed a post-traumatic stress disorder and put her on medication. In time her dosage had increased to the point that it hindered her memorizing her scripts. She sought a second opinion.

I was intrigued by the three-year lapse between the actual trauma and the onset of symptoms. What happened during those three years? For one thing, prior to the symptoms starting, she purchased her own apartment. Did leaving her family create a separation anxiety that triggered the hitherto dormant traumatic reaction? A better question was, why did she move out?

She said the primary reason was that her success finally allowed her to purchase a dream condo in the city. I was struck by the word "primary." Was there a secondary reason? There was, but she didn't want to talk about it. Bingo!

When a patient says they don't want to talk about something, they're saying how painful it is for them to confront it. They're also saying how powerful, and probably symptom-producing, the issue must be.

Tamara moved out because she had woken up one night and found her father, drunk, naked and aroused, in her bed. Physically, Tamara had only been raped once, at age 17. Emotionally, she had been raped twice. It was the second rape that had precipitated her overwhelming rage and, in turn, her equally overwhelming guilt, which caused her obsession. She didn't need medication; she needed to deal with her anger towards her father.

Fear and anger are two sides of the same coin. As such, they are always in proportion to each other. As much as, God knows, we might want to take that coin out of circulation, we can't. Our anger is a permanent stain, that as Lady Macbeth[24] discovered, no amount of washing can remove.

The reality is we will all sometimes have scary moments. The reality is that we will all occasionally be frightened by anger. The reality is we will (almost) all pray to God to relieve that dark fear. The most important reality of all is that usually we can do much more than just pray. By understanding our fear, we can also begin, God help us, to illuminate that darkness.

> *"He best keeps from anger who remembers that God is always looking upon him."*
> —Plato, (427-347 B.C.E.)

Notes

---

[1] *Genesis* XVIII: 30.

[2] In times of emergency, or even perceived emergency, blood flow is

diverted from non-essential functions like digestion. The gastrointestinal tract's sudden loss of blood will frequently result in involuntary urination, defecation or vomiting.

[3] *Macbeth*, William Shakespeare.

[4] Oral reassurance is the primary reason that smoking is so addictive. It would be significantly easier, for example, to withdraw from drinking nicotine than to stop putting a cigarette in your mouth continuously. Chances are that your colleague who chews on straws is a former smoker.

[5] These measurable somatic manifestations of anxiety, such as pulse, respiration rate and galvanic skin response are what comprise so-called "lie detectors." Since they measure nervousness, rather than truthfulness, their usefulness is limited, and they are inadmissible in court.

[6] *Through The Looking Glass, Alice in Wonderland* (1862), Lewis Carroll.

[7] "I went to Fenway for a series against New York, and I'll never forget listening to Sox fans chant, 'Yankees suck! Yankees suck!' Thing was, it was an interleague series. The Red Sox were playing the Mets."—Sports Illustrated, July 1, 2002.

[8] William Walsh (1663-1708).

[9] *Poor Richard's Almanack*, from whence this quote appears, contains Ben Franklin's philosophy of life expressed in pithy memorable adages.

[10] *The Ego and The Id* (1923), Sigmund Freud.

[11] When in the throes of passion, someone acknowledges that "a stiff dick (or a lubricated vagina) has no conscience!," they are unrealizingly invoking both Freud and Plato.

[12] *Phaedrus*, Plato.

[13] *Henry VII*—Act I, Scene 1, William Shakespeare.

[14] Mark is a real name. The first. The others have been pseudonyms, for the sake of confidentiality.

[15] The whimsical comic strip, *Calvin and Hobbes*, about a boy and his tiger doll, by Bill Watterson, was ironically named after two notably unwhimsical philosophers, John Calvin and Thomas Hobbes.

[16] Bjorn Borg and John McEnroe were contemporaneous tennis champions. Though their records were similarly brilliant, their

court demeanor could not have been more different. Whereas Borg was cool as ice, never betraying any emotion, McEnroe was "super-brat," better known for his tantrums than his victories. Not coincidentally McEnroe would only control himself for one opponent: "Against Borg I'll always behave" because of "the respect I have for Bjorn."

[17] *The New York Times Magazine,* August 30, 1981.

[18] *The Expression of the Emotions in Man and Animals* (1872), Charles Darwin, D. Appleton and Co.

[19] *Deuteronomy* XI:17.

[20] *The Dybbuk* was a famous play by Shalom Ansky that was a staple of the Yiddish theater. The theme of Dybbuks is recurrent in Jewish literature.

[21] *The Exorcist* (1971) William Peter Blatty, Harper Collins Press was made into a successful movie in 1973 directed by William Friedkin. It was so popular that it was released again 25 years later.

[22] *Obsessive Acts and Religious Practices* (1907), Sigmund Freud, The Hogarth Press

[23] Dr. Eugene Carragee, director of Stanford's Orthopedic Spine Center, has reported that patients suffering from anxiety or depression are far more likely to find diagnostic discography painful.

[24] *Macbeth,* William Shakespeare.

PART II

LIGHT ONE CANDLE

PART II

CHAPTER ONE

And Cain was Very Angry

Feeling the Anger

"And Cain was very angry, and his face fell. And Cain rose to his brother Abel and slew him." [1]

I hate soap operas. I despise them. I cannot abide contrived melodrama wherein the virtuous heroine is clueless to prevent the painfully obvious, dastardly deed of the villain.

If Terry's life had been a movie, I would have walked out. Terry was the kind of person who made everyone proud. She was a devout Catholic who reflected well on Catholicism. She was a pediatric nurse who gave nursing a good name. She was a devoted mother and wife whose children and husband understandably cherished her.

Unfortunately, Terry had a younger sister. Sherry had always been indulged by their parents. Terry's parents were farmers who didn't have the time or the ability to supervise Sherry. It was Terry's responsibility. If Sherry's homework was unsatisfactory, it was Terry's fault. If Sherry did poorly on a test, it meant that Terry had failed. When Terry went away to college, Sherry dropped out of high school.

Terry escaped to the big city. Sherry got pregnant. She married the father. Her parents built them a house next door.

For their parents' twenty-fifth anniversary Terry and Sherry decided to purchase them the big screen television they had always wanted. Terry bought it on her credit card.

Sherry was supposed to reimburse her. She never did. On Terry's next visit home, the TV was nowhere to be found. Terry asked why. Her parents explained that they had allowed Sherry to take it, "for the grandchildren." The TV was only the beginning. Every time Terry visited she noticed another prized possession gone. She didn't bother to ask why or where.

Sherry wasn't just stealing from her parents. She would promise one of Terry's children an expensive toy. Terry's child would be elated. In front of the child Sherry would ask Terry to purchase and deliver the toy, and, "of course" Sherry would reimburse her. Terry would buy the gift. She didn't want to disappoint her child or to destroy her relationship with her only aunt. Over the years Sherry owed Terry over $20,000.

It got worse. Sherry needed $2000 for an abortion. She couldn't ask her husband because he would know it wasn't his child. If Terry didn't give it to her, Sherry would ask their parents. Terry knew that they would be devastated. They, like Terry, were adamantly opposed to abortion. She "loaned" Sherry another $2000.

Sherry announced that she was coming to stay with Terry for two weeks, alone. She didn't come alone. She came with a waiter ten years her junior. They didn't stay with Terry. They spent their two weeks in a "honeymoon" hotel. For the sake of Sherry's children and her own parents, Terry provided the alibi. She didn't comprehend why Sherry had bothered to visit her in the first place, until she got the hotel bill. Sherry had "borrowed" a credit card.

Had enough? Can you see the soap opera analogy? Can you understand why Terry sought psychiatric help?

Guess again. In her first session Terry never once mentioned Sherry. Instead she complained bitterly about her own husband, Sean. He was insensitive. He was unreasonable. He was complaining about all the money that Sherry had borrowed. He didn't understand Terry's love of her parents, how she needed to protect them. If not for their children, Terry would divorce Sean. She couldn't live with his pressure. She hated Sean.

The more she spoke, the more it became obvious that there was nothing wrong with Sean. If anything, he was too generous. (No wonder Terry married him. He was just like Terry.) He wasn't asking to retrieve the money, though they needed it. He wasn't asking to press charges for the stolen credit card, though he had to pay for Sherry's "honeymoon." All he wanted was Terry's assurance that she wouldn't "loan" Sherry any more money.

Terry was furious. It was amazing to behold how much anger was inside this quiet angel of mercy. It was frightening to realize how inaccessible that anger was. "There is no passion that so shakes the clarity of our judgment as anger."[2]

If I tried to defend Sean, Terry would get angry at me instead. Terry was too polite to express it directly. Instead she would say things like: "I should expect that men would stick together," or "You just don't get it." Her remarks wouldn't be said with venom, but rather with a resigned condescension, like Ronald Reagan saying "Now there you go again" in the 1980 Presidential debate. The venom would appear if I dared to question, no matter how delicately, the behavior of her sister, or worse, her parents. "When you're in their shoes, then and *only then*, can *you* second guess them!" "Let he who is without sin cast the first stone!" At that point she emulated not Reagan, but Munch[3].

I even half-heartedly attempted a single fruitless session of marital therapy. It succeeded only in proving G. K. Chesterton's observation that "the full potential of human fury cannot be reached until a friend of both parties tactfully intervenes."[4] That disaster, full of sound and fury, persuaded me to recommend group therapy to Terry. I wasn't sure it would work; I didn't expect her to agree, but frankly I couldn't think of any other option. To my grateful surprise she did agree.

What options do we have, when we, like Terry, are consumed by anger? The simplest, quickest, most cost-efficient solution, drugs, are *not* an option. Dr. Myrl Manley[5], and many other psychiatrists, have pointed out that anger is the only emotion that we can't medicate[6].

The most common approach is complete **DENIAL**. No matter how extreme the provocation, no matter how obvious our ire, somehow it seems more civilized, more mature, not to get angry. No matter how hard the slap, we are admonished to turn the other cheek. "Blessed are the merciful: for they shall obtain mercy."[7] "Good to forgive; best to forget!"[8]

Denial is familiar to every physician. It's the worst part of our job. I remember the mother of a comatose college girl pointing out to me how "thrilled" her daughter was to see me. I can't forget the wife who had seen her husband shot dead in front of her, beating my chest with her fists irate that I was lying to her, telling her that her husband hadn't survived[9]. I'll always remember my father, on his deathbed, asking me to take care of his first child, who had been murdered by the Nazis 50 years earlier. Fortunately, outside the hospital, examples of denial are more mundane:

> Your son has just "borrowed" your brand-new $100,000 car that the dealer delivered today. He's driven it into the lake. "Dad/Mom. I know how angry you are." "I'm not angry at you, son. I'm just very disappointed."

> "Senator Smooth, your opponent accuses you of income tax evasion, wife beating, treason and child molestation. Do you have any comment?" "Yes. I feel very sorry for him that he's reduced himself to this."

What do you think the Senator said in private when he first heard his opponent's charges? "Oh, I feel so sorry for him." Or "That blanking blank! I'm going to make him sorry he was ever born!"?

What was *your* instantaneous reaction when you heard that your new car was in the lake? An expression of disappointment in your son? Or a single word with four letters and several exclamation points?

Whom are we kidding? Of course we're angry. Not only that, we have every right to be. There's nothing wrong, uncivilized or immature in expressing it. Yes, we *eventually* have to move past our anger. *Eventually* we have to accept the fact that the rich Corinthian leather upholstery, that we paid through our nose for, will always smell of mildew. Right *now* however, we're angry. As unhealthy as it would be to remain perpetually angry over an accident which damaged only an inanimate object, it is equally unhealthy to deny the emotion entirely.

The anger is there. If we try to deny it, it will only come out in a far more destructive manner: "I told you son, I'm not angry at you, only disappointed. However, as an expression of my disappointment, I've decided not to pay for your college education after all."

Alternatively: "Where the hell were you? How could you let him take the keys to the car? It's all *your* goddamned fault! You should have put the keys away! I can't count on you for anything!" When we blame our spouse for our children's irresponsibilities, (or in Terry's case for our sibling's), we're displacing the anger that we have denied.

DISPLACEMENT, our second option, can go in any direction. Just as often we displace onto our kids the anger that we're feeling for our spouse. God save any child who innocently knocks on his parents' bedroom door while they're in the midst of a fight.

Clichéd textbook displacement examples tend to be "trickle down" in nature. My boss' boss is angry at his wife, so he yells at my boss. My boss is angry at his boss, so he yells at me. I yell at my spouse because I'm angry at my boss. My spouse yells at our kid because she's angry at me. My kid kicks the dog[10] because he's angry at my spouse. The dog barks at the cat because he's angry at my kid. The cat scratches up the furniture, ultimately getting even with all of us.

Alysa's father was a teacher. Their town was so small that for two years Alysa was in his class. Frequently the class would get so rowdy that even her father's yelling couldn't quell the noise. On occasion her father would get so frustrated that he would slap a student across the face. The student was always Alysa, though she had been the only one sitting there quietly.

Obviously Alysa was the only student whose parent wouldn't complain about corporal punishment. Just as obviously Alysa's father was engaging in displacement.

In the public arena displacement is clearly apparent both during and following sporting contests. During the game the object of ire is usually the umpire or referee. Managers or coaches who have been famously ejected from games because they couldn't control their temper include Earl Weaver, Lou Piniella, Bobby Valentine, Red Auerbach and, of course, Bobby Knight. In reality, the manager who always remains calm[11] is more the anomaly than the rule.

Even more striking is when the manager or player lashes out at the press after a game. In one televised meltdown Kansas City Manager Hal McRae started violently flinging anything he could get his hands on all over his office bloodying the face of a reporter. It need not be mentioned that these displacement tirades only occur after a team loses.

Our third option is almost as common, and almost as bad, **SUPPRESSION**. Rochelle, in our last chapter, was a perfect example. We're aware of our anger. We acknowledge it to ourselves, possibly to others, but we don't do anything about it. We suppress it. We push it back. We sweep it under the carpet. In the short run, it usually works.

In the long run, it never does. Like Rochelle, we wind up directing our anger inwards. We become symptomatic. Our symptoms might include anxiety, obsessions, compulsions, depression, even phobias. An example of a phobia, an exaggerated fear, is the dog phobia mentioned in our last chapter.

It would make perfect sense for someone to have a dog phobia if they had been traumatized by a dog. As we said, getting burnt creates a fear of fire. Interestingly, most people who have been bitten by a dog do *not* have a resultant phobia. They have instead a healthy respect. More interestingly, most people who *do* have dog phobias have *never* been attacked by a dog. Then why do they have it?

Because a dog is unlike a cat, a mouse, a gerbil, a rat, a cockroach, a horse, a parakeet, a cow, a goat, a pig, or a chicken. Unlike any other animal that man commonly comes into contact with, dogs express anger. If you're overly frightened of anger, then you'll probably have, to some degree, an exaggerated fear of dogs. You will probably also have a phobia of other angry animals. Fortunately, unless you're a park ranger, you never come into contact with mountain lions, grizzly bears or wolves, so you're probably not even aware of it.

Obsessions, non-constructive thoughts that continue to bother us, most commonly involve either anger directly or the fear of something bad happening to us. My classmate Eduardo was a good example of the former. Evander, the family therapist, was a perfect example of the latter. Compulsions are, in a sense, obsessive acts. We check the gas, the locks, the alarm, etc., because we're convinced that if we don't, as a result, something bad will befall us. We're convinced that if we shake a hand, or drink from a water fountain, we will become infected. Understandably obsessions and compulsions frequently occur simultaneously.

Anxiety's relationship with anger was explained in "A Bitter Price," (Part I, Chapter 2). Depression's relationship to anger is even more illuminating.

You are angry at me because I treat you poorly. You are aware of your anger. You feel it is justified. Nevertheless, to avoid the unpleasant consequences, you suppress it. You don't express it to me. What's going to happen? I'm going to continue treating you poorly. How is that going to make you feel? What is that going to do to your self-esteem? One need not be a psychiatrist to realize that the most direct cause of depression is decreased self-esteem. Repeating the aforementioned insightful observation of St. Thomas Aquinas: "If a peasant is insulted by a nobleman, anger does not ensue, but only sorrow."

In theory, your suppressed anger is irrelevant to this equation. The key ingredient is my abusive treatment of you. Emotional abuse can be every bit as traumatic as physical abuse. No one should tolerate it, whether it comes from a stranger, an authority figure, a cleric, or a loved one. Every religion believes in the Golden Rule. "Do unto others as you would have them do unto you."[12] "Love (treat) thy neighbor as thyself."[13]

If the Golden Rule is true, so must be its contrapositive— Don't allow others to do unto you, what you would not do unto them. It's not right for your friend to treat you in a manner in which you would not treat them. If you don't abuse me, why should I abuse you? There are only two possible answers. Either there is something wrong with you, i.e. you deserve to be treated this way, or, there is something wrong with me. Either you stink, or I stink.[14]

Silence is acquiescence. If you suppress your anger, if you don't say anything to me, if you allow my abuse of you to continue, then you are clearly indicating the first answer. You *deserve* to be abused this way. You stink. A stinking piece of crud obviously deserves to be depressed as well. Thus, suppressing your anger creates your depression.

Confirming this, studies[15] have shown that depressed patients have "significantly higher levels of anger"[16] than healthy controls, anxious patients and even patients with psychosomatic disorders. This is one reason why previously popular Valium, Librium, Xanax and the entire category of anxiolytics known as the Benzodiazepines, was largely supplanted by Prozac, Zoloft, Paxil, Effexor and the category of anti-depressants known as the Selective Serotonin Reuptake Inhibitors (SSRI's).[17] Anti-depressants can pharmacologically relieve the depression that inevitably accompanies the suppressed anger.

If the consequences are so severe, why would anyone allow themselves to be repeatedly abused? The answer is, as with Terry, you feel there is a higher priority. You allow yourself to be abused by a parent, or an older relative, because you feel it would be disrespectful to complain. You allow yourself to be abused by a supervisor or colleague because you feel you would be jeopardizing your job otherwise. You allow yourself to be abused by a neighbor, sibling or playmate because you don't want to rock the boat, creating waves.

You convince yourself that it's not really abuse. When your mother keeps on calling you at the office on a daily basis, even though you've repeatedly asked her not to, it's not abuse. It's an expression of her love. She can't help herself. When your supervisor keeps on calling you "honey" instead of your name, it's not abuse. He thinks he's being friendly. He says that women's names are hard for him to remember. When your poker buddy keeps on rubbing your bald head for good luck, though he knows you don't like it, it's not abuse. It's his way of being friendly.

"All animals, except man, are not subject to anger, for while it is the foe of reason, it is nevertheless born only where reason dwells."—Seneca[18] Whatever our rationalization, if we suppress our anger, we will pay a price. Like its fecal metaphor, anger is toxic and must be expelled. Either it comes out voluntarily, at a time and place of our choosing, or it comes out involuntarily.

Our fourth option is the usual result of having unsuccessfully used the third option, suppression. **EXPLOSION.**

Cain was very angry. His face fell. He said nothing. He murdered his brother.[19]

San Francisco. 1979. Dan White resigns his seat on the Board of Supervisors. Shortly thereafter he changes his mind. Nevertheless political adversary Mayor George Moscone gives his position away. White barges into City Hall, through a window to avoid metal detectors, and kills Moscone as well as opposing supervisor Harvey Milk.[20]

Texas. June 20, 2001. Andrea Yates methodically drowns her five children, seven-year-old Noah, five-year-old John, three-year-old Paul, two-year-old Luke, and six-month-old Mary, one by one in their bathtub. Each child struggled or begged for their life, but their deeply religious mother was convinced that they needed to be saved from eternal damnation.[21]

Sadly, Andrea Yates is not a rarity. Anger is extremely common in postpartum depression[22] with up to one third experiencing infanticidal, homicidal or suicidal thoughts.[23] Nor is postpartum depression limited to postpartum women. It has been seen in men, parents who adopt, even new pet owners, indeed anyone who feels overwhelmed by anger at an unremitting stress.

You suppress your anger. You build up steam. Eventually something's got to give. Finally the proverbial straw breaks the camel's back. You explode. You prove Horace's observation two millennia ago that "Anger is a brief madness."

Your mother calls you at the office one time too many. She says: "Did you hear that the postman's wife died?" You say: "I wish *you* would die! Get out of my life already." Your supervisor patronizes you one time too many. You curse him out and quit. Your friend rubs your head one time too many. You punch him in the mouth.

The explosion serves its purpose. It finally expresses your pent-up anger. For a few seconds it makes you feel incredibly better. "Take this job and shove it!" was a great title for a mediocre song. It proved so popular that it was made into a movie. Unfortunately, popularity fades, and so does your satisfaction.

Your explosion was over-kill. You don't really want your mother dead. You feel terribly guilty about what you said to her. You didn't really mean to quit. You don't have another job and you need one. By impulsively quitting, you threw away both the severance pay that you had earned and the unemployment benefits that you would have received had you been fired. By punching your friend you got yourself thrown out of a card game that you had enjoyed for years. Worse, everyone is talking about what you did, how he had to go to the hospital, how he lost his two front teeth. You and your family have become pariahs in the neighborhood you've lived in your entire life.

Your explosion has made life untenable. You have to undo it. You wind up having to apologize profusely to the very person with whom you were so furious. You pay a heavy price for your explosion.

To make amends, not only do you still speak to your mother every day in the office, but now *you* have to call *her*. You got your job back after apologizing to your supervisor both orally and in writing. You lost your seniority and this year's bonus however, and now he calls you "Sweet Cheeks," in addition to "Honey." You beg your friend's forgiveness. You pay his hospital bills, his dental bills and in addition you give him your power tool set that he always coveted. You're allowed back into both the game and the community. For good luck your friend now both rubs your head and pinches your cheek.

Life has become even worse than it was before. You're convinced that your original instinct was right. You should have kept your anger suppressed.

It's reminiscent of a Persian fable. A poacher, caught fishing in the King's lake, is offered a choice of punishments. He can either eat the six fish he caught which are now putrid, or be whipped one hundred times, or pay a fine of a thousand drachmas. The poacher opts for the fish. He eats five of them, throws up and can eat no more. He's whipped ninety times. His skin is lacerated. He can take no more. He pays the thousand drachmas.

It's the converse of having your cake and eating it too. In the end, the poacher suffered all three penalties. Exploding produces the same result.

The fifth option is better than the first four, but still far from ideal. **PASSIVE-AGGRESSIVE**. You express your anger, but you do it passive-aggressively. It still results in the termination of the relationship, but with less severe consequences.

You take your mother's phone calls at work, but you stop calling her. After you ignore her on her birthday, she gets the message. You become estranged. She has stopped calling you at the office, but it was at the price of your relationship with her. The more your supervisor patronizes you, the more you avoid him. Inevitably your evaluation reflects that. Eventually you're fired, albeit with severance and unemployment benefits. Alternately, you take another job, despite the fact that, in all other respects, it's worse. Either way your supervisor's behavior has stopped, but it was at the expense of your job. Your card playing pal's behavior bothers you so much, you avoid activities at which he'll be present. As a result he never again rubs your head, but you never again play cards with your friends.

Passive-aggressive behavior is ubiquitous. A wife is angry at her husband. She becomes too "tired" to have sex. He starts "dining" with his secretary. She starts sleeping with the milkman. Ultimately, there need not be a divorce, or even on overt expression of anger, for the marriage to come to an end. Clichéd or not, passive-aggressive behavior always provokes a passive-aggressive reaction, deteriorating into a vicious cycle.

I was once consulted by a Russian mobster. (He didn't mention his vocation before we met.) In describing his workday, he proudly demonstrated his signature collection technique. "Make believe you owe me money. I explain to you, you have two choices." He held up two meaty closed fists in front of me. "Pick one." I attempted to decline. "Come on Doc, you pick, or I pick for you. Same difference."

I pointed to his right fist. He turned it over and unfolded it. There was a large calibre bullet inside. My visceral reaction made him laugh. "Doc, here's the best part. You know what your other choice was?" He opened his left fist revealing another bullet. This Hobson's choice amused him no end.

It might appear that these five options similarly contain five bullets differing only in calibre size. They all arrive at the same undesired destination, differing only in the route. No wonder Terry's situation was so hopeless. No matter which option she took, she would have to bite the bullet.

Fortunately, for her, and for us, there is another option.

"Believe me, I have not the least sense of resentment in my heart for all the evil they speak and publish against me."
—Rabbi Jacob Joseph in 1888,
Chief Rabbi of New York City.

Notes

---

[1] *Genesis* IV: 5, 8.

[2] Michel Eyguem de Montaigne, a 16th century philosopher.

[3] In 1893 Edvard Munch created his signature painting, "The Scream."

[4] Trying to intervene in a lovers' quarrel is as wise as intervening in a dog fight. At best you'll get bitten; at worst you'll get mauled. As you lick your wounds, the realization that your injuries were unintentional is of little comfort.

The only thing worse is attempting to intervene in an internal conflict. "I don't know if I should marry him or not." "I think you should." "Of course you do, you would love for me to spend the rest of my life with a loser." Or "I don't think you should." "Of course not. You want me to be alone and miserable for the rest of my life." Intervening in an internal conflict is the best possible example of no good deed going unpunished. While you've succeeded in externalizing the conflict, you've simultaneously made yourself the object of the conflicted individual's wrath. You've accomplished nothing, and you've made yourself the scapegoat.

Questions to be avoided at all costs include: "Do I look fat in this dress?", "Would shaving my beard make me look younger?", "Do you think my husband is too heavy?", "Should I invite my despicable sister?", "Do you think I should ask for a raise?", "Should I get my breasts/penis enlarged?', and innumerable others.

[5] Dr. Myrl Manley is the director of psychiatric education at the N.Y.U. School of Medicine.

[6] It is debatable whether we can, (or should), medicate grief. While drugs can ameliorate the tears and other surface manifestations, the visceral emotion underneath remains. It is similar to prescribing Inderal to pianists or singers with performance anxiety. The superficial symptoms, like sweaty fingers or tremulous voice, are lessened, but the underlying nervousness remains.

[7] *Matthew* V:7.

[8] *La Saisiaz*, Robert Browning (1812-1889).

[9] Singer Rosemary Clooney witnessed Robert. F. Kennedy's assassination by Sirhan Sirhan in person. Nevertheless she subsequently convinced herself that the news reports of his death were a hoax, and that, in fact, he was still alive.

[10] "If you pick up a starving dog and make him prosperous, he will not bite you. That is the principle difference between a dog and a man."—Mark Twain. Dogs never displace onto man, but too often we displace our anger onto our dogs.

[11] "I used to throw my bat after striking out... Then, when I was catching, I'd see the other guys do it... It looked so silly... The thing to do is to keep your cool." Multi-World Champion New York Yankees Manager Joe Torre—*New York Times*, Oct. 5, 1981.

[12] This version of the Golden Rule is most commonly ascribed to the

Talmudic scholar, Hillel. When a skeptic demanded that he summarize the Bible succinctly, Hillel responded: "Whatever is hateful unto thee, do it not unto others. This is the whole Bible, the rest is explanation."

[13] *Leviticus* IX:18.

[14] The first thing that new lawyers are taught when they start at the Manhattan District Attorney's office is that "nuts tend to gather at the same place and time," i.e. when citizens complain about each other, often they're both crazy. In other words, in reality, frequently both you *and* I stink. As Ambrose Bierce ironically defined an "egotist": "a person of low taste, more interested in himself than in me."

[15] Department of Psychiatry, Yonsei University College of Medicine, Korea.

[16] Journal of Clinical Psychiatry, June 2002.

[17] Other important reasons for the popularity of Selective Serotonin Reuptake Inhibitors (SSRI's) are that they are more advertised, more promoted, less addictive, less dangerous and have fewer side effects.

[18] Lucius Annaeus Seneca was a Roman philosopher who wrote "On anger" and also "On self-control."

[19] *Genesis* IV:5-8.

[20] At Dan White's trial his lawyers argued that his excessive consumption of junk food had caused a "diminished mental capacity." Incredibly enough, what became known as the "Twinkie Defense" was accepted by the jury who convicted him of the lesser charge of voluntary manslaughter which carries a maximum sentence of only 7 2/3 years. This verdict was highly controversial and was particularly vilified in the homosexual community since the victim Harvey Milk had been one of the first openly homosexual political representatives.

[21] Andrea Yates' conviction on two counts of murder was highly controversial as well. She had pleaded not guilty by reason of insanity. The jury deliberated less than four hours and she was sentenced to life in prison. The verdict was particularly vilified in the feminist and psychiatric communities.

[22] *British Journal of Psychiatry*, 1968, 114:1325-1335.

[23] In Andrea Yates' case, as in many cases of postpartum depression, her anger might have been largely towards her husband, but displaced onto her children. Indeed many in the feminist community expressed the opinion that Andrea Yates' husband, who had encouraged five children in quick succession, was the true culprit, and that Andrea Yates herself was the sixth victim. The jury disagreed.

PART II

CHAPTER TWO

EXTAR

Resolving the Anger

"And God said: If you choose wisely, your anger will be lifted."[1]

"It's not so simple."
Though I use them myself, how I hate those words. More often than not I hear them in response to an obvious solution to a problem.

> "You can't hit your wife because she embarrassed you, even if it was deliberate." "It's not so simple."

> "Your eyes are yellow. You have cirrhosis, an inflammation of your liver. You need to stop drinking. Immediately." "It's not so simple."

> "The reason you can't climb the stairs is because you weigh over 350 pounds. If you don't lose weight, you'll die." "It's not so simple."

On the one hand I know they're right, to some degree. Life is never simple. On the other, I also know that when they're saying it, they're using it as a rationalization to postpone changing their behavior. It was always Terry's first line of defense.

If she said instead: "It's not so easy," she would be correct. "Simple" and "easy" are not synonymous, though they're invariably inextricably linked. Many difficult tasks in life are in fact simple, though they're never easy. Confronting our own anger is one of them.

There is, in fact, a healthy approach. You express your wishes, and your anger, directly. If necessary, you do it repeatedly. Most importantly, you make certain that your behavior corroborates your words.

It's not enough to tell your mother that you're angry that she keeps calling you at work. If you take her phone calls, if you keep talking to her, then your actions belie your words. She'll say to herself, and eventually to you, that you gave her a mixed message. She'll say if you really didn't want her to call, then why did you continue to talk to her?[2] She's right.

Consider this *simple* five-step approach:

STEP 1: Explain to your mother why it is a terrible imposition for you to talk to her at work. Explain to her that it deleteriously affects your performance. Explain to her that your boss considers it unprofessional. Explain to her that personal phone calls are explicitly forbidden in the company's written rules.[3] Explain to her it jeopardizes your job. Ask her as nicely as you can to please stop. This should be a relatively pleasant conversation. Anger need not be expressed.

STEP 2: If she persists, tell her that her continued calling is inconsiderate. Let her know that you are angry at her for ignoring your request. Let her know she is disrespecting you. Anger *need* be expressed. This conversation should not continue beyond that point. It should *not* be pleasant. If it is, it belies your expression of anger.

STEP 3: If she still continues, inform her succinctly that she leaves you no choice but not to take her phone calls at work, unless it's an emergency. Terminate the conversation immediately thereafter. This is a unilateral declaration, not a dialogue. Your ending should be abrupt. Your anger should be self-evident.

STEP 4: The next time she calls, you, or preferably your assistant, ask if it's an emergency. If she says no, you don't take the phone call. If she says yes, you take the phone call. If then, it turns out she was lying, you inform her that in the future you will not take her phone call, whether she says it's an emergency, or not.

STEP 5: The next time she calls you don't take her phone call, no matter what she claims. If you pick up the phone inadvertently, you hang up at the sound of her voice. There is nothing more for you to say.

(What happens if it really is an emergency this time? It's unfortunate, but all parents are aware of the story of the boy who cried wolf. Furthermore, your mother is not totally dependent on you. She is an adult, not a child. If she truly *is* totally dependent on you, that means she can't take care of own needs, and either she should have a full-time attendant, or she should be in a nursing home.)

Rather than translate each of the five steps to the alternative scenarios with your boss or buddy, it's more helpful to describe them generically.

STEP 1: Explaining why you don't like the manner in which they're treating you, and politely, explicitly requesting that they stop. This gives them the benefit of the doubt. It assumes that they didn't realize that they were bothering you. It allows the person to terminate the behavior without any expression of anger on either side. It is clearly the ideal way to resolve the problem.

Should you take this step even if you're 100% sure that they implicitly know that they're bothering you? Yes. Number one, people are not as sensitive to your feelings as you think they are. Number two, it avoids any recriminations or excuses when you go on to STEP 2. They can't say they didn't know it bothered you.

STEP 2: If the behavior is repeated, you express your anger, directly and unequivocally, to the person. You tell the person how angry you are, (not disappointed, not sorry), that they have persisted in this behavior after you had requested that they stop. You point out how disrespectful they are being to you.

STEP 3: If the behavior still continues, you inform the person that you will no longer tolerate it. You will take whatever steps are necessary to prevent it.

STEP 4: If the person calls your bluff, you take the action you had threatened, *no matter what.* If you don't, you will be far worse off than had you done nothing.

STEP 5: If it happens again, you respond again. Occasionally people who have known you a long time assume that when you took STEP 4, it was an aberration. They think you were proving a point, but you would never do it again.

Too often we forget that our actions speak louder than our words. When the two contradict each other, it's only our actions that are remembered. If our actions are decisive, our words can afford to be as conciliatory and generous as we choose.

Shortly after our marriage, my wife and I arranged to drive to her parents, 100 miles away, for the weekend. We were both looking forward to it until Thursday night when my wife received a phone call from her Aunt Henrietta that left her ashen-faced. I wondered what could have been said. While Henrietta, a misanthropic spinster, was loud, opinionated and judgmental, generally she had always been civil to us.

My wife said that Henrietta wanted to hitch a ride with us. I wasn't thrilled, but I still didn't understand my wife's reaction. Two hours with Henrietta in a claustrophobic compact car was not something to look forward to, but neither was it something to dread so acutely. My wife explained that Henrietta's company was not what she was dreading. *Waiting* for Henrietta was the issue.

Henrietta was notorious for always being late. We had arranged to leave at 3 P.M. to beat rush hour. If Henrietta was her usual tardy self, we wouldn't leave till after 4. As a result we would arrive after 8, rather than at 5, as we had planned. Not only would a pleasant two-hour trip turn into a four-hour nightmare, but we would also come late to a festive family dinner that we had both eagerly anticipated.

What could we do? We couldn't refuse Henrietta a ride on the basis of her reputation. We couldn't even lie if we wanted to. She knew exactly where we were going and when. My wife called her parents who commiserated. They themselves had often been delayed by Henrietta as well, but they could offer no solution.

Forewarned is forearmed. We sat down and devised a plan.

I called Henrietta back, ostensibly to tell her how happy I was that she would be joining us. She was similarly polite. I got to the point. I informed her that we would be leaving at exactly 3 P.M. to avoid traffic. Since there were other ways that she could travel (other relatives' cars, train, bus), my wife and I would assume that if she wasn't there by 3, she had changed her plans and would be coming some other way.

"No, no!" Henrietta interrupted. She was definitely coming with us, although she "might conceivably be a few minutes late." If so, we should wait for her.

I repeated our intentions. I reiterated how we hoped she could join us, but how we understood that something might come up unexpectedly and she might not be able to reach us. (This was well before cell phones.) Either way I said, we looked forward to seeing her that evening.

Friday 3 P.M. came and went. Predictably Henrietta was nowhere to be found. Finally at 3:10 P.M. we took a deep breath and, with a great deal of trepidation, pulled out of the garage. The trip was quick and pleasant, but not enjoyable. We were both too worried about the impending consequences.

When we arrived at her parents, we were pleasantly surprised at the reaction. Everyone expressed how thrilled they were that someone had finally left without Henrietta, something that every one of them had always wanted to do. We both felt better, but not good. There was still Henrietta to contend with.

She wound up taking the 4:30 train. She got to the house at 7. When she walked in, the tension was palpable. All dinner table conversation came to an abrupt halt. She angrily informed us that she had arrived at 3:01 and that the attendant had informed her that we had just left. I responded, perhaps foolishly, that we hadn't left until 3:10. She said that maybe her watch was a few minutes slow. She was still furious. We apologized for her inconvenience, to no avail.

From the time that she arrived, until she left, it was torturous for my wife and me. After her departure, the rest of the family again reassured us that we had done the right thing. We weren't sure. We were young and no match for Henrietta's anger. The fact that we subsequently discovered from the garage attendant that Henrietta, in fact, didn't arrive till 4:05, over an hour late, didn't erase our discomfort.

Several months later, the identical situation recurred. We didn't know what to do. We didn't want a recurrence of the tension. Even though we felt that we had been right, we decided that this time we would wait for her. We brought some magazines with us to the garage prepared to make the best of a bad situation. Henrietta was sitting there waiting for us.

Following that incident, Henrietta treated us with greater respect than she did any other relative. In the years before she passed away, she even started bemusedly telling the story of the time we "taught her a lesson." With everyone else however, she still came late.

To summarize the five steps:

1—(**E**)xplaining (what's bothering you)
2—E(**X**)pressing (your anger)

3—(**T**)hreatening (what you will do)
4—(**A**)cting (i.e. doing it)
5—(**R**)einforcing (i.e. doing it again)

An acronym for these five steps would be **EXTAR** which is appropriate since its effect is to EXTARnalize (creative spelling) the anger that you've been carrying around with you.

"EX"[4] is a Latin prefix which means "from." With EXTAR you've effectively *ex*pelled the anger *from* you. That, in turn, is infinitely better than beating the TAR out of yourself, which is the unfortunate alternative.

Expressing the anger is critical in every crisis, from the mundane to the sublime. Following *September 11, 2001,* a representative sample of 1,000 Americans[5] found that nine days after the attack those who felt angry were significantly more optimistic than those who felt fearful. Two months later the same sample was studied again. Half the people were exposed to anger-inducing media reports, the other half to fear-inducing media reports. Once again the angry half was significantly more optimistic. In other words, whether naturally occurring, or artificially induced, perceiving and appropriately expressing anger is healthy.

The courageous religious iconoclast Martin Luther wrote in the early 16th century: "When I am angry I can write, pray and preach well, for then my whole temperament is quickened, my understanding sharpened, and all mundane vexations and temptations gone."

A half millennium later his namesake Martin Luther King Jr., equally courageous, religious, and iconoclastic, delivered his seminal speech now familiarly know by four simple words, "I have a dream." His language that day in Washington D.C. was eloquent, indeed poetic. Yet his voice was incongruously angry. What made his delivery that day so powerful was not only the constructive aspirations in his text, but also the frustrated rage in his heart. As another Washington revolutionary, Ben Franklin, had observed: "The heart of the fool is in his mouth, but the mouth of a wise man is in his heart."

Martin Luther King Jr.'s adversarial contemporary, Malcolm X, had expressed that philosophy more candidly when he wrote[6]: "They called me 'the angriest Negro in America'. I wouldn't deny that . . . I believe in anger." As Jack Hawkins said to Charlton Heston in *Ben Hur*[7]: "Your eyes are full of hate . . . That's good. Hate keeps a man alive."

Athletes, professional as well as amateur, will often use their anger towards their adversary to motivate their training. You train harder and longer visualizing your opponent gloating in victory, then if you visualize the two of you going out for dinner afterwards, even if the latter is more realistic than the former. The strategy is identical to that of a student posting a disappointing grade above his desk to motivate harder and longer studying.

What differentiates the healthy constructive expression of anger in EXTAR, or the Martin Luthers, from the unhealthy destructive expression of anger of Eduardo or Pancho Gonzalez?

Two things. One is focusing on changing the future, rather than ruminating on the past. Two, is having a finite end point after which the anger ceases, rather than continuing interminably. A good run is healthy, a treadmill without an "off" switch is not.

Moses had every right to be angry when he saw his people enslaved and abused in Egypt.[8] With God's help, his healthy anger helped liberate them. Unfortunately, like the burning bush[9] he had witnessed, his anger would not naturally extinguish. His unhealthy pertinacity cost him the Promised Land.[10]

What distinguishes the prophet from the mere madman? "I want all of you to get up out of your chairs. I want you to get up right now and go to the window, open it and stick your head out and yell, 'I'm mad as hell, and I'm not going to take this anymore!' "– Peter Finch, *Network[11]*. Sometimes the only definitive answer is history.[12] Most of us are neither Moses nor madmen. Yet we still have the choice of ceaselessly ruminating on the past, or using EXTAR to change the future.

Is EXTAR a sure-fire solution to all anger-provoking situations? Of course not. There are an infinite variety of situations for which it won't work. We'll be discussing two alternative approaches in the following chapters.

EXTAR assumes many axioms that aren't always true. It assumes that you're aware of your anger and its real cause. It assumes that your anger is justified. The fact is, if Terry had bought this book instead of entering therapy, she undoubtedly would have applied "EXTAR." Unfortunately, it would have been to her husband, not her sister. That is most regrettable, but as mentioned in the Introduction, it remains an unavoidable problem with any self-help book. The problem can be lessened, if we're wise enough to listen.

Cal was a high school senior who batted clean-up for his school's baseball team. Yet, he was also a schizophrenic taking a medication which had as its side effect, diplopia. Cal saw two of everything. I asked Cal, if he always saw two balls coming at him simultaneously, how did he know which ball to hit? His answer was simple, yet profound. "I hit the ball that everyone else sees."

What if there really are two balls, but they look like one?

Rob was a young, brilliant CEO who had started his own successful company. The world was truly his oyster, yet he was uncharacteristically perturbed. There had been a very minor incident at his parking garage that morning, and he couldn't stop obsessing about it.

Rob had called his garage to get his car.[13] Despite it being the morning rush hour, when many people pick up and drop off their cars, the beleaguered attendant had promptly obtained Rob's car for him. Rob only needed to remove his cell phone from within. He retrieved it and informed the attendant that he could take the car back. The attendant, previously professionally polite, was irate. Though other customers were standing around, some of whom undoubtedly recognized Rob, the attendant started yelling at Rob:

"Why didn't you tell me that you weren't going to take your car out? You made me bring your car all the way up for this? I don't believe this! Do you have any clue how busy we are at this hour? God almighty! What a piece of work!"

Even with the expletives deleted version, the tirade was disrespectful at best, humiliating at worst. How to respond? Many options suggested themselves to Rob:

1—He could ask the attendant to step outside and resolve this in the traditional physical confrontation.

2—He could yell back at the attendant, at the same volume and with the some obscenities, and point out that:

a) He needed the phone urgently.

b) He doesn't have to justify to an attendant why he needs his car.

c) He had never been informed that he should distinguish between needing his car and needing to remove something from his car, when calling for his car.

d) Considering how much he pays to park his car, (on a monthly basis more than the rent on many studio apartments), he should be able to get his car whenever he wants, and as often as he wants.

e) How dare this employee speak to him, a valued customer, in such a disrespectful manner, in public no less.

3—He could demand to speak to the manager and repeat (2) a-e.

4—He could write directly to the owner about his incident.

5—He could combine (3) and/or (4) with a threat to remove his business unless this incident was resolved to his satisfaction, i.e. fire the attendant.

6—He could simply move his car to a different garage without explanation. Let them wonder why.

Ironically, even while the attendant was yelling at him, and the first six options came to mind, two other paradoxically opposite options came to mind as well:

7—Rob could mutter a quick, albeit insincere apology.

8—He could give him a few bucks for his extra work, and to terminate his tirade.

In the end, which of the eight options did Rob choose at the time? None of the above.

Uncertain of what his correct response should be, he simply turned his back and walked out on the attendant in mid-tirade. He could still hear the attendant yelling as he hurriedly exited the garage.

Did this ninth approach bring Rob any satisfaction or closure? Quite the contrary. Rob still felt frustrated and humiliated by the incident. On top of that, he was worried what subtle (spitting), or unsubtle (stripping the gears) damage the obviously still frustrated attendant would wreak on Rob's expensive new car.

What makes Rob's dilemma extraordinarily difficult is that it's not merely a question of degree. Rob knows that both he and the attendant are angry, but he doesn't even know what direction his response should be—vengeful, or conciliatory. Questions of degree are fine-tuning. Questions of direction are seismic shifts.

To analyze this trivial, albeit tenebrous, incident and arrive at the correct response, it is most helpful to theorize the ideal world. In the perfect, insightful, self-aware world, how would the attendant have handled the situation?

He would have quietly, privately explained to Rob that in the future, if he only has to remove an item from his car, it's easier on all concerned, including Rob's car, to bring Rob to his car than to bring his car to Rob.

How would Rob have reacted to that explanation? Intellectually honest in general, Rob would have apologized, this time sincerely, for having caused the overworked attendant the unnecessary inconvenience. Generous by nature, Rob would undoubtedly have tipped him as well. It would have worked out perfectly. But it didn't. Now, how to resolve this mess?

The solution is to realize that there are two balls, two separate issues. The first is the fact that Rob called for his car unnecessarily only to remove an item. The second, by now more important, is the disrespectful manner in which the attendant addressed him.

Rob returned to his garage, sought out the attendant and informed him that he needed to talk to him privately. The attendant complied, albeit sullenly. His demeanor was defensive. He obviously knew what this confrontation was about. To the attendant's pleasant surprise however, Rob started by apologizing for the inconvenience that Rob had caused him. Rob explained that he hadn't realized that he could obtain an item from his car without the car being physically retrieved. As he spoke, Rob could see the anger on the attendant's face melt away. He actually started nodding sheepishly, even smiling, for the first time that Rob had ever seen.

Rob wasn't done. In the same reasonable tone, Rob explained to the attendant that the manner in which he had publicly berated Rob that morning was unacceptable. He started to invoke EXTAR, i.e. if it ever happened again, Rob would take it up with the manager. Before Rob could even spell out the threat, the attendant was apologizing. Although not well spoken, his contrition was palpably genuine. He explained that he had been having an impossible day because one of the other attendants had called in sick. He volunteered that he had been bothered by the incident since it happened. Rob confided that so had he.

Before the incident, Rob and the attendant had been barely aware of each other's existence, though they had seen each other hundreds of times. Since they expressed their anger, they actually looked forward to seeing each other. No attendant gave Rob quicker or more respectful service; no attendant received a warmer greeting in return, or a bigger gratuity.

EXTAR always assumes that your relationship with this person, be they your mother or your garage attendant, has intrinsic value. Therefore, you want to preserve it. The relationship is worth the time and effort of the five steps. Otherwise, you're better off using the original fifth option, passively aggressively ending the relationship.

> "Hello, I'm sorry if I woke you up. You don't know me, but I'm authorized to offer you an incredible investment opportunity . . ." "CLICK."

Even if you apply it perfectly, EXTAR is no guarantee that the situation will be resolved to your satisfaction. There's always a possibility that the final result will be the same as if you reacted passive-aggressively, the termination of the relationship. In the short run, it's even likely. You expressed your anger. So will your mother.

As the mother exclaims in Stephen Sondheim's *Into The Woods*: "What about my anger?!" *Into The Woods* revisits every familiar fairy tale to conjecture a never-ending cycle of revenge. When anger is expressed destructively, nobody lives happily ever after. This is as painfully obvious in Northern Ireland, the Mideast, or the India Pakistan border as it is in the woods.[14]

After you stopped taking your mother's phone calls at work, did you really think that everything would be immediately hunky-dory? Of course not. Your mother was hurt. In all probability she not only stopped calling you at work, but she stopped calling you period. It's even possible that to prove a point, that you need her too, she stopped taking your phone calls.

If that's the case, what have you accomplished? What was the whole point of EXTAR? Why did you have to go through that unpleasant confrontation, if the result is identical to your passive-aggressively ignoring her?

Two reasons. First and most importantly, you did the right thing. You were honest. You were direct. You were constructive. Even if your mother doesn't immediately appreciate that, *you* will. When you second-guess yourself, (everyone does,) you won't do so as harshly, or as frequently. That holds true for anyone else (your father, siblings, spouse, children) who is aware of the situation and second-guesses you as well.

The second reason is pragmatic. It's easier and more likely for your mother to make peace with you in the future, if she knew what the problem was in the present. She knew you asked her nicely at first. She knew you explained why. She knew you warned her. Eventually she'll swallow her pride and come around.

How should you act when she does? As magnanimous and gracious as you would want her to be, if the roles were reversed. If she calls pleasantly and acts as if there had never been any unpleasant incident, you act the same. The issue has been resolved. There's nothing wrong now with letting by-gones be by-gones. There's no constructive reason to rub her face into an episode that she would just as soon forget.

What if she starts calling you at work again? Unless she's senile, it's unlikely. If worse came to worse, you could always go through EXTAR again, although frankly, you won't get past STEP 1. You won't even have to explain. A simple request will be more than sufficient to jog her memory.

In reality, STEP 1 is as much Requesting as it is Explaining.

I summarize it as Explaining for two reasons. Reason number one is fatuous. The alternative acronym, "RETAR," sounds too much like "RETARD."

Reason number two is cogent. The explanation is as critical as the request. It shouldn't be overlooked. We *owe* the important people in our lives an explanation of our feelings and actions. "Never explain. Never apologize[15]." was a popular, oft quoted business maxim of the generation that inspired Gordon Gekko[16]. It was designed to inspire awe in one's underlings.

Frankly, speaking as a business consultant, I hate it. If it inspires anything, it's confusion and resentment. It might be appropriate for a monarch and his subject, but it clearly has no place in the relationships of relatives, colleagues or friends. In terms of anger, it can only serve an inflammatory function. I was unpleasantly surprised that people quoted it, and worse, adhered to it as often as they did.

On the other hand, I was pleasantly surprised to discover that Terry flourished in group. Though she didn't like the fact that the group, as well, defended Sean and attacked Sherry, somehow she was able to accept it. The reason was partially because it's harder to disagree with several heterogeneous peers' unanimous conclusion, than with a single opinion, however educated. More importantly, the group gave her something in return that I never could.

They were family. They gave her the support, the encouragement, the nurturing that she had never gotten at home. She looked forward to the weekly sessions like no one else. Invariably, she was the first one in the waiting room.

There were many highlights to Terry's stay in group. There was the time she informed her parents that since her gifts were all winding up in Sherry's house, she would no longer bring any presents. She would take them to a show and dinner instead. There was the time when she demanded and received some money she had loaned Sherry. Sherry's threat that, because of the repayment, Terry would be responsible for Sherry's divorce was duly ignored. Best of all, was the time both Terry and Sean informed me that they had never been happier together. Apparently, Terry was finally seeing the right ball.

When Terry eventually "graduated" from group, the champagne that we all shared couldn't have been more appropriate. There were tears in everyone's eyes. Especially mine.

Maybe I could learn to like soap operas after all.

> *"I was angry with my friend;*
> *I told my wrath, my wrath did end.*
> *I was angry with my foe;*
> *I told it not, my wrath did grow."*
> -William Blake, (1757-1827)

Notes

---

[1] *Genesis* IV: 7.

[2] John McEnroe pointed out, after his retirement, that a critical reason that he never restrained himself from his temper tantrums on the tennis court was that no one ever disqualified him. The tennis establishment always complained about his behavior but they never threw him out of a game. They should have taken lessons from Bjorn Borg's parents.

[3] You might be tempted to send her a copy of the company rules forbidding personal phone calls. Don't. It infantilizes you. She should be willing to stop calling you at work out of respect for you, instead of respect for your boss.

[4] Most words containing the "ex" root, e.g. excavate, except, excise, exclude, exempt, exhale, exhaust, exhume, exile, exit, exodus, even Ex-lax, refer to the meaning "from."

[5] The study was conducted by Jennifer Lerner, Ph.D., et al from the

    Carnegie Mellon University in Pittsburgh and funded by the National Science Foundation and the American Psychological Association.

[6] *The Autobiography of Malcolm X* (1966), Malcolm X, Grove Press.

[7] *Ben Hur* in 1959 won an unprecedented 11 Oscars, including Best Picture and Best Actor for Charlton Heston.

[8] *Exodus* II:11-12. When Moses saw an Egyptian flogging a slave, he killed the Egyptian.

[9] *Exodus* II:2. "the bush burned with fire, but the bush was not consumed."

[10] *Numbers* XX:8-12. Because Moses struck the rock, rather than speak to it, God punished him by denying him entry into the Promised Land. As is often the case with uncontrolled anger, Moses got the rock to release its water, but did so at an expensive price to himself. Unbridled anger is often successful in the short run, but in the end a Pyrrhic Victory.

[11] In 1976 Peter Finch won the only posthumous Best Actor Oscar for his portrait of Beale, the newscaster gone mad.

[12] Many heroic historical figures from biblical prophets to Joan of Arc have been conjectured to have been hallucinating paranoid schizophrenics.

[13] In Manhattan garages you don't have your own parking spot. Rather your car is buried behind innumerable others. Hence you need to call in advance to get it.

[14] Stephen Sondheim commonly incorporates psychological insights into his work. In *Into The Woods*, the woods represent the dark fearsome Id where sex and violence are permitted. It is similar to the phenomenon of the loyal spouse who finds it permissible to philander on a business trip, as seen in another Broadway hit, *Same Time Next Year*. Other manifestations of Superego on vacation are apparent in college students on spring break, expressed and augmented by massive ingestion of drugs and alcohol.

[15] Unbeknownst to most, the expression "Never explain. Never apologize." was first recited by John Wayne in 1949 in the western *She Wore A Yellow Ribbon*: "Never apologize and never explain—it's a sign of weakness."

[16] Gordon Gekko was the Oscar winning performance of Michael Douglas in the 1987 movie *Wall Street*. The homophonically named Gekko was a reptilian character whose best-known quote was: "Greed is good! Greed is right! Greed works!"

PART II

CHAPTER THREE

Revenge is Mine, Saith the Lord

Silencing the Anger

"And the Lord was provoked to anger by the actions of his children: 'They have enraged Me . . . They have lit a fire in Me which will devour the Earth and set ablaze the mountains.'"[1]

One of the better comedies in the history of television was *TAXI*. It spawned the careers of its ensemble cast: Judd Hirsch, Danny DeVito, Christopher Lloyd, Tony Danza, Marilu Henner and the late Andy Kaufman. Its creator, James L. Brooks, went on to direct *Terms of Endearment, Broadcast News* and *As Good As It Gets*.

Does any TV series have a "best episode" or "biggest laugh"? Probably not. Nevertheless, there was one particular episode and one climactic moment that might qualify.

In it, Elaine Nardo (Marilu Henner) scrimps and saves to go to a "society" hairstylist because of an all-important upcoming event. He butchers her. He makes her head look like a collaboration of Buckminster Fuller and Pablo Picasso. Elaine is humiliated. With her friends' encouragement, she goes back to complain. She asks the high priced stylist (Ted Danson[2]) to rectify the mess. Instead, he mocks her and embarrasses her in front of the entire salon. She leaves in tears.

Finally, she returns with reinforcements, Alex Rieger (Judd Hirsch) and Louie DePalma (Danny DeVito). Alex is the moral leader, the conscience of the cabbies. Louie, on the other hand, is an unabashed sleazeball, (the prototype for most future Danny DeVito roles.[3])

The stylist is again snide and condescending. This time, however, Elaine is able to stand up to him. She tells him off. He tries to ignore her. She gets his attention by holding a pail full of orange dye over his head. Alex intervenes: "Elaine, if you do that, you're no better than him. Put it down. It's beneath you."

Elaine sighs and removes the pail. The stylist is deeply relieved. Alex and Elaine leave with their moral victory.

Suddenly, Louie grabs the pail. With his pathognomonically gleeful smirk he announces: "It might be beneath her, but it's not beneath me!" and pours the goo all over the stylist. The studio audience responds not only with the longest protracted laugh ever heard on a sitcom, but also, spontaneous applause. Why?

They wanted revenge. Their anger hadn't been appeased. They wanted this unrepentant jerk punished. When Alex and Elaine started to leave, having done the politically correct thing, the audience felt cheated. Because of Alex's merciful appeal, Elaine had chosen to forgive Ted. The audience hadn't. Why not?

It is not human nature to forgive someone who shows no contrition whatsoever.

Yet, many argue we should rise above our human nature. "To err is human; to forgive divine." is one of the first proverbs that all children learn. "Forgive us our trespasses, as we forgive those that trespass against us."[4] "Forgive us our debts, as we forgive our debtors."[5] A similar maxim was invoked by Terry: "Let he who is without sin cast the first stone!" Since none of us is without sin, that means that no stones, (or pails of dye), should ever be cast.

Religious leaders of all faiths suggest to us that the avenging God of the Old Testament, "A life for a life." "Eye for eye, tooth for tooth, hand for hand, foot for foot. Burning for burning, wound for wound, bruise for bruise."[6] should *not* be taken as a role model. They teach us that when we read "Revenge is mine, saith the Lord!,"[7] it means that revenge belongs exclusively to God, and is not permissible by man.

While an apology is always audience pleasing, the enlightened view has been to forgive all trespasses against us, no matter how cruel, no matter how destructive, no matter how unrepentant the sinner remains. That point of view might be "enlightened," but it is neither natural, nor healthy.

The fact of revenge being natural has always been self-evident. The Bible, for example, goes into lengthy detail describing the establishment of six isolated, guarded communities to serve as cities of refuge ("Orey Miklat").[8] These enclaves were designed to protect those who had accidentally killed from being avenged by the deceased's relatives.

Mind you, these were accidents. If it were murder, or even negligence, then the appropriate punishment, capital or otherwise, would be administered by the courts. The Bible goes into exquisite detail to distinguish between murder and accidents[9]. Only accidental killers would be protected.[10]

In a sense these enclaves served two purposes. Firstly, they, of course, protected the innocent party. Secondly, however, they effectively imprisoned that person as well. No doubt this served to allay the vengeful wrath of the deceased's family. If the accidental killer chose to leave the city of refuge, he became fair game for the deceased's family.[11]

Vengeance of course is not limited to the Bible. Blood feuds transcend all geographical and temporal boundaries. One cannot study any country's history, or any region's culture, without finding innumerable examples. They are as obvious in the plays of Shakespeare as they are in the tribal warfare of Africa. They can be as highbrow as the Tudors and the Stuarts or as lowbrow as the Hatfields and McCoys.

The gang warfare of the Wild West was replaced by the *Gangs of New York*, which were replaced by the Crips and the Bloods. The gunfight at the O.K. Corral was modernized to biker brawls at malls. *Romeo and Juliet* was updated to *West Side Story.*

Modern technology has replaced the theater of Shakespeare's era with the cinema. The special effects have increased, but the audience-pleasing theme has remained the same.

It has been estimated that over ninety percent of today's movies not only involve revenge, but indeed revolve about it. The actors evolve, from Charles Bronson, to Clint Eastwood, to Arnold Schwarzenegger, to Steven Seagal, to Jean Claude Van Damme, to Jet Li, to Vin Diesel but the revenge remains the same. As discussed in "A Looney Tunes World," the need for revenge is the raison d'etre of the entire movie. Not only is the act of revenge the climax of the movie, but in most viewers' minds, it's the only memorable moment.

One hundred minutes of their attention has been repaid by a few seconds of cathartic violence. Not surprisingly, directors often attempt to increase the payoff by filming the death in slow motion, or in some cases, a freeze frame, or even repeating the sequence a second time. If the opera isn't over till the fat lady sings, the movie isn't over till the villain dies. The hero may or may not die, but the villain surely must.

This avenging moment has become so important in the viewer's mind that it comes to define the movie:

> "Was *Dirty Harry* the one where Clint Eastwood blows the guy up with a bazooka?"

> "No, in *Dirty Harry* he blows the guy's head off with his magnum after he says 'Do ya feel lucky, punk?'."[12]

> "Oh, that's right. Great flick. The other one I

like is when he says 'Make my day'[13] before he blows
him away."

The act of vengeance is so critical that the hero's quote
as he performs it becomes a part of popular culture. For
example, *Terminator II*, which grossed hundreds of millions
of dollars, made "Hasta La Vista, Baby!" a catch phrase. What's
the origin of the phrase? It's what the hero terminator
(Arnold Schwarzenegger) mutters as he blows to
smithereens the villain terminator (Robert Patrick). Every
time it's uttered on screen the audience responds with
laughter and spontaneous applause. (Maybe it shouldn't be
surprising that Arnold Schwarzenegger and Danny DeVito
co-starred as *Twins*.)

The act of vengeance need not even be performed by a
hero to be audience pleasing. In 1991, *Silence of the Lambs*
swept the Academy Awards, including Best Picture, Best
Director, Best Adapted Screenplay, Best Actor and Best
Actress. What is the final climax of *Silence of the Lambs?* At
what point does the audience spontaneously applaud
through their laughter? When Dr. Hannibal Lecter (Anthony
Hopkins) informs Clarice Starling (Jodie Foster) that he's
about to "have a friend for dinner."

Think about that for a second. The audience, including
you and me, is applauding a psychotic murderer announcing
that he's about to cannibalize an innocent psychologist. Why?

Because we know that the psychologist, Dr. Chilton
(Anthony Heald), isn't so innocent. He's arrogant, selfish,
deceitful, cruel, patronizing, sexist and stupid. Nevertheless,
none of those crimes, or even all of them put together, merit
the death penalty, much less being cannibalized. Why do
we still approve?

Because this hateful man has never been punished for
his crimes. If, during the course of the movie, this obnoxious
psychologist had been punished, e.g. if he was fired from

his powerful position and publicly humiliated, then Lecter's revenge would have been overkill, and we would feel differently. In our minds, quite naturally so, unpunished sins demand retribution. As in *Silence of the Lambs*, better the punishment exceed the crime, than the crime go unpunished. More importantly, Chilton had never expressed even a scintilla of regret for his many despicable actions, or the pain and damage that they caused.

Imagine for a second the following scene. After Lecter's escape, Chilton visits Clarice . Rather than making a pass at her, as he did in their first encounter, or interfering with her work, as he did in their last encounter, or condescending to her, as he did continually, he has come to apologize, confess and make amends. Imagine him sitting there movingly expressing his regret and guilt. In retrospect, he is disgusted not only by his unforgivable treatment of Clarice, but also by his sadistic treatment of Lecter. His tears are genuine as he begs Clarice's forgiveness.

Furthermore he confesses to Clarice a fact that hitherto only the audience knew. It was his negligence, in forgetting his pen in Lecter's cell, that allowed Lecter to open his handcuffs, murder and mutilate the guards, and escape. He informs Clarice that he holds himself accountable for Lecter's actions. Accordingly, he has publicly acknowledged his mistake, he has voluntarily resigned from his position, and he has used his own life savings to recompense the guards' families. The entire scene would require no more than a few minutes. Yet, it would completely change the aforementioned climax.

No longer would we be rooting for Chilton to get his just dessert, serving as Lecter's dessert. On the contrary, we would be rooting for Dr. Chilton. Why? Because Chilton had repented. He had made amends. He no longer needed to be punished. In fact, he was no longer the villain.

Interestingly, his reformation left Lecter as the most villainous character remaining. In the absence of Chilton's villainy, Lecter is no longer a brilliant, chivalrous, avenging angel. Though his character hasn't changed one iota, from the audience's perspective, he is now a psychotic murderer. With the addition of one short scene not involving him at all, Dr. Lecter the charismatic hero, has become Hannibal the Cannibal, the despised villain.

Thus it is the villain who defines the hero, and not vice-versa. It was Chilton's villainy and our consequent anger that made us root for Lecter, not Lecter's good taste. Unfortunately, it is only effortless to go from villain to hero in professional wrestling, sports and the movies.

In professional wrestling many icons have been transformed from "face" to "heel" and back again. If one's performing career is long enough, like Andre the Giant, Hulk Hogan, The Rock or Jesse "The Body" Ventura, it's inevitable.

Even in legitimate sports, a change of venue turns a villain into a hero. Patrick Ewing was vilified in New York when he led Georgetown against St. John's. The instant that the Knicks won first place in the draft however, and selected him, he automatically became a Big Apple idol. In baseball, Roger Clemens' transformation, from New York's perspective, was identical. From Boston's perspective, it was reversed.

In real life, on the other hand, an apology is required. An effective apology is neither simple nor easy. Furthermore, not all apologies are equal. Saying "I'm sorry you were upset by what I did" is not remotely the same as saying "What I did was unforgivable. I will be forever sorry and ashamed of my actions."

In fact, there are at least six discrete levels of regret.

Level 1—"I'm sorry that you're upset."

I acknowledge that you're upset. I acknowledge that I'm sorry that you're upset, i.e. I care about your feelings. I don't however acknowledge that I regret my actions. Neither do I acknowledge that I did anything wrong. Consequently, I neither apologize nor ask for your forgiveness.

Level 2—"I'm sorry I did it."

While I regret my actions since it obviously upset you, I still don't think I did anything wrong. When, sixteen months later, President Clinton finally expressed regret for pardoning Marc Rich as Clinton left office, it was on level 2. "It wasn't worth the damage to my reputation. But that doesn't mean the attacks were true." i.e. I did nothing wrong. Revealingly, while Clinton didn't say that was the reason for the pardon, he did acknowledge, "I was just angry . . ." As he insightfully acknowledged: "I don't know that anyone is 100 percent aware of his motives."

Level 3—"I'm sorry I did it. I was wrong."

Finally, I acknowledge that I did something wrong. I express my regrets, but I have yet to apologize. This kind of statement is usually made by someone too proud and/or insecure (aren't the two synonymous?) to add the logical conclusion, i.e. the apology, to the observation, i.e. "I screwed up."

Level 4—"I'm sorry I did it. I was wrong. I apologize."

Finally, a real apology. The first three weren't. It would be even better if a response was solicited, i.e. "Please forgive me."

Level 5—"I'm sorry I did it. I was wrong. I apologize. Please forgive me."

The ultimate apology. If genuine, (a big if), it's hard to resist.

Level 6—"What I did was unforgivable. My apologies are insufficient. I will be sorry and ashamed of my actions for the rest of my life."

In most instances, this would be overkill. Unfortunately, in the cases when it really does apply, it isn't enough.

With these six totally different levels of apology, is it any wonder why there's so much confusion and miscommunication on the subject?

"I apologized! What more can I do?"

"You never apologized!"

"I certainly did! I said I was sorry!"

"You're sorry when the home team loses! That's not an apology!"

"What should I do? Get down on my hands and knees? Nothing's enough for you!"

The Level One regret, "I'm sorry that you're upset," is in some ways, yet another insult, i.e. "I'm sorry that you're so incredibly sensitive that you would over-react and get upset by my actions, even though there was nothing at all wrong with what I did. A normal person wouldn't have even raised an eyebrow." Obviously, it can make matters even worse.

If all Chilton had said in our imagined scene is "I'm sorry Lecter got away," it wouldn't have assuaged our anger at all. On the contrary, it would have reinforced our negative impression of him as someone so arrogantly stupid that he can't acknowledge his own mistake.

Just as the punishment has to fit the crime, the apology has to fit the sin. Just as the audience and the victim prefer a punishment that's too harsh, rather than too lenient, so do we prefer an apology that overstates the sin, rather than understates it.

That doesn't mean that the Level One apology always does more harm than good. It does mean that the misdeed should have been commensurately slight.

If, for example, after STEP 1 of EXTAR in our last chapter, your mother had responded: "I'm sorry that by my calling you at work, I upset you," it would have been perfectly acceptable. Even if it means that she believes that you're too sensitive, you're over-reacting, and she did nothing wrong, it's still helpful for her to say it.

Why? Number one, she's acknowledging that she cares about your feelings, i.e. she loves you. That's good to hear from anyone, (especially your mother). Number two, calling someone at work is in fact a very slight misdeed. Number three, as we discussed last chapter, whatever she says is far less important than what she does, i.e. stop calling you at work.

In understanding our anger, it is crucial that we realize the qualitative difference between actions that annoy us and actions that are fundamentally wrong. Both anger us. We have a right to demand that both cease and desist. We *don't* have a right to demand an apology for the former. We have every right to demand a profound, sincere, abject apology for the latter. Indeed, we have a responsibility to demand it before we even consider restarting the relationship.

How can we differentiate between the two? How can we recognize behavior that is inherently wrong, and not merely annoying? One is tempted to quote Supreme Court Justice Potter Stewart's definition of pornography: "You know it when you see it." Unfortunately, recent history has taught us that it's no longer the case with either pornography or misdeeds.

A better definition would be that the deed is so immoral and unethical, that the overwhelming majority of disinterested observers would never do it themselves or accept it in others. Consequently the three examples of annoying behavior from our last chapter, calling someone at work, referring to them as "honey," or rubbing their head, do *not* qualify. Insensitive and inconsiderate are not the same thing as immoral and unethical. We need to differentiate between the two because while "EXTAR" is an excellent approach in dealing with the former, it is woefully inadequate in dealing with the latter.

Cliff's newest film was an eagerly anticipated sequel on which he had invested incredible time. After its completion, but prior to the whirlwind of activity inherent in its release, he took his wife and kid on a vacation. As always, he left his house in the care of his neighbor, Peter, who watered his plants and walked his dogs. Peter, a handsome, charismatic actor, had been in many of Cliff's movies, although not this one, and was a trusted friend.

The vacation was wonderful. The return wasn't. Cliff was met at the airport by studio representatives who informed him that apparently there was a bootleg copy of the movie circulating. They needed to know if he still had his copy of the movie. Cliff rushed home and was relieved to see that his copy was still there. He called Peter who assured him that there had been no worrisome activity.

After an extensive, expensive investigation a copy was traced back to an actress. This actress hadn't been in the movie. In fact, Cliff had never worked with her. He had only met her once. When she was dating Peter.

He asked Peter if he knew anything about this. Peter swore he didn't. The studio interrogated the actress who acknowledged that it was Cliff's copy. Cliff called Peter who confessed that he had entertained the actress in Cliff's house. Before she left, the actress had asked if she could copy a tape. Peter hadn't bothered to look at which tape she was copying.

Cliff was upset that Peter #1 had invited someone else into his home, #2 had been negligent in allowing Cliff's movie to be copied, and #3, worst of all, had lied. Still, Peter was guilty primarily of stupidity, and he did apologize. In the end, there was minimal harm done, since the studio had been able to retrieve the copy. Several weeks later Cliff saw the actress at an industry function. She came over to apologize for any inconvenience. Cliff refused to accept her apology. He told her that she should have known better than to copy an unreleased movie.

The actress was shocked. She had never copied anything. In fact, she had never been in Cliff's house. Peter had *sent* her the copy. Furthermore, Peter had sent copies to other ex-girl friends as well. Subsequently, the studio confirmed her story.

Cliff confronted Peter. Peter admitted it, acknowledged he was sorry, then expressed how angry he was that Cliff hadn't given him a part in this sequel. Cliff was furious. How should Cliff deal with his anger? Would EXTAR suffice? Of course not.

Cliff had been betrayed by someone he had trusted and helped for years. Peter had stolen from Cliff, made copies that he knew would hurt Cliff's movie, and had lied to Cliff, *again* and *again*. Though the movie was still ultimately successful, Peter had cost the movie a significant amount of money, and had repeatedly made Cliff look like a fool in the eyes of anyone who knew about the incident. Cliff demanded revenge. He expunged Peter from his life. That meant not only no longer socializing with him, but also, more importantly, no longer hiring him for his movies.

Yet Peter, in the end, *did* say he was sorry. As Robert Browning said: "Good to forgive; best to forget."[14] Should we be so cynical as to never forgive anyone? No. Being cynical *is* unhealthy. Being skeptical however, is not. Mark Twain said: "Fool me once, shame on you. Fool me twice, shame on me." Peter's so-called apology was more an expression of regret than remorse, Level 2 at best. While he was sorry he got caught, he justified his action. He was angry that Cliff hadn't cast him. This was his way of getting even.

Why was Cliff's anger justifiable where Peter's anger wasn't? Both angers were justifiable. Peter's anger at not being cast justified his expressing it. It might even have justified EXTAR. It didn't justify stealing and lying. Cliff's behavior had certainly been annoying to Peter, and perhaps even insensitive. Peter's behavior on the other hand, had been unequivocally immoral and unethical. He had committed a grievous misdeed against Cliff. It was healthy for Cliff to avenge it.

In 1992 a 17-year-old girl suffered a fatal post-operative stroke. Her parents sued for malpractice. Ten years later the case was still pending[15]. This wouldn't be worth mentioning, but for two facts: 1) The girl's parents were both physicians, her father, in fact, a surgeon. Indeed, all five of their children had intended to become physicians. 2) It took place in Japan where malpractice suits are virtually non-existent[16]. Yet, the anger of the parents was so overwhelming that they dared to defy convention and authority. Interestingly, in this case, both the family and the medical establishment each felt betrayed by the other. The family demanded revenge, no matter the cost to their careers.

Another incident might be termed "A Tale of Two Sisters." Sharon and Judy had been close growing up. Sharon had followed her father into his construction business, while Judy had pursued her studies in art. By the time their father passed away, Sharon had been working in the business over ten years. Accordingly, he left her the business in his will. The estate was substantial. Neither sister was left wanting. Eventually however, Judy decided that art could not provide her the manner to which she had become accustomed. After discussions with Sharon, she came to work in the family business.

The first few years went well. Judy received a handsome salary. Sharon appreciated having her sister working with her. Eventually however, Judy decided, with the support of her then boyfriend, that she was entitled to more. After all, this was a family business and she was half the remaining family. It was only fair that she be a partner, not an employee. Sharon demurred.

Privately, Judy consulted a lawyer who could find no legal basis on which to pursue a claim. Judy decided to get Sharon's attention. While Sharon was on a vacation, Judy proceeded with her meticulous plan. As co-signer on Sharon's bank accounts, (in the event of Sharon's death), Judy emptied them and put the money into her own name. With the key to Sharon's apartment, Judy (and her boyfriend) cleaned out all of Sharon's jewelry, silver and art. Upon Sharon's return, Judy laughingly informed her of what she had done. Judy estimated the total cache to be two million dollars, approximately one half the worth of the company, what Judy was "entitled to" in the first place.

Sharon was devastated. This was not only her only relative in the entire world, but also her best friend. This had been her sole heir, the person who would bury her. She felt at a complete loss, totally helpless. She also felt angry. She had been betrayed. After a few days her depression converted to rage. She wanted to get even.

She did. She called the police to report a robbery. The police duly contacted Judy and arrested her for the theft from Sharon's apartment. At this point every distant relative that the two sisters ever had suddenly contacted Sharon. How could Sharon do this? Put her own sister on trial, possibly send her to jail? How could Sharon treat her like a common criminal? This was a family matter. You don't wash your family laundry in public. "The family" and Judy were outraged that Sharon would call the police. Sharon didn't care.

Eventually, willy-nilly, Sharon was able to recover most of her bank accounts. Judy, and her boyfriend, however had managed to sell and spend all of Sharon's personal assets. The case was settled. Sharon estimated her losses at a quarter million dollars.

Today, two decades later, Judy's boyfriend is long gone. Judy has never apologized to Sharon, since in her mind, she did nothing wrong. On the contrary, she still informs people that Sharon cheated her out of her inheritance.

Nevertheless, now indigent as well as indignant, she has magnanimously offered to resurrect their relationship. Sharon continues to decline.

Virtually all religions have guidelines for forgiveness. They tend to be extensive and well thought-out. They usually include at least three separate elements, confession, contrition and penance. Not coincidentally, neither Peter nor Judy had expressed *any* of the three.

CONFESSION means revealing *everything* you have done wrong, not just acknowledging the bare minimum with which you were caught. If, for example, Peter had confessed before he was caught, perhaps Cliff might have felt differently. Concession is *not* confession. Acknowledging each step only as each step is revealed is the antipode of true confession. If anything, it attests to the fact that this person is *not* trustworthy, as was the case with Peter.

It is similar to the legal concept, "negative pregnant." When Cliff asked Peter: "Do you have a copy of my movie?" and Peter replied: "*I* don't have a copy," his words were literally true. Nevertheless he was guilty, since his girlfriends had copies which he had given them. Peter was being literally honest, but in reality duplicitous.

CONTRITION means remorse. Your every word and action should reflect how badly you feel about what you did. Furthermore, it's not merely the consequences of your actions that bother you so terribly, it's the very act itself. Even if nothing unfortunate ensued, what you did was inherently wrong, and you feel justifiably guilty. *Your* anger, your reasons for doing it, are, at most, of heuristic value. They in no way justify your actions and are therefore irrelevant to the process of forgiveness. Focusing on them belies your contrition.

PENANCE is last, but certainly not least. Since it has religious associations, it seems foreign to someone without a religious background. Penance means more than fasting, or saying "Hail Mary"s. It means trying to make amends for your actions. It means rectification. Even if your actions or their consequences can never be totally undone, you can try.

Penance was our imagined scenario where Dr. Chilton insists on sharing his wealth with the families of the prison guards. Penance would have been Peter volunteering to recompense the studio the cost of the investigation that he had necessitated, obviously something he never remotely considered. Penance would have been Judy offering to repay Sharon the $250,000 she had stolen, instead of still complaining that Sharon had cheated her. Penance comes from within, rather than being imposed from without. Begrudging, willy-nilly penance is an oxymoron. It's not penance. It's punishment.

Taking all three steps only creates the possibility of forgiveness. It doesn't insure it. The ultimate decision to forgive lies exclusively with the victims. Only they can decide when and if. Society of necessity proscribes specific punishments for specific crimes. If you assault someone, you will serve six months in jail. If you rape someone, you will serve three years. If you negligently kill someone, you will serve six years.

Upon your release, your debt to society is repaid. Neither confession, contrition nor penance are demanded or expected. Rarely are they given.

It should not be surprising then, that punishment rarely includes forgiveness. Most victims, and their families, are, at best, sorry when their respective miscreant is finally released. At worst, they are scared. Without confession, contrition or penance, it is virtually impossible for a victim to forgive, or for a screen audience.

It should not be surprising therefore, that most people favor the death penalty. Movie audiences demand it. An astute viewer can immediately tell from the crime committed what the perpetrator's cinematic fate will be. Certain injustices are so heinous that only death will begin to propitiate the audience. In fact, if the crime is vile enough, and the criminal loathsome enough, death won't be enough. The audience will demand a sufficiently cathartic death. It's not enough for the villain to die. It has to be in a particularly painful way. It helps considerably if the audience sees that the villain realized his fate, and suffered painfully. The successful film satisfies the audience's subliminal need for revenge.

In Julie Taymor's cinematic version of *Titus Andronicus*, it isn't enough for Alan Cumming's despicable despot to die torturously as a large serving utensil is slowly forced down his throat. Subsequently the avenger's saliva is captured mid-air in an extended, computer enhanced, freeze frame, lest we miss the point that insult was added upon injury. Had it been filmed in real time, the audience might not have realized that Anthony Hopkins spat upon Cumming's cadaver. Finally, in literal over-kill, the avenger pulls out a revolver and adds some lead seasoning to the previous mixture of blood and saliva. The audience might wince, but it doesn't complain.

The Harrison Ford movie, *Patriot Games*, returned to the studio, at enormous expense, to refilm the killing of the villain because preview audiences were not sufficiently satisfied by the original underwater death. In the final version the villain is painfully skewered by an anchor and then further disintegrated in a fiery explosion. The result? Significantly improved audience appraisals.

Similarly, in the Sylvester Stallone movie, *Cliffhanger*, preview audiences demanded two extra shots. In one, they wanted to know that an innocent bunny had in fact escaped a villain's gunfire. In the second, they wanted to see the arch-villain, John Lithgow's terror at his impending death. They weren't satisfied that he died. They needed to know that he suffered as well.

In the blockbuster hit *Independence Day—ID4*, it wasn't enough for the test audience that all the alien invaders die. There had to be a reaction shot, in which the two aliens in the control tower realize that they are about to die and turn to each other and say the alien equivalent of "Oh shit!" How much did this expensive two second add-on shot increase the final multi-hundred million dollar gross? We'll never know.

Even in movies based on real life wars, the audience demands a personification of the villainy. In *The Patriot*, *Saving Private Ryan*, and *Behind Enemy Lines*, the enemy is a faceless mass. While Mel Gibson, Tom Hanks and Gene Hackman are predictably our heroes, in real life the British, the Germans and the Serbs are no longer our enemy. Consequently each film provides at least one fictional, recognizable, unequivocally evil character so the viewer will feel satisfied when he is killed at the climax.

Are there crimes that can never be forgiven? Is there anger that can never be appeased? Will any American ever forgive *September 11, 2001*? Recapitulating President Roosevelt's description of the Pearl Harbor attack, it will always be remembered as a day of infamy. As Senator John McCain, a Vietnam war hero, said at the time: "May God have mercy on their souls, because we won't." Talk to Armenians about Turkey. Talk to Blacks about slavery. Talk to Jews about Nazis. Talk to Cliff about Peter. Talk to Sharon about Judy.

The crusade against drunk drivers was started by parents who had lost their children in traffic accidents caused by them. Nothing could bring their children back, but neither could anything make them forget that the perpetrators rarely got substantially punished. It's no accident that they call themselves "M.A.D.D."

It was unheard of years ago, but today victims' families frequently attend the trials of their assailants. If they are found guilty, the family and friends will often unabashedly exult in glee. Is it barbaric? Is it uncivilized? On the contrary, just as Clarice Starling needed to silence her lambs, victims need to silence their anger. Sometimes the only way to do it is by vengefully expressing it.

Forgiveness might be divine, but in certain instances, revenge is a Godsend.

> *"Speak to them, bid them rage . . .*
> *Demand the retribution for the shamed,*
> *Of all the centuries and every age,*
> *Let fists be flung like so many stones,*
> *Against the heavens and the heavenly throne . . .*
> *And you, son of man, be part of these,*
> *Believe the heart's pang, not their litanies."*
> -Chaim Nachman Bialik, (1874-1934)

Notes

---

[1] *Deuteronomy* XXXII:19, 21-22.

[2] Ted Danson went on to star in his own shows, *Cheers* and *Becker*.

[3] Danny DeVito has made a career playing variations on the character of Louie DePalma in *Romancing the Stone*, *Throw Momma From The Train*, *Ruthless People* and *Tin Men*, among many others.

[4] *The Lord's Prayer*.

[5] *Matthew* VI:12.

[6] *Exodus* XXI:23-25.

[7] *Deuteronomy* XXXII:35.

[8] *Numbers* XXXV: 11-15.

[9] *Numbers* XXXV: 16-32.

[10] Though the Bible goes to great lengths to protect only accidental killers, other ancient societies were more forgiving, usually to their detriment.

"In ancient Greece and Rome, shrines that gave asylum to murderers were nurseries of criminals. In the time of Tiberius, the swarms of desperadoes at shrines had become so dangerous that the right was limited to a few cities. Conditions were not much better when the Medieval Church began to offer 'sanctuary' to criminals of every description."—The Pentateuch, Dr. J.H. Hertz—Editor, page 721, Soncino Press 1977.

[11] *Numbers* XXXV, 26-27.

[12] "I know what you're thinking. Did he fire six shots, or only five? Well, to tell you the truth, in all the excitement I've kinda lost track myself. But being this is a .44 Magnum, the most powerful handgun in the world, and would blow your head clean off, you've got to ask yourself one question: do I feel lucky? Well, do ya, punk?"—Clint Eastwood, *Dirty Harry,* 1971.

[13] "Go ahead, make my day!"—Clint Eastwood, *Sudden Impact,* 1983.

[14] *La Saisiaz,* Robert Browning (1812—1889).

[15] *The Wall Street Journal,* June 10, 2002.

[16] In the year 2001 only 805 malpractice suits were filed in all of Japan. By way of comparison, many American cities had more suits than this entire populous country.

PART II

CHAPTER FOUR

A Time To Make Peace

Avoiding the Anger

*"To every thing there is a season,
and a time to every purpose under the heaven:
A time to be born, and a time to die;
a time to plant, and a time to pluck up that which is planted."* [1]

To support myself through college and medical school I took many and varied jobs. One of the more interesting (and lucrative) was working as a waiter.

Being young, inexperienced and insecure, it was very important to me that my patrons liked me. Given a choice, I preferred a generous compliment to a generous tip. (Given my druthers, I preferred both.)

One slow evening I was waiting on a silent couple who ordered a full three course dinner, alas without alcohol. [2] Since it was a quiet night, I had no trouble giving them all the attention that they required. They were perfectly gracious in return, though I couldn't help but notice that the lady seemed uncomfortable. At the end of the meal the lady asked me for the check which I promptly gave her. When I returned her credit card and slip, she asked me to wait as she filled it out. She handed it back to me as if she wanted me to read it. I smilingly obliged, since that unusual gesture always indicated that the tip was overly generous.

I looked at it. I was stunned. She had stiffed me. There was no tip whatsoever. Not one red cent. It had never happened to me before. I stood there looking at her. She looked me in the eye, even more uncomfortable than she had been before. I didn't know what to say. Finally she broke the tense silence. "I didn't leave you any tip."

She didn't say it as much with anger, as I would have expected, but rather with defiance. I subsequently learned from more experienced waiters that the correct response would have been: "Was there something unsatisfactory with the service?" At the time, however, I was at a complete loss for words. She seemed pleased at my lack of response. She triumphantly got up and left. For the first time all evening she had a smile on her face. I, on the other hand, had tears in my eyes. (Yes, I know that was a very childish response, but, as I said, I was young.)

A few minutes later her husband returned. He appeared rather sheepish, looking for something he had left behind. I gave him wide berth. After a few seconds he approached me. Furtively, he stuck a ten-dollar bill in my hand and whispered under his breath: "She's taking an assertiveness training course. This is an exercise. Don't take it personally."

Since that episode I have noticed many similar examples of assertiveness training, involving not only waiters, but cabbies and other gratuity-expectant service personnel as well. Unlike my experience, most of them do not end happily.

Several years ago E.S.T.,[3] now defunct, would conduct their weekend seminars in a building adjacent to our garage. It was deja-vuish to see them defiantly block all vehicular traffic as they would exit the building. Their triumphant smiles as they walked deliberately in front of our car, despite their red light, always reminded me of the confrontation between the uncomfortable lady and her insecure waiter.

Do these assertiveness training exercises really make sense? Their supporters argue that going through the actual experience in real life is the only way to make you comfortable confronting other people's anger. I can't agree. Surgeons don't become comfortable with appendectomies by removing healthy appendices. While it's important to be able to deal with anger, we don't learn to do that by *unjustifiably* provoking other people's anger. Examples like these serve only to ridicule our field.

Being comfortable with anger doesn't mean having to be angry all the time. On the contrary, it is more like the peace loving person who deliberately possesses a black belt to *avoid* having to fight. As much as we must learn when and how to express our anger, we must learn when and how not to, as well. There is a time for EXTAR and a time for revenge, but much of the time, we have other priorities.

We recently purchased a piano. We arranged for a weekend delivery, so I could be there when it arrived. Three burly deliverymen removed it from the truck and uncrated it on the sidewalk. The foreman asked me if I wanted them to take it upstairs to the apartment. I said of course.

With a barely concealed smile, he informed me that he would require $150 cash, in advance, for the service. I told him he was mistaken. I showed him that it stated explicitly on the bill that "delivery and set up *in the home*" was included. He replied that "in the home" actually meant the sidewalk in front of the home. If I wanted the piano in my apartment, I had to fork over the hundred-fifty bucks. As he said it, one of his partners couldn't prevent himself from giggling at my obvious frustration.

I was livid. I immediately understood what was happening. Their office was closed. I had no options. I couldn't call their boss. I couldn't move the piano myself. I couldn't leave it on the sidewalk while I tried to round up friends on a Sunday morning. They had me and we all knew it. I felt like yelling at them, or even worse, but what would it accomplish? If angered, they could pulverize me. They knew that, the same way they knew that if I could afford the piano, I could afford the $150. The fact of my wife and three children standing there already playing the piano further exacerbated the situation. I sent them all upstairs, and then turned to the foreman.

"You know. I'm really angry about this."

"Oh yeah? You want to do something about it?"

"Oh no, I'm not angry at you. I'm angry at your boss. He lied to both of us. He told me that I would get the piano delivered to my apartment, but he told you that you only had to deliver it to the sidewalk."

"Yeah, that's tough, but that's the way it goes."

"Well, I'm going to teach him a lesson. I'm refusing delivery. I paid with a credit card. When the bill comes, I'm not paying it. That'll teach him for lying to us that way."

"Whaddaya mean?"

"I mean, take the piano back. Your boss shouldn't be allowed to take advantage of both you and me this way. If he has a problem with it, tell him to call me tomorrow."

Was I telling the truth? Of course not. I wasn't angry at their boss. He knew nothing of this. I was angry at them. Yet the priority here wasn't my anger, or my need for revenge. It wasn't my relationship with them, or my need for EXTAR.

The priority was the piano. I knew that they couldn't afford to take the piano back and have their boss call me and find out about their scam. (I also knew that I had already paid the credit card bill, but I assumed that they didn't know that.) Sure enough, the foreman conferred with his confederates.

"You know what. You seem like a nice guy. Your kids really liked the piano. Why should they be disappointed? We'll take it upstairs for free."

"Gee, that's really very kind of you. I appreciate it."

Benny and Michelle decided the time was right to renovate their master bathroom. Since they both had demanding jobs, they hired a neighbor who was an architect to oversee the project. As he explained to them, in return for his 15% fee, he would coordinate and oversee everything. He would take care of the headaches. They wouldn't have to worry about anything.

Benny and Michelle moved out. When they returned the bathroom was complete. It was breathtaking. It was so spectacular, it took several minutes before Michelle noticed something was wrong. The shelf above the sink was gone. There had been one in the old bathroom. It had been explicitly specified with the architect, yet, it wasn't there.

"Maybe they just haven't put it in yet," Benny offered hopefully. "Where would they put it?" Michelle responded. "They didn't leave any room for it."

Benny called the architect. He started to ask him about the shelf. The architect interrupted him: " . . . But how do you like the overall effect? It's awesome, isn't it? You're going to knock people's eyes out. I've already taken photographs for my portfolio. I can't tell you how proud I am."

Benny persisted about the shelf. The architect explained apologetically that the vanity that best complemented the pedestal sink didn't allow clearance for a shelf. He assured Benny that "the right decision had been made in terms of the big picture."

Benny conveyed the architect's message to Michelle. Initially they were mollified. They liked the architect and overall, they were happy with the bathroom. With each succeeding day however, they became increasingly bothered. Benny had no place to leave his razor and brush. Michelle had no place to put her makeup when she was using the mirror. When the architect came over, they conveyed how much they needed the shelf. The architect explained that at this point, there was nothing that could be done, short of ripping out the entire wall, vanity and marble, and starting from scratch. His unspoken implication seemed to be that it would be prohibitively expensive to do so.

Neither Benny nor Michelle was prepared for an angry confrontation. As Benny put it, he felt he would have to "go to the mat" on this, and he didn't have the stomach for it. Unfortunately, the easy way in the short run, wasn't the best way in the long run. Long after the architect was out of their lives, they would still be stuck without the shelf. Every morning that Benny would have to shuffle back and forth between the bedroom and the bathroom in order to shave, as he was currently doing, it would bother him yet again. The absence of a shelf would be like a pebble in a shoe, unignorably bothersome, ultimately eliminating any possibility of pleasure. Furthermore, knowing that they don't have it because they couldn't confront their architect, would impinge on their own self-respect. Benny understood that, but simply couldn't go to war with his neighbor.

He didn't have to. The issue here wasn't Benny's anger. It was the shelf.

There was no need to express his anger, as in EXTAR. There was certainly no need to extract revenge. This wasn't an intentional slight. It wasn't a scam, like the piano man. It was only a mistake. The only need was for rectification. Benny met with the architect.

"I'm sorry, but Michelle and I have decided that we simply cannot live without a shelf. You're going to have to put one in."

"But aren't you satisfied with it otherwise? Don't you love the over-all appearance?"

"We do. We think you've done a wonderful job in all other respects, but we absolutely need a shelf."

"But I'll have to rip out the whole wall."

"We're sorry, but that's not our problem."

"It's going to cost a lot of money."

"That's not our problem either. We agreed on a price. We agreed on a shelf. We're entitled to both."

"You know I was only trying to make your bathroom more beautiful. I was only trying to help you."

"We know that. That's why we'll recommend you to our friends. That's why we'll use you again. *After* we get our shelf."

Benny and Michelle got their shelf. True to their word, they used the architect to renovate their kitchen. On that project he didn't make any unilateral decisions. Apparently, both architect and client had grown.

Part of growing up is learning that just because we're

angry, it doesn't always make sense to express your anger. We have a right to demand rectification if we're entitled to it, as Benny was. We don't have a right to be obnoxious about it, which is what expressing it angrily would have been.

If I buy a defective television, I have a right to demand it fixed. I don't have a right to berate the repairman because I missed the Super Bowl. There will be times when we will be angry and there will be no one to blame. Unlike what contingency lawyers would like us to believe, just because something went wrong, it doesn't necessarily mean that someone is at fault.

Our plane sat interminably on a runway at New York's La Guardia Airport. In and of itself that's hardly an unusual occurrence. What made it so, was the fact that we weren't waiting to take off. We had already landed.

The only gate that could accommodate our plane was broken. We waited over two hours for it to be repaired. One "gentleman" couldn't wait. After a few minutes, he informed the stewardess that he absolutely had to disembark immediately. He had an urgent appointment that could not wait, under any circumstances. The stewardess informed him that it was not possible. He pointed out the emergency exits. She pointed out that this wasn't an emergency. He insisted that it was.

He got angrier and angrier demanding to speak to the Captain, promising to sue, using any threat that his frenzied mind could think of. When that didn't work, he tried to physically push his way off the plane. He would not take no for an answer. In the end, he got his way. He did indeed disembark before the rest of us. Thirty seconds before the rest of us got off, he was escorted off the plane in handcuffs by airport police.

If "maturity" had to be defined with one word, that word would be "acceptance." As we grow emotionally, we learn that while life is not always perfect, or just, our best option is usually to accept it and make the best of it. Our maturational stage can be defined by our ability to tolerate such frustrations. Growing up is learning what the rules are and then playing by them.

Simon was a high school student with a bad temper. Mr. Crawford was his chemistry teacher who was as volatile as the reagents with which he experimented. The two of them together were bad chemistry. Simon had been suspended a dozen times. Yet Simon had legitimate gripes against Crawford, who at times was deliberately provocative. Nevertheless, Crawford was in charge. Simon wasn't. Whether the rock hits the glass, or the glass hits the rock, the glass loses[4]. Simon was the glass. The authority is always the rock.

What could Simon do? When Crawford would make one of his typically witty remarks such as: "Simon, when you yawn, it smells like someone lifted a sewer manhole cover.," Simon couldn't control his anger.

In reality there was nothing wrong with Simon feeling angry, or even expressing it, with one caveat. He couldn't let Crawford hear it. There was an alternative. He learned to sit in class with a smile on his face, taking notes furiously as Crawford spoke. In fact, he took more notes than anyone. While everyone else was merely writing down Crawford's words, Simon was adding commentary. They ranged from "you are the stupidest asshole on the face of the Earth," to "I hope you die from cramps." The messages assuaged his anger, brought the smile to his face, and, most importantly, avoided his getting suspended.

We often overlook how helpful the written word can be in dealing with anger. First and foremost, it gives us the luxury of time. It takes time to write a letter. We write it. We re-read it. We add a paragraph or eliminate one. We change a word or a phrase. We get an envelope and address it. We look for a stamp. Then, even after all of that, we still have to wait till we get to a mailbox.

All the while, we have the opportunity to cool down, to

censor, to reconsider. Most of the angriest letters ever written are never sent. The act of writing the letter was cathartic enough. Crawford doesn't have to see it. Even if the letter is sent, at least we had the opportunity to say precisely what we mean. We weren't interrupted. We weren't provoked further. We didn't get caught up in an escalating argument. Not only can the letter assuage our anger directly, but it can also assuage others' anger indirectly, in the process avoiding an unnecessary confrontation.

Efrem was a well-known author and lecturer. His friend Jerry, a corporate president, paid him a generous honorarium to give the keynote address at his company's meeting. The meeting went well. The address went well. The review however, left something to be desired.

A *New York Times* reporter in the audience had written an article about the meeting and Efrem's address. Albeit accurate, her review quoted primarily Efrem's most controversial points. Both Efrem and the company were mocked. Being used to reviews, Efrem took it in stride. Jerry had a cow. He was livid beyond reason, demanding that Efrem write a letter of protest to the editor.

What was Efrem to do? His friend and benefactor was demanding a letter which could jeopardize his future with a powerful reporter and newspaper. Whether he wrote it or he didn't, he would be burning an important bridge behind him. If he tried to compromise and write a reasonably argumentative letter, he would still probably satisfy neither and alienate both.

In the end Efrem wrote the letter. It pulled no punches, sarcastically denouncing the reporter in a merciless ad hominem attack. He sent a copy to Jerry. He discarded the original.

A week later Jerry, by now mollified, called Efrem. "I knew those gutless bastards at the *Times* would never print your letter."

Efrem replied: "So did I."

In that sense, the inventions of the telephone, and the internet (and to a lesser degree, the fax) were the worst things to ever happen to anger. A telephone to an angry person is like a spark to gasoline. It facilitates our impulsiveness. It exacerbates the confrontation, often irreversibly. A keyboard is an improvement only because it takes longer to type than to talk. Nevertheless, e-mails, instant messages especially, can be as destructive as that ill-advised phone call. There are at least four objects that one should never pick up while under the influence of alcohol, drugs or anger: A weapon, a car key, a telephone and a laptop.

What can we do when we didn't initiate the angry phone call, but merely answered it?

Larry was a young professional basketball coach. He was struggling with a moderately talented team, but that wasn't what was bothering him. What was bothering him were the phone calls he was receiving from his general manager, Stretch, the man he reported to, the man in charge of extending his contract. Stretch wasn't calling to discuss the team, or even Larry's performance. He was calling to complain about Cash, the team's owner.

Stretch would interminably recount to Larry every last, picayune detail of every stupid thing Cash said. As soon as Stretch got off the phone with Cash, he would call Larry to repeat the conversation. Stretch was angry at Cash and he was using Larry as a sounding board, in effect his therapist. These phone calls would relieve Stretch's anger, but they were driving Larry crazy.

It wasn't just the monumental waste of time that bothered Larry about the phone calls. It was also the content. Larry liked Cash. Cash had always been not only nice, but indeed generous to Larry. While Stretch was correct that Cash was not that bright, he was paternal to Larry, doting on him like a son.

Stretch's phone calls frustrated Larry no end. They reminded him of his mother complaining to him about his father, when he was a kid. Then like now, he was in a no-win situation. If Larry defended Cash to Stretch, Stretch would get angry at Larry and imply that Larry must be as stupid as Cash. If Larry insincerely agreed with Stretch, it just encouraged him. If he said nothing, Stretch would go on forever. If he said he was busy, Stretch would call back later.

What was Larry to do? EXTAR, expressing his own anger to Stretch would only succeed in alienating Stretch and getting Larry fired. Besides, Larry had no threat to make. Larry couldn't tell his boss that he wasn't going to take his phone calls. Stretch wasn't making sexist, or even offensive remarks, as in our EXTAR work example. Revenge would be squealing, telling Cash what Stretch said about him. It was unthinkable. Besides betraying Stretch's trust, it would guarantee that Larry would never work again in the league.

My advice to Larry was simple. I told him to stretch. Hold the phone away from your ear. Put Stretch on the speakerphone, and turn the volume way down. The fact that we occasionally have to take an unpleasant phone call doesn't mean that we have to listen to it. It wasn't the fact of Stretch's calling that angered Larry. It was the content. By distancing himself from the content, he eliminated his own frustration. He was even able to continue working through Stretch's monologues.

I learned this precious piece of advice not from a psychiatrist, or a textbook, but ironically enough from my own basketball coach, Norm, who was conducting a practice before a big game, keeping us overtime. The phone on the gym wall rang. It was the principal. He was screaming at the top of his lungs at our belatedness. Norm let the phone hang from the wall. It was clear that this was to be a one-sided conversation anyway. We concluded our drill to the accompaniment of our principal yelling in the distance. We finished at the same time that he did. Norm picked up the phone, winked at us, apologized and told the principal we'd be right there.

Norm was right. There was nothing to be gained from listening to the tirade. The principal needed to vent. That didn't mean that Norm needed to listen. Larry didn't need to listen to Stretch. Larry didn't need to listen to his mother complain about his father. You don't need to listen to your bitter sibling complain about your parents. You don't need to listen to your colleague complain about his salary. You don't need to listen to your neighbors complain about their in-laws. In all these cases, and many more, the most constructive approach to an angry phone call is to pick up the phone and hold it as far away from you as possible, both physically and emotionally.

Sometimes you can even go a step further. You can safely express your anger back, no matter who the caller is. Just make sure you press the "Mute" button first. Like Simon with Crawford, you receive the cathartic release of expressing your anger, without the repercussions. It doesn't eliminate the injustice that precipitated your anger. It just makes it easier to tolerate.

Injustice is an inherent part of life. That doesn't mean we have to allow ourselves to be upset by it. It wasn't an iceberg that sank the Titanic. It was the ship's inability to isolate the leak. It's their inability to isolate the anger that sinks people like Dean or Eduardo, rather than the actual breach.

We define psychotic as a person who has lost touch with reality. He thinks that two plus two equals five. By that definition, a neurotic, (all of us at times), is someone who knows that two plus two equals four, but can't stand it. If we choose to get angry about something, we are choosing to make a significant investment of time, energy and emotion. It only makes sense to choose things that are worth getting angry about. If not, we're being neurotic.

Years ago my wife and I attended a party at the invitation of Jack, a new friend. We were sitting at a table with others engaged in conversation when a matronly lady approached. She cheerily introduced herself as Jack's mother. We all warmly responded. With a smile on her face, she turned to me. "Jack mentioned that you're a psychiatrist."

"Guilty as charged. Do you have an interest in the field?"

"Very much so. I believe in (a certain cult). Have you read (title of deceased cult leader's book)? He says that psychiatrists are the lowest form of life. You're worse than a murderer. A murderer kills quickly. You kill slowly."

She still had the smile on her face. The rest of us had a look of shock. Part of me wanted to respond. I could insult her back, argue with her, perhaps even explain or persuade. A larger part of me was angry.

How dare she! She was deliberately insulting me, trying to publicly humiliate me, despite the fact that she had never met me before in her life. I felt my wife's reassuring hand under the table in nervous anticipation of what I was going to say. I stood up. I turned to the others at the table. I lifted my water glass and said: "Excuse me. I'm going to get a refill."

I left. My wife joined me. Several minutes later Jack's mother approached me again. I excused myself again. Since then, she and I have attended many of Jack's celebrations together. She has learned that the minute she approaches me, I excuse myself. Jack has apologized to me and thanked me for "handling the situation so adroitly." Apparently his neighbor, also a psychiatrist, will not attend any function at which Jack's mother is present.

Truthfully, that option had occurred to me. If I did that however, she would have won. Why should I allow her ignorance to prevent me from enjoying a friend's celebration? Do I have a right to be angry at her? I think I do. I just don't think she's worth it. Even when she bothers me, I don't want to give her the satisfaction of knowing it.

One of the nurses at Bellevue Hospital was dating a doctor at another hospital. The relationship intensified. For a while they lived together, until she accidentally discovered that he was simultaneously sleeping with another woman. She eventually got over him, but was still bothered by how utterly dishonest he had been.

It bothered her worse to discover months later that he was scheduled to do an elective at Bellevue. She knew what he was like. This egotistical bastard wouldn't let sleeping dogs lie. He would definitely go out of his way to make some embarrassing remark to her, probably in public. She considered begging him or threatening him, but didn't want to give him the satisfaction of either. She asked me for a suggestion.

True to her prediction, he approached her at lunch his first day there. She was sitting at a table with several of her aides when he came over. He stood there smiling at her in his characteristically patronizing way until he had her attention. "I hope that my presence isn't going to make you uncomfortable. Whatever happened between us shouldn't prevent you from acting professionally."

She smiled back. "No problem. I'm sorry, what's your name again?"

He left in a huff as the table erupted in laughter. He never approached her again.

Was she being honest? Not at all. Of course she remembered his name. Was she being passive-aggressive? Absolutely. Then why did I recommend both here, when I advised against both in EXTAR? Because in EXTAR, we were discussing relationships that we wanted to continue. This was a relationship that she wanted to end. Ending a relationship, or our memory of it, can be even harder than maintaining it, as we saw with Eduardo and his interminable obsessions.

Yet, if, as in *A Beautiful Mind*[5], we can ignore psychotic hallucinations and delusions[6] and not let them destroy our life, we can certainly do the same with neurotic obsessions. Even if the annoying thoughts come knocking at the door of our mind, we don't have to let them in. One humorous lady when bothered by recurring memories of a scoundrelous boyfriend would say to herself sprightly, out loud if necessary, "Go away! There's nobody home." It made her laugh, rather than cry.

The most eloquent speech that President Reagan ever gave was to the American hostages when they finally returned from Iran. These poor men, through no fault of their own, had been imprisoned, humiliated, and both physically and mentally tortured for a period of years. Anyone could readily understand both their anger and their desire for revenge. The President spoke instead of "turning the page." He advised them to "start a new chapter" and get on with their lives, instead of dwelling on their suffering. Any of us who have ever treated a former hostage would readily agree with the President's advice.

It doesn't matter if we were held hostage by an enemy in a far-off country, or by our toxic parent in our own home. At some point, we have to get on with our life. We have to take responsibility for our problems and not conveniently blame them all on our parents or our previous trauma. Ultimately, to the degree that we blame our problems on our parents, we remain children.

A critical part of growing up is learning to deal with our anger. In these three chapters we have discussed three different methods—EXTAR, Revenge and Peace. Despite their trivergent approaches, the three methods share a critical common denominator. They confront the anger. They stop the cycle.

The anger-fear cycle is like a pendulum. It sequentially swings back and forth, with the momentum of one extreme inevitably bringing it back to the other extreme. When we try to stop it, we usually try to stop it at either extreme. We can't. A pendulum can only be stopped in the middle.

We can only stop our obsessions by expressing our anger. Sometimes, expressing it to our spouse or close friend is enough. Sometimes, expressing it to our psychiatrist is enough. Sometimes, we have to express it to the person who made us angry.

A seemingly trivial example is possibly the most ubiquitous catalyst of resentment, the insulting joke. As discussed in A Looney Tunes World, all jokes have some anger in them. Nevertheless, some jokes have more anger than others. Many a truth is said in jest. So is many an insult. How should we handle them? EXTAR, revenge or peace?

The answer, of course, depends on the circumstances. We have to examine the details of the incident, other people's reactions, as well as our own feelings.

Was the joke really funny, or was it a thinly veiled insult that was only ostensibly facetious, because the teller was smiling? Was the teller a genuinely funny person, who makes fun of everyone, most importantly, himself, or does she tease you purposefully? Did the other people laugh heartily without apparent discomfort, or did they titter nervously, looking at you expectantly? Did you feel warmly, appreciative to be included, even flattered to be the center of attention, or did you feel attacked, even humiliated, like someone was spitting in your face?

Examine not only the verbatim content of the comment, but also the tone of voice—affectionate, or reeking with sarcasm? the surroundings—a boisterous bar, or a quiet home? the perpetrator's behavior both before and after the comment—solicitous, or contemptuous?

Try to imagine how you'd react if the same comment, in the same tone, in the same circumstances had been made by someone of whom you're unequivocally fond. Would you be equally angry? Would you be angry at all? If not, why not? Are you overreacting in this case? It might seem impossible to evaluate so many variables so quickly, and perhaps it is. Yet, we need to, if our conclusion is to be accurate.

What are our options once we reach our conclusion? The most common option is also unfortunately the worst.

We do nothing. Denial. No matter how humiliated we feel, we grit our teeth, smile politely, perhaps blush, but say nothing in response, for fear of appearing to be a bad sport. Then we vividly recall the embarrassing moment for the rest of the day, and probably for many days to come.

Depending on our state of stress or intoxication, we might resort to the second worst option. We overreact. We hit the joker, or throw our drink at them, or curse them out. With any of these acts, we announce to all that we have lost control. We have been goaded into doing something that we subsequently regret.

The best options, of course, are the aforementioned three. If you feel that you have been deliberately insulted, take revenge. Let the punishment fit the crime however. Make an insulting joke back.

The story has been often repeated of the society matron who told Winston Churchill: "If you were my husband, I would feed you poison." On paper, that might seem too confrontational to be a joke, but it would have sounded like one if she was smiling when she said it, as she probably was. No doubt Churchill was similarly smiling when he replied: "If you were my wife, I would take it."

Can't think of a joke quickly enough? Respond sarcastically. "That's *very* funny." "I find that *so* amusing." "Thank you for *such* a compliment." *What* you say is less important than *how* you say it. Don't smile. Let the joker and everyone else know that you're nobody's fool. You realize that you've been insulted, you don't like it, and you hold the joker accountable. The joker will quickly learn that you are not someone to be trifled with. More importantly, you will feel better about yourself afterwards.

If, on the other hand, the joke, albeit insulting, was not meant maliciously, use EXTAR instead. Take the joker aside and explain to them that you prefer that others not make fun of your weight, age, toupee, handicap, spouse, etc.

Other times it is wisest to make peace. A medical student

used to periodically correct his Unit Chief on rounds. Whenever he did, the Unit Chief would respond by joking about the thickness of the student's glasses reflecting how much he must read. On the surface the joke was a compliment, referring to the student's scholarliness. Nevertheless, the student was embarrassed. His glasses were indeed of the proverbial Coke bottle thickness, and he didn't appreciate the reminder.

What could he do? Revenge would be self-destructive, EXTAR inappropriately presumptuous. The best option was to make peace, i.e. stop correcting the Unit Chief on rounds since she obviously didn't like it.

In a variation on the same theme, Sanford, a law firm partner, phoned Ken. Ken, also a partner, was not only disturbed to note how angry Sanford sounded, but also that Sanford had three associates on the line with him. In a patronizing tone Sanford reprimanded Ken. Ken felt so infuriated he couldn't even focus on Sanford's words. What were Ken's options?

Option one is the path of least resistance, total capitulation. Its advantages are it would alleviate Sanford's anger and shorten the unpleasantness. Its disadvantages however are far greater. Not only would it exacerbate Ken's own anger, not only would Ken be dishonest, but most importantly, Ken would be positively reinforcing Sanford's behavior.

Option two is the path of least action, say nothing. First and foremost, it would negatively reinforce Sanford's actions. It would probably frustrate him to some degree. The disadvantages are it might prolong the agony of the phone call and it still wouldn't express Ken's anger.

Option three is the instinctual path of retaliation. Yell back at Sanford. Give it back to him as loudly, and as insultingly as he was dishing it out. Only now does Ken begin to adversely condition Sanford, and, more importantly, express his own anger. However, on the negative side, Ken is not only prolonging the confrontation, he is escalating it. Furthermore, he is guilty of the same sin as Sanford, deliberately insulting a colleague in front of subordinates.

Option four is passive-aggressive, ending the conversation politely without prejudice or explanation. "I'm sorry Sanford, I can't talk to you right now." Sanford however, might well not accept that reply: "Why the hell not? This is more important than anything you're doing." It could easily escalate to Option three.

Option five is curtailing the conversation with prejudice, but without explanation, i.e. hanging up. Ken has expressed his anger. Sanford has been put in his place, albeit in a rude, unprofessional manner. Arguably, he deserved it.

Option six, the best, is terminating the conversation with prejudice, but with explanation. "Sanford, I'm not having this conversation with you with associates on the line. If you want to discuss this further, come to my office, alone. Good bye."

Some find these inevitable business confrontations so unpleasant, they do anything to avoid them. Wendy was a successful investment banker who gave up a generous salary because she couldn't say no when her boss made unreasonable demands. Fortunately her husband was able to support them. She became pregnant and moved to the suburbs. Never again would she have to deal with people taking advantage of her.

Then her next-door neighbor time and again dropped her kids off at Wendy's. Another neighbor repeatedly asked Wendy to substitute for her in the car pool. Her daughter's teacher asked Wendy, the class mother, to call all the class parents because the teacher hadn't bothered to send a note home. Finally, Wendy came to realize that she couldn't find peace by running away from confrontations. There will always be people who will take advantage, given the opportunity, no matter the location.

Tragically, but thankfully rarely, sometimes the price of peace is ending an important relationship.

Clucky, as his mother called him, dutifully called his mother at dinnertime every day. Clarence, as his friends called him, had a hectic schedule, being Chairman of Anesthesiology at a major hospital. Still, he never missed his dinnertime call. After dinner, he regularly sat down to play war games. After a few beers, he would start to name and even label certain soldiers "Mom." Soldiers labeled "Mom" were treated differently from the others. They couldn't merely die. They had to die slowly and painfully, preferably after losing several body parts.

Clarence had innumerable stories to justify his hatred of his mother. There was his fifth birthday party when she pushed him into his birthday cake for a laugh. There were the times she threw him to the ground, kicked him, cursed him, and spat on him, because he dared to disobey her. There was his wedding that she "accidentally" came late to, and "mistakenly" put on the wrong dress, because she didn't approve of his bride. There were the times she would mock him in front of his children. It was easy to understand why Clarence hated her. It was harder to understand why he still called her daily.

When I asked him that question, his outraged response was: "What kind of son do you think I am!?" I replied: "The kind of son whose after dinner activity is torturing his mother to death."

"But *she* doesn't know that."

"But *you* do."

"That's because I also know that she's a fucking bitch who is as spiteful as she is obese!"

Talking to him was like witnessing a one-man debate. One second he would attack her without mercy. The next he would defend his continued relationship. His attempt to displace his maternal anger onto toy soldiers was as successful as tying off the sternum's artery to displace blood to the heart.[7] He would probably still be vacillating, if not for an incident in the operating room. The patient was, not coincidentally, a demanding, overweight lady his mother's age.

As the surgeon started to operate, he repeatedly informed Clarence that the patient was looking blue. Clarence repeatedly checked the tubing never noticing that he had connected the unfortunate lady to Nitrogen, instead of Oxygen. Finally, the surgeon himself had to rush back to rectify Clarence's mistake. In another minute, the lady would have been brain dead.

Clarence described the episode to his mother. She found it amusing. She told all her friends how Clucky was still a bonehead. Then she told his children. That was the last straw.

Clarence stopped talking to her. She blamed it on his wife. She called both of them and cursed them out. Clarence could hear her spitting over the phone. He hung up on her. He soon lost interest in his war games. It took five decades, but Clarence finally was able to turn the page and close an unpleasant chapter.

In contrast, my friend Elie Wiesel, a Holocaust survivor whose profound work has earned him not only universal respect but also the Nobel Prize, wrote in his memoirs:

> "Tell your stories, even if you have to invent a language. Communicate your memories, your doubts, even if no one wants to hear them. It is incumbent upon survivors not only to remember every detail but to record it, even the silence. Celebrate the memory of silence, but reject the silence of memory."[8]

There is something to be said, as Ronald Reagan did, for not living in the past. There is equally, if not more, to be said, as Elie Wiesel continually has, for not forgetting the past either.[9]

As the Bible teaches us, there is a time for all emotions.

There are times to get angry and express it; there are also times to overlook slights. There are times we should eternally remember; there are also times to forget. There are times we are right to take revenge; there are other times we are wiser to make peace.

"Revenge is a kind of wild justice;
which the more man's nature runs to,
the more ought law to weed it out."
—Francis Bacon (1561-1626)

Notes

---

[1] *Ecclesiastes* III: 1-8.

[2] Waiters universally prefer imbibing customers for two reasons. Number one, drinks and wine precipitously jack up the bill and thus the tip. Number two, alcohol begets good will towards all, including waiters.

[3] Ehrhart Sensitivity Training.

[4] Sancho Panza sang of the plight of the pitcher hitting the stone in *Man of La Mancha*, the story of Cervantes and Don Quixote.

[5] *A Beautiful Mind* was a book by Sylvia Naser and a Best Picture winning movie directed by Ron Howard describing the life story of John Nash. John Nash was a Nobel Laureate who was also a paranoid schizophrenic who managed to defy the generally horrendous prognosis of his disease. *A Beautiful Mind* (1998), Sylvia Naser, Simon & Schuster.

[6] There was much controversy associated with *A Beautiful Mind.* Many psychiatrists question if it is accurate or helpful to suggest that John Nash was able to overcome his schizophrenia with a combination of intelligence, will power and love. It might even be inadvertently insulting to the vast majority of schizophrenics, and their families, who are less successful.

[7] In the 1950's many patients with coronary artery disease underwent surgery in which the artery that runs under the sternum was tied

off. The theory was that the blood would be deflected into the coronary arteries and would perfuse the heart. The theory was wrong. It was as ineffective as increasing the pressure on a hose with a closed nozzle. The operation persevered so long only because so many patients had reported post-operative improvement. Double blind studies eventually proved that all the improvement had been purely a placebo effect. The operation was discarded.

[8] *All Rivers Run to the Sea* (1995), Elie Wiesel, Knopf.

[9] On one important occasion President Reagan and Professor Wiesel disagreed strongly on precisely this issue. On his controversial trip to Bitburg, President Reagan chose to honor German war dead at a cemetery where Gestapo members were buried. Professor Wiesel sought privately to dissuade the President from this visit, spoke out publicly against it and finally, in protest, resigned from the Presidential Holocaust Commission.

PART III
SPOT LIGHTS

PART III

CHAPTER ONE

It's Only a Temper Tantrum

Anger In Children

"And his brothers envied him. And they said to each other: 'Let's kill him now.'"[1]

Professor Hans Heinz was a well-known, highly respected psychoanalyst. He looked the part, balding, dignified, and always immaculately dressed. He had written a famous book on the art of listening to a patient. I was privileged to have him as a supervisor. By tradition, at the end of the year, I and his other supervisees, were invited to his home for dinner.

I remember the evening well. I particularly remember his six-year-old son, Otto. I sat next to him. Otto was impossible. Throughout the evening, whenever his father was making a serious point, Otto would accompany him with his singular imitation of passing gas.

Professor Heinz, seated at the far end of the table, ignored him. So did Mrs. Heinz, seated at the other end of the table. The only person who would occasionally reprimand him would be the maid as she was serving a course. "No, Otto. Not nice. No make noises." Otto ignored her.

During the entree, Otto decided that playing with the food on his plate no longer amused him. He started to play with the food on mine. I looked to his parents to see if they would choose to intervene. They chose not. Otto only stopped when I smilingly gestured to him that if one of his fingers strayed onto my plate again, I would slice it off. Subsequently he started to bother the lucky guest to his left.

Dessert was the climax of the meal. It was lemon meringue pie with boysenberry sherbet on the side. Otto was delighted by the consistency of the meringue which he repeatedly punctured with his stubby little fingers. He then would take his pie-encrusted finger and see how far he could flick the pie across the formal dining room. When a piece of pie came flying in Professor Heinz's direction, he finally took notice of his son.

"Otto. A civilized person does not play with his food."

Delighted by finally achieving a response, Otto flicked another piece of pie in his father's direction.

"Otto! I am not pleased with your behavior!"

The gauntlet had been lain down. Professor Heinz glared at Otto. Otto glared back. Finally Otto picked up a gob of boysenberry sherbet and flung it at his father. Otto's eye hand coordination was apparently his strong suit. The purple slush-ball landed squarely on Professor Heinz's high forehead. The silence was thick with tension as the Professor slowly removed his horn-rimmed glasses to clean his face with his napkin. We all nervously awaited how the world renowned psychiatrist would react. Everyone at the table was scared.

Except Otto.

Finally, the professor spoke: "Otto."

"Yeah."

"You're very angry. Very angry indeed."

Otto smiled. The maid hurriedly removed any remaining ammunition from Otto's range. The meal then proceeded as if nothing untoward had happened.

As I walked home that evening I decided that I had just learned two valuable lessons.

Number one—Children can be very angry.

Number two—In their home, children need a parent, *not* a psychiatrist.

The job of a parent is both more demanding and rewarding than the job of a psychiatrist. The responsibilities are greater, but so are the privileges. As a parent, we always remain an irreplaceable figure in the lives of our children, a realization simultaneously frightening and thrilling. For the most part, we don't need any so-called expert to give us lessons in parenting. Our instincts are perfectly fine. Parents don't need instructions to know to hug their children, or play with them, or talk to them. The most important lesson of all *can't* be taught. Loving your child is God given.

In this chapter, and the next, the infinite love that we each have for our children is, of course, beyond question. The questions that we do confront, address the best methods of expressing that love. Unfortunately, sometimes we love our children too much. When we think *only* with our heart, our children inadvertently suffer.

Thinking back to the evening with Professor Heinz, I should have learned a third lesson as well. Even the most brilliant psychiatrist will have a blind spot when it comes to their own child. In fairness, it seems that every parent has that same blind spot. At a wedding, or funeral, a toddler continually interrupts the sanctity of the occasion, yet the parents are firmly convinced that everyone is as amused as they themselves are. A pair of twins are using a restaurant's aisle as their private race course. When the Maitre 'd finally asks the parents if they could keep their children at the table, they reply: "Oh, they're not bothering anyone." Several patrons immediately point out that, in fact, that is *not* the case. The parents are insulted. They leave in a huff.

Other parents have deaf spots. In a concert, show or movie you have to put up with a crying or whining child whose parent is totally oblivious to the racket that is being created. The parent assumes since they have the capacity to tune their child out, everyone else should as well. When, an usher finally forces the parent to remove her child, her parting remark is: "Obviously, you don't like children." Liking children is not synonymous with liking their misbehavior, nor tolerating their disruptiveness.

Professor Heinz was right. Children are at times very angry. He was also right that Otto was expressing his anger by misbehaving. He was wrong to tolerate that misbehavior. Why? Because a child should be encouraged to express their anger constructively and verbally, *not* destructively or disruptively.

One of the most precious things about children is their natural candor, their innate desire to express themselves. They are born honest and open, until unfortunately, we teach them otherwise. In some cases we do it for good reason. It is inadvertent, but still cruel, when a child gets on a train and loudly proclaims to his mother, "Why is that lady so fat?" or "Look at that funny looking man." In other cases however, we do it for the wrong reasons. Our children see us lie to the bus driver about their age to avoid paying the fare. Our children see us lie to our neighbors, or even to each other, to avoid a confrontation. They learn.

Worst of all, they learn that they're not allowed to express their anger. We deem it disrespectful, or unseemly. When a child says: "I'm very angry at you!," they hear in response: "Oh, yeah? I'll give you something to be angry about!" Alternatively, not much better, they might hear: "You don't talk that way to your mother. Go to your room this instant." Less punitively, they might hear: "You're a spoiled brat. You have no right to be angry."

All three responses have negatively reinforced the child expressing his anger. The child has learned that nothing good will come out of verbally expressing his anger. He will be beaten, punished or, at best, insulted. The next time, the child will keep his anger in. It will grow, until it can no longer be kept in, and then it will explode, in a gob of boysenberry sherbet, or worse.

What's the alternative? Do we want to *encourage* our children's anger? No. But we want to encourage their expressing it. When our child tells us he's angry, the best thing we can do is to positively reinforce his telling us. "Thank you for telling me."

What if he's wrong? What if he's angry about the game being rained out, or about the TV show being a rerun, or a movie being a disappointment? It doesn't matter. The issue is *not* that he's wrong or right. The issue is not even that his anger is displaced. The issue is that he has a *right* to be angry. Every human being does, of any age. It doesn't mean that he's going to get his way. Seneca[2] pointed out two millennia ago: "A child should gain no request by anger; when he is quiet let him have what was refused when he wept." It doesn't mean that he's going to change your mind. It does mean that he's going to feel better for being able to speak his mind.

Many years ago our twin daughters wanted to stay up late to watch *E.T.*. We wouldn't let them. As I came into their room to kiss them goodnight, the older one refused to talk to me. When I kissed her scowling face anyway, she melodramatically wiped it off. When I went over to kiss the younger, she asked me not to. I respected her wishes. She then informed me: "Daddy, I'm very angry at you." I replied: "I understand. Thank you for telling me."

I expected that. I was prepared for it. I wasn't prepared for the follow-up. "Daddy, I don't love you any more." That floored me. I didn't really believe it, but it still hurt like hell to hear it.

I was tempted to give her a lecture about how precious and sacred love is, how love is not a commodity to be bartered for television viewing privileges. A part of me was angry myself that she had cheapened our relationship with her comment. Instead, I managed to mutter: "I still love you."

Ten minutes later I was lying in bed, still upset, when she scurried in. She smiled, leaned over and hugged my neck. "I changed my mind, Daddy. I love you again." She gave me a kiss. "I'm not angry at you any more either."

What happened to her older sister? An hour later she came into our bedroom crying. We asked her what was wrong. She said she had a nightmare. She wanted to lie down with us. She proceeded to tell us that, in her nightmare, we had been in a car accident and died. It frightened her so much that she needed our presence to reassure her that we were all right. We were happy to comply. She didn't mention her previous anger at us. Neither did we.

Did I explain to her that her nightmare was her way of expressing her anger at us by killing us? Of course not, for two reasons.

Number one—At the age of four she wasn't old enough to understand that whatever happens in her dreams is her creation. *I* understand that she wrote the screenplay, she directed it, and she produced it. *She* doesn't. Instead, she would argue with me that we were killed by the truck. She tried unsuccessfully to save us. In her mind, she had nothing to do with our death.

Number two—As Hans Heinz taught me, I'm her father, not her psychiatrist.

In his influential book *The Uses of Enchantment,* Bruno Bettelheim[3] pointed out that fairy tales[4] are popular because they vicariously express the children's repressed anger. As but one example, the ubiquitous wicked stepmother unconsciously represents the child's actual mother when she isn't being nice. Thus a child is able to split[5] his bad mother from his good mother, and be angry at the former without jeopardizing his relationship to the latter.

Every time our children express their anger to us, as painful as it feels at the moment, we need to remind ourselves that it's a compliment. It means they feel secure enough to say what's on their mind. They know that their relationship with us is safe enough for them to express an uncomfortable, unpleasant thought.

Will it still bother us? It probably will, in the short run. In the long run however, it makes them feel better about themselves and their relationship with us, and that should more than compensate for our momentary discomfort.

Besides, to be perfectly candid, my kids' anger is *nothing* compared to what mine was like at their age. One of my temper tantrums was witnessed by my entire school. I was in third grade. I had won the lead in the school play. We rehearsed for months. Finally, the big night arrived. At the time I considered it the single most important moment of my life. I was nervous, but prepared.

They put on my make-up. They started to put on my costume. Suddenly, they realized it was torn. It couldn't be repaired. It couldn't be used. I would have to go on without a costume. It wasn't a great option, but it was the only option. It made perfect sense. I didn't care. I refused to go on without my costume.

The teachers explained that I was still the star. I would still be front and center for the whole play. No one would blame me for the lack of costume. After a few minutes, no one would notice. Was I really going to waste all those months of memorization and rehearsal? Yes. Reasoning with your child in the midst of a temper tantrum is like reasoning with your pet in the midst of a dog fight. It's wasting your breath.

They tried to persuade me. They begged me. They argued with me. They threatened me. In the end, I cried and ran away. I never went on. Like Dean at his daughter's wedding, the single most important moment of my life was destroyed.

Why was I so stupid? All I could think of was that it wasn't fair! All the other kids had costumes and I didn't. I couldn't accept that. As in all temper tantrums, I couldn't stop myself from cutting off my nose to spite my face.

Why do children have temper tantrums? For one thing, it's because they lack perspective. If they were promised and expected the whole pie, they can't appreciate the logic that half a pie is better than none. It's all or nothing. A child has so little control over his destiny. Consequently, when his destiny appears optimistic, and then he's cheated, or so he feels, he can't accept it.

Ironically, the incident is usually dismissed with the phrase: "It's only a temper tantrum." A temper tantrum deserves the respect accorded any other natural disaster, like an earthquake or a hurricane. After all, it is natural, and it *is* a disaster. It would be far more appropriate to say, "Oh my God! It's a temper tantrum!"

Temper tantrums aren't limited to children. Did you see Roger Clemens, then Boston Red Sox's premier pitcher, get thrown out of a championship playoff game? Did you hear Richard Nixon's concession speech in 1962? Did you witness Dennis Rodman get ejected any of his innumerable times? Did you watch Mike Tyson bite Lennox Lewis' leg when he felt frustrated at a press conference? They all felt similarly cheated. They all lashed out, irrationally and uncontrollably. They all hurt themselves, and their reputations, to some degree irreversibly.

Jimbo, a brilliant mathematician, was a patient in group. When still a young child, his mother committed suicide. The unfortunate result was that he was raised by a succession of stepmothers and surrogates. He didn't have a choice but to be a perfectly behaved boy. He didn't have the luxury of a single temper tantrum in his childhood. He made up for it in his adulthood.

One week Jimbo was awarded a major honor that he had sought for years. To celebrate, he bought champagne to share with the group, his surrogate family. When he arrived he discovered that some members had canceled. Jimbo was incensed. He had looked forward to this moment for years. This wasn't the way he had envisioned it. The whole family was supposed to be there. It wasn't fair!

Jimbo expressed his anger. The group was sympathetic, but tried to point out to him how unreasonable he was being. He could not be mollified. He wouldn't open the champagne. He refused to speak further. He sat through the group in sullen silence. He didn't return for several weeks. Like me, because of an unexpected annoyance, he turned his moment of triumph into disaster. Eventually and inevitably, he left the group.

Jimbo's anger in group, as in all temper tantrums, was transparent. Fortunately, that is usually the case with children. Unfortunately as we get older we learn to hide our anger, behind the guise of politeness.

Several years ago I delivered a lecture to a psychiatric group in Israel. Although I understand Hebrew, I spoke in English. When I finished, I welcomed comments. A young, angry psychiatrist took the microphone and, addressing the audience in Hebrew, thinking that I didn't understand, called my entire speech "a colossal waste of time." After calling me an "amiable fool" in Hebrew, in English he asked me a minor question.

I had my revenge. After I answered his question in English, as he returned to the audience, I remarked in Hebrew that his comments hadn't been very generous. The audience laughed at his obvious embarrassment.

He had his revenge on me as well. When, the following day, I concluded my lecture at another hospital, he burst in, grabbed the microphone, and warned the audience: "Be careful! He understands Hebrew!"

Not coincidentally, when he had questioned me, he had started his question with, "With all due respect . . ." Invariably any question that starts, "With all due respect . . . ," never is. Similarly, anyone who starts off by saying, "I hate to disagree with you . . . ," really doesn't.

Ask a child, on the other hand, what he thinks and he'll tell you. As in *The Emperor's New Clothes*, the child hasn't learned to be polite. When it comes to dealing with his parents, he never should.

"What did you think of Mommy's dinner?"

"It didn't taste good."

"That's not very nice! Mommy worked hard to make you that dinner. You should be ashamed of yourself for saying that!"

Why? He was asked a question. He answered it honestly. The question was *not*, "Do you appreciate how hard Mommy worked on dinner?" He wasn't being cruel. He didn't volunteer the information. He was asked a question. In the end, he was given a choice of either lying or being insulted.

Should children *never* be reprimanded or punished? Of course they should. When they misbehave, there should be consequences for their actions. The more serious the misbehavior, the more serious the consequences should be. However, they should be punished for their actions, *not* for their expressions of anger.

Should Otto Heinz have been punished for giving his father a boysenberry shower? Absolutely. What if, instead of throwing the sherbet, the little brat had hurled invectives instead? What if he insulted his father? What if he loudly proclaimed how much he hated him? He should still be punished, not for expressing his feelings, but for deliberately embarrassing his father. Just as it's wrong for a parent to embarrass his child by reprimanding him in public, it's equally wrong for a child to do it to a parent. Otto should have been sent to his room within minutes of our sitting down.

Reprimanding the child should always take place in private, without anyone else present, especially siblings. Ideally, if it's possible, both parents should be present, so there's no miscommunication. The parents should be united, clear, firm, sober, possibly stern, but above all else, not angry. If they're angry, the anger will be the only thing that parent and child subsequently remember from the interchange. The parent will often over-react and consequently rescind whatever punishment was promised. The child will be frightened and therefore won't learn any lesson from the entire, unpleasant episode.

The parents obviously shouldn't be cheery either. Otherwise, their attitude belies their words. The most common example of this is how parents react to their child cursing. They reprimand them verbally, but simultaneously they're laughing because it's so cute to hear a four-year-old saying a four-letter word. Which will the child remember longer, the words or the laughter? Children are like dogs in that regard. The tone of voice is far more important than the content.

Experience teaches us that anything we do angry, we do worse. An angry driver is headed for an accident. An angry machine operator is commonly headed for an emergency room. How would you feel about getting on an airplane with an enraged pilot? How would you feel about having your procedure performed by an apoplectic surgeon? If a cabbie pulled up ranting and raving, shaking his fist at another driver, would you get in? To do something well, do it calmly. Few things in parenting are more important than disciplining our children. For our sake, as well as theirs, we should do it when we're even-tempered.

Furthermore, where do we think our children learn their temper tantrums in the first place, but from us? They fear us for our outbursts; they resent us, but in the end, they copy us. What a terrible inheritance. If we hit our children, in time they will hit our grandchildren. We'll try to tell them that we were wrong, but by then, it will be too late.

Why do we get angry at them in the first place? Ironically, it's often because we failed to discipline them when we should have. Because of our love for them, we indulge them. We give in to them. We fail to enforce the limits that we had previously announced. Finally, when they push the envelope too far, we explode.

Last week our family was eating out. At the next table was a similarly composed family. Their children however, were anything but composed. They were screaming; they were fighting; they were throwing food; they were running around. The father sounded like an unbroken record: "If you don't sit down this instant!," "If you don't stop throwing your food!," "I'm warning you for the last time!," "If you don't shut up this second!"

Finally it happened. I didn't see the straw that broke

this father's back. I did hear the slap. I did see the girl burst into tears. I saw the fear in the face of all the children and the embarrassment on the face of the parents. As the family hurriedly left a few minutes later, the father murmured to me, (I think by way of apology): "What's your secret?"

I don't have a secret. Indeed, my children's restaurant behavior has little to do with me. Instead, it's the result of an incident that had occurred many years earlier with my wife. Our kids had acted exactly like these children. She similarly warned them: "If you don't sit down and stop misbehaving, we're leaving." She warned them a second time. The third time, she left. She apologized to the waiter and had the food sent home. By then of course, the children were apologetic. "Mommy, we promise. Please give us another chance. Come on, we didn't know you meant it." My wife refused to relent. Since that day, and precisely because of it, dining out with our children has been a pleasure.

Early on, I developed my own warning: "If you don't do it (whatever it is they're supposed to do, e.g. turn off the light/TV, get up, etc.) by the count of three, you're going to be very sorry."

I don't specify the threat for three reasons:

1. I can't think that fast.
2. I don't want to commit myself to a punishment when I'm angry and then subsequently regret it.
3. Their imagination will conjure up something far worse than anything I could have come up with.

Early on they called my bluff. They deliberately waited till after I said "three." By then I had to follow through on my threat, or the next time, the threat would have been pointless. I roughly picked them up. They were crying, pleading for another chance before I ever touched them. I carried them up to their room, equally roughly, so there would be no miscommunication. I didn't want them thinking this was a game or a joke. I threw them each on their respective beds and told them in no uncertain terms that they were to do nothing but breathe for the next half hour.

I'm not sure for whom it was more difficult, them or us. Every few minutes my wife and I would find some excuse to walk past their room and surreptitiously peek in. Part of it was we wanted to make sure that they weren't disobeying us. Part of it was we wanted to make sure they were alive. Finally at the end of the accelerated half hour we walked into their room and discussed what had happened. They readily acknowledged that they had been wrong and promised that it wouldn't happen again. After that day I never got past the number "one."

Is it always so easy? Of course not, but it is simple. If done consistently and persistently, straightforward behavioral reinforcement always works.[6] It works with single celled paramecia, laboratory guinea pigs, barnyard animals, as well as Nobel Laureates. Yet, people swear that with their children, it doesn't work. Why not? I remember witnessing a friend discipline his son: "Scott, put that down! Scott, I'm warning you! I'm going to count to three. One . . . Two . . . This is the last time, Scott! One . . . Two . . . Are you listening, Scott? One . . . Two . . ."

I got so frustrated just listening that I wanted to go over and yell in his ear: "Three! Goddamn it! Three!" Subsequently I had to bite my lip when he soberly explained to me how threats don't work with Scott. Of course they don't. He had quickly learned how empty they were.

Yet, the father is a seasoned pediatrician. Why doesn't he realize his own mistake? Because Scott was born with a congenital malformation. He spent the first year of his life in a hospital undergoing several major surgeries. Despite the fact that he's now fully recovered, his parents are still trying to make it up to him.

Our tendency to indulge our child is invariably exaggerated if we perceive our child to be a special case.

Common examples include: only children, handicapped children, children who underwent a life-threatening illness, and children who lost a sibling or a parent. Special circumstances also include children born after the death of an older sibling or miscarriage, children born to older parents who perceive the birth as miraculous, and children adopted after a struggle.

The indulgence is exacerbated even more if the parents feel guilty. The two most common examples involve parents who feel that they haven't spent enough time with their children, and parents who get divorced. If custody is an issue, then indulgence serves the practical purpose of affecting the child's parental preference as well.

When the issue is confronted in a clinical setting, the parent will ultimately acknowledge their indulgence, but insist that the extraordinary circumstance justifies an extraordinary response. Scott suffered terribly. It wasn't fair. What's so wrong with trying to make it up to him?

The sad reality is *nothing* can make it up to him. His traumatic infancy can never be rectified. Nothing can erase the scars, both physical and emotional. We can only try to make the rest of his life as normal as possible. By indulging him, we're not making him healthier, but quite the contrary. We're penalizing him by teaching him inaccurate rules of life. The rest of the world will not show him the preferential treatment his parents do. As a result, his adjustment to school and peers will be more difficult. Furthermore, his parents are weakening him by not allowing him to learn to tolerate frustration. Like Elsa the lioness in *Born Free*, when the time comes for him to enter the outside world, Scott will be at a disadvantage. By avoiding his anger, and theirs, now, his parents will only increase both in the future.

As difficult as these issues between parent and child are, at least they're accessible. You the parent are one of the players involved. That is why many parents find that the most difficult anger issue in raising children is the one that's *not* accessible to them, sibling rivalry. If you have more than one child, you've experienced it. The only question is, have you had it bad, or have you had it worse? What factors make it worse?

1. Other factors being equal, the worst rivalry will be between the eldest child and the next to eldest. The eldest child was the only child to ever experience exclusivity. Consequently they're going to resent their loss of it the most. All the other children[7] had to share their parents' attention from the get-go, so while they might resent their loss of the spotlight, they had learned to share from day one.

2. The closer the children are in age, the worse the sibling rivalry will be. Children vastly separated in age become less of peers and more a separate generation. Consequently, they don't compete athletically, or for boys, or for friends. Ideally, you'd like your children to be at least four, even five, years apart. Of course practically, we tend to have our children two to three years apart which is probably the worst time gap. Children born really close together, less than 12–18 months, can develop the less competitive relationship of twins. Perhaps the older has no recollection of exclusivity, life without the younger.

3. Children of the same sex will have worse rivalry than children of the opposite sex. There's more competition if they're interested in the same things, as same sex children tend to be. This effect will be more pronounced as the children get older. Opposite sex siblings can be terribly competitive in childhood. Yet they become fiercely protective of each other once when they turn puberty. In a sense, they each moved to a different territory and the competition between them correspondingly decreased.

4. The more children there are in the family, the worse the rivalry will be. If each child is getting a smaller piece of the pie, their parents' attention, there inevitably is going to be a fiercer struggle for it.

5. The less the parents are available, the worse the rivalry will be, for the same reasons as 4.

What practical use are these five factors? They don't help the parent currently struggling with sibling rivalry. Practical suggestions would be at least twice as helpful. Accordingly, here are ten:

1. Spend more time with your children. Yes, this is so obvious it's almost patronizing. Yet, it's amazing how many parents still argue about quality of time versus quantity of time. Both are important. A helpful rule is to never go out two nights in a row. The children will learn the rule and appreciate it. It will help mollify them on the night that you are going out.

2. Spend time alone with each child. This too may seem obvious and insulting. Yet, many parents argue that everything should be done "as a family." Not true. At times it's useful to split up and take individual children out for a walk, a movie, a meal, etc. We naturally do this in response to a crisis, but if we habitually do it, we can avoid the crisis. This is particularly critical with twins, who tend to be treated as a pair.

3. Don't compare children. Nowadays most parents know *not* to say something like "How come you're not as smart as your brother?" Yet, parents will still say "Gee, your sister really loved French" or "Your brother didn't have any problem with this teacher." For the same reason, never look at report cards simultaneously. Even if the report cards come the same day, open them separately, in front of each child privately. Similarly, try to encourage each child into different extra-curricular activities. Even though it's less convenient for you, it's better in terms of their rivalry, *not* to send your three daughters to the same dance school. Even though there's a discount, don't bring the same piano teacher home to give lessons simultaneously, or even sequentially. If you help each child develop a world of their own, though it's impractical for you in the short run, it's rewarding for them in the long run.

4. Don't make older children responsible for younger ones. Even if you have your own fifteen-year-old, pay someone else's fifteen-year-old to baby sit. It might not make sense in terms of dollars, but it makes sense in terms of not having to deal with the arguing when you get home, or the bitter feelings the next day. Even if you're willing to pay your eldest to baby-sit, he'll still resent his sibling(s) taking away his freedom. He'll also be less equitable about putting them to bed. Similarly, older children should never be forced, or even encouraged, to help their brethren with homework, or tests. (Remember Terry and her sister?) If they wind up doing it on their own, they should of course be applauded, the same way you would if they helped anyone else. It's important that they understand however, that it's not their responsibility.

5. Force your children to resolve their own disputes. If the resolution involves death or dismemberment, you can intervene. However, once you impress upon them that might does not make right, allow them to reach their own solution. Better for them to work out a compromise over two hours, than for you to impose the identical compromise in two minutes. With the latter, they have more respect for you, but they still hate each other. With the former, they'll have more respect for each other, and for themselves. It won't be easy. They'll come to you to judge their disputes. They'll ask you to take sides. They'll complain bitterly about each other. Be prepared with your responses:

"I wasn't there, so I can't judge."

"It's your problem. You solve it."

"I can't tell who's right or wrong, so I have to let you work it out on your own."

Think of it as the equivalent of no fault insurance. Since you can't determine who's responsible for the damage, the consequences will be the same for everyone. This promotes an "us" versus "them" mentality, "us" being the kids, and "them" being the parents, which in turn lessens their rivalry.

6. Don't force them to be perfect siblings. Your efforts will only backfire and breed more resentment than if you hadn't done anything. If Hank is playing in a game, the whole family should *not* be forced to come watch him. *You* should go of course, the same way you would for Hannah's recital, but each child should have their own choice. Knowing that, if they do come, Hank will appreciate it more. Paul was always forced to attend his younger brother's basketball games. Paul himself had never made the basketball team and he felt humiliated having to be his brother's cheerleader. Is it coincidental that Paul has nothing to do with his younger brother today?

7. Allow your children to express their anger, even hatred of their siblings. Every child will sometimes feel and say: "I hate my sister," "I wish my brother had never been born," or "I wish my sister was dead." All too often we instinctively respond, "God forbid!," "Don't you ever say that!," or "You should be ashamed of yourself."

Instead, we should be saying matter of factly, "Why do you say that?" The more that the child has the opportunity to ventilate his perfectly natural competitive feelings, the less consumed he'll be by them. As it's good to encourage our children to express their anger towards us, it's equally good to encourage them to express their negative feelings towards their siblings. The principle is the same. Anger expressed is relieved. Anger suppressed grows.

8. Don't make an older child sacrifice for the younger. All too often, an older sibling is forced to move out of her room to a less desirable location, because her room has become "the baby's room." How does that make her feel about the baby?

Give the baby the lesser room. The baby won't know the difference, but the older sibling will. Even if it means that you have to take a few extra steps for the nightly feeding, you will be more than compensated by your elder sibling's increased interest and affection for the baby.

The same principle holds true for seating protocol in the dining room. Don't move an older sibling away from you to make room for the baby. If necessary, change your own seat, so you can be next to both. If it means that you can no longer be at the head of the table, so what? The head of the table is defined by where you sit, not by a geometrical configuration.

9. Don't allow the youngest to dominate the spotlight. Yes, the younger a child is, the cuter they are. There's nothing the older children can do about that, except regress. Try to divide your attention between all your children equally. This will be even more of a problem when you entertain relatives or guests. They will naturally focus exclusively on the youngest. Be as active as you have to in shifting their focus. When attending a birth celebration (e.g. a christening, circumcision, etc.), always bring presents for the older siblings as well as the "guest of honor." The older siblings often feel like "a fifth wheel" at these celebrations. Similarly encourage your friends and relatives to focus on the older siblings when you're the one hosting a party for the baby.

The same principle holds true with a handicapped or sickly child. Inevitably he tends to dominate our time and attention. It's not fair to the other children. They did nothing to deserve this loss of attention. One way or the other, you have to make it up to them, or they too will be handicapped or made sick by their childhood experience.

10. Most importantly of all, try not to develop a favorite. This is a step beyond what everyone already knows, not to play favorites. Not playing favorites means treating everyone equally, which is, of course, only fair. Unfortunately, sometimes even parents who treat their children equally develop a favorite. The child might be their favorite because it's the youngest, the oldest, the best looking, or the only one of that sex. It might have to do with their name, (e.g. named after you, or a favorite parent), or the fact they remind you of you. It doesn't matter. It's always bad.

Invariably, you tell it to your spouse and eventually, sworn to secrecy, to the favorite child themselves. Inevitably, it isn't long before the whole family knows about it. The other siblings claim that it doesn't bother them, but how do you imagine they really feel? You don't have to be familiar with the biblical story of Joseph and his brothers, whose quote opened this chapter, to realize the inevitable consequences.

If you're finding it particularly difficult to like a specific child, work on it. Spend more time with that child until you can find something about them that appeals to you. You *can* have a favorite child, only as long as it's a different child at different times. While it's true, as Freud said, that a parent's favorite has tremendous self-confidence for life, don't forget what happens to the other children. Don't condemn your child, through no fault of their own, to feeling like a loser. If you do, you might find that it becomes a self-fulfilling prophecy.

Will following these "ten commandments" eliminate sibling rivalry? Of course not. Sibling rivalry has been around since Cain and Abel, and it will continue to be around long after our children are no longer raising cain, and we're no longer able.

A patient waxed nostalgic of playing "hide and seek" with her younger brother. I sensed resentment of him, but she denied it. Years later, she mentioned that she had once been punished severely for playing "hide and seek." It piqued my curiosity. Why would someone be punished for playing "hide and seek"?

It turned out that in her version of "hide and seek," she would mischievously hide the baby and then her parents would have to find him. This particular time she hid him on the roof. Since the roof sloped, the baby rolled down, but mercifully became lodged in a rain gutter, from whence the fire department rescued him. To her it's still an amusing story. She can't understand why her parents were so upset and no, she still insists, she was never angry at her brother.

The comic strip *Peanuts* was probably the first public

acknowledgment of how angry and cruel children can be[8].
Big sister Lucy is always angry and makes no attempt to hide
her resentment of her brother Linus[9]. Similarly, Charlie
Brown's younger sister Sally angrily advertises her frustration
if something doesn't go her way. Before *Peanuts,* we liked to
believe that children were always loving, as on *Donna Reed* or
Leave It To Beaver. While Dennis was a menace, it was never
with malice. By the time *Calvin and Hobbes* and *Boondocks*
came around, we accepted that our children are merely
smaller versions of their parents, anger and all.

Whether they express themselves in boysenberry sherbet
or in playing "hide and seek," all children are angry at times.
Our choice is to either help them express their feelings, or
clean up their mess afterwards.

> *"Let dogs delight to bark and bite,*
> *For God hath made them so;*
> *Let bears and lions growl and fight,*
> *For 'tis their nature too.*
> *But children, you should never let*
> *such angry passions rise;*
> *Your little hands were never made*
> *to tear each other's eyes."*
> —Isaac Watts, (1674-1748)

Notes

---

[1] *Genesis* XXXVII: 11, 19-20.

[2] Lucius Annaeus Seneca lived from 5 to 65 A.D.

[3] Sadly, Bruno Bettelheim's reputation was tarnished when it was
discovered that he himself had unresolved anger issues. Allegedly
he had physically and verbally abused many of the disturbed
children who had been under his care. Though extremely
regrettable, his behavior in no way invalidates the insights of his
writings.

[4] In *From the Beast to the Blonde,* Marina Warner focuses on the misogynistic anger in fairy tales.

[5] Splitting is a Freudian principle whereby we separate our conflicting feelings about the same person, and, if necessary, transfer them onto someone else.

[6] Try this famous experiment. Before engaging in a protracted conversation, pick an arbitrary word that you will positively reinforce with a smile. Don't make it too obvious, but be consistent. Before too long your companion will be unconsciously increasing their usage of the word you chose.

[7] To avoid the painful loss of exclusivity, a wonderful involuntary method of reducing sibling rivalry is to have twins first. Unfortunately having twins later makes life even more difficult for the preceding child.

[8] Charles Schulz perceptively reflected the isolated world of children by never allowing an adult to appear in *Peanuts.* Even when the strip was animated for television and movies, adults' voices were conveyed by cacophonous musical instruments, much the way they often sound to children.

[9] In one particularly sagacious series of *Peanuts* strips, Charles Schulz had Lucy "fire" her brother Linus and bar him from the house. She relented and allowed him re-entry only because her parents brought home yet another sibling, Rerun, so she couldn't be an only child anyway.

PART III

CHAPTER TWO

Leave Me Alone!

Anger in Adolescence

"And Saul was furious with Jonathan:
"You son of perverse rebellion!"[1]

"Come mothers and fathers throughout the land. Don't try to criticize what you can't understand. Your sons and your daughters are beyond your command. There's a battle outside and it's raging. The times they are a changing."

How I loved that song. It spoke to me. It spoke for me. It seems like yesterday. In fact, it was the Sixties. I still remember nevertheless at the time some reviewer called the song by Bob Dylan "the anthem of this angry young generation."

Right on! I didn't know a fellow teen[2] who didn't love it, or an adult who did. The song captured our angst, our rebellion, our dissatisfaction with the establishment which was screwing up everything. Today I still enjoy hearing the song. Today however, it provokes nostalgia, not self-righteous outrage. Today, I question its accuracy.

Were the times really changing? We thought at the time that we had created the very concept of adolescent rebellion. We had undeniable cause: the assassinations of the Kennedys and Martin Luther King, the Civil Rights marches, Viet Nam. We knew that no one before, and no one again would ever be as estranged from their parents' generation as we were. We were sure we would remain the generation of outsiders.

We called ourselves "the Counter-Culture." We promised ourselves we would never "sell out."

Instead, *we* became the parents whom our children now criticize as being out of touch. *We* became the authorities who don't understand what's it like to be a teen. *We* ourselves became the dreaded "Establishment."

Furthermore, our notions of exclusivity, our imagined uniqueness, has turned out to be a delusion of grandeur. Every adolescent generation since ours, without exception, has been equally self-righteous, equally outraged and equally rebellious. The reasons change with the season. Nixon. Agnew. Watergate. Grenada. Reagonomics. Dan Quayle. Somalia. Haiti. AIDS. Monica. Marc Rich. Kosovo. The Persian Gulf. The Middle East. The Florida ballot. Hard time. Soft money. Osama. Saddam. The anger remains constant.

We console ourselves by taking pride that at least we started something. After all, we the children of Woodstock, were the *first* to rebel. Every subsequent generation followed our lead. In reality, even that isn't true.

Adolescents have been rebelling as long as there have been adolescents. Adults' complaints about teens' lack of respect transcend all geographical and temporal boundaries. Socrates, in ancient Greece, was apoplectic about the behavior of this "new generation." He could have written the lyrics from the 50's musical, *Bye Bye Birdie:* "Kids! What's the matter with kids today? Why can't they be like we were, perfect in every way?" Four decades later, three decades after Dylan, another "angry young man"[3], Billy Joel wrote a song[4] listing every establishment injustice from 1949 to 1989, from Walter Winchell to Bernie Goetz. The chorus proclaimed: "We didn't start the fire. It was always burning since the world's been turning."

Why is the fire always burning? The answer lies in a lyric in Dylan's defiant anthem: "There's a battle outside and it's raging." The verse is right on line, but 180 degrees in the wrong direction. There *is* a battle; it is raging, but it's not outside. It's *inside* every teen who's struggling to come of age.

You can't become an adult without declaring your independence from the adults who raised you. As long as you continue to obey them, to agree with them, to go along with them, you're not your own person. You're still their child. To define yourself, you have to distinguish yourself from them. You have to go your own way. You have to confront them. You have to rebel.

On a different continent, in a different century, Goethe wrote of adolescence: "In trying to oppose Nature, we are, in the very process of doing so, acting according to the laws of Nature." Every teen, on every continent, in every century loudly proclaims the same thing. Like Greta Garbo, they want to be left alone. If only adults would stop bothering them and making demands upon them, everything would be fine.

They have a point. By the time they enter adolescence, as they turn puberty, they are capable, both physically and intellectually, of most adult functions, including reproduction. Our closest evolutionary relatives, the chimpanzees, enter adulthood five to seven years earlier, roughly the length of adolescence. It would appear that our species has chosen to artificially prolong childhood beyond puberty.[5]

When teens fantasize, they imagine the same universal dream, a world without adults. Movies geared for teens, (*The Breakfast Club, Risky Business, Adventures in Babysitting, Clueless, Ten Things I Hate About You,* Leo's *Romeo and Juliet, Road Trip,* and countless others), incorporate variations of that fantasy.[6] Ironically, if that fantasy came true, if an adolescent actually found himself in a situation devoid of adults, then he would no longer be an adolescent. He would, of necessity, become an adult himself, albeit a very young one.

Sadly, we see that very scenario too often. An adolescent

boy who has lost his parents and must support his family, doesn't have the luxury of being rebellious. An adolescent girl who has a baby to take care of, doesn't have the time for self-righteous outrage.

That's not the case with most adolescents. They're still supported by their parents. They're still going to school. Their primary interests in life seem to be "sex, drugs and rock and roll." They're angry and looking to disagree. Paradoxically, they simultaneously avoid and invite their parents' anger. The parents feel like they can't win.

"It ain't necessarily so."[7] After all, what every teen ultimately wants is independence. The more we deny it to them, the angrier they become, the more they fight us for it. By giving it to them, we avoid much of the acrimonious struggle. Keep in mind however, that giving them their independence is *not* synonymous with giving them everything they are asking for. In fact, the pair can be mutually exclusive. The former is advisable, the latter is not.

For example, the first power struggle is usually over the child's room. This will even predate adolescence. The parent will complain that the child's room is a mess, the child doesn't put anything away, the child takes no responsibility for their things. The parent will be simultaneously absolutely right, and incredibly wrong. The complaints are, from an objective perspective, accurate. Nevertheless, the fact that they are complaining is completely ill-advised. Worse yet, even while they're complaining, they're simultaneously positively reinforcing the child's irresponsibility by continuing to clean the child's room. (When a housekeeper, being paid by the parents, cleans a child's room, it's as if the parents themselves are doing it.)

An endless series of arguments could be avoided if the parent simply took a hands off approach to the room. The child's room is their castle. It's their privilege to keep it in whatever state of tidiness they choose to. It's their responsibility however, to take care of it. Out of necessity, very quickly the child will become responsible, without the necessity of any intervention by the parent. When the boy can't find his baseball glove, he will learn to put away his things. When the girl can't find her favorite top, she will learn to hang up her clothing. When they can't have their friend sleep over, because they can't open the trundle bed, they'll clean the floor.

Of course if the parent is short sighted enough, they can still manage to snatch defeat from the jaws of victory. When the child says, "I can't find my notebook!," the parent replies: "Well, if you cleaned your room, you wouldn't be always losing things." It is smart for the parent to realize that. It is stupid to say it. Far wiser to respond: "I haven't seen it, honey." The child will sooner learn the lesson if he draws his own conclusion, then if it's spelled out in a condescending put-down. Is that being honest? Yes. You haven't seen it. It's not however, being candid. While honesty is always advisable, candor is rarely so[8], especially with an adolescent who is looking for an argument.

The next power struggle is commonly the phone. The teen wants to use the phone without limits. They want to be able to talk to whomever they want to, as long as they want to, as late as they want to. In a previous era the parents effectively lost the use of their own phone. In the modern era the parents get the teen their own phone line. That solves the problem of the phone being tied up, but exacerbates the problem of the phone bill.

Instead, let the *teen* get their own phone number. It becomes the adolescent's privilege to talk to whomever, whenever. It's their responsibility however, to pay for it. If they're on the phone too late on a school night, it's their problem. They will be exhausted the next day, not you. If their exhaustion affects their schoolwork, it's their problem. Their performance, their attendance, even their grades, should be strictly an issue between the school and them.

You'll still be seeing their report cards. There is nothing wrong with congratulating them on a good performance. It is terribly wrong however, for them to have to perform well for your sake. It creates a constant state of tension between parent and teen. The home becomes an exercise in surveillance and deception, if you have to constantly check their homework, make sure they have prepared for their exams, and oversee the productive use of their time. Their schoolwork is their responsibility, not yours. How and when they choose to deal with it, is their privilege.

The more we succeed in increasing the commensurate responsibilities and privileges of our adolescents, the more quickly they mature. Even better, the less we have to fight with them. Conversely, there are two ways we can regress them. We can take away the privileges and responsibilities that are rightfully theirs, or worse, we can give them privileges they haven't earned and responsibilities they can't handle. The largesse we bestow upon them might be great for our egos, but not theirs.

Grant, 28, had been angry, uncommunicative and unproductive since his early teens. He had barely graduated high school. He had flunked out of college. His father offered him any position he wanted at any of the companies that his father owned. He refused. He would never work for his father. His father then offered to get him a job at another company. He refused again. He didn't want any job through his father's connections. He would only take a job that he had gotten on his own merits, through his own efforts. Since neither his merits nor his efforts were apparent to anyone, Grant had never worked a day in the decade since his dishonorable discharge from academia.

Grant's relationship with his parents could, at best, be described as a peaceful coexistence. He lived in the same mansion as them, but never spoke to them. He obligatorily attended family functions, but did so begrudgingly. He lived the proverbial life of Riley. He slept till noon, lunched at their country club where he would partake of golf, tennis or the health club, depending on the season. He returned home to change for his evening activity, a night on the town with an ever changing flavor of the month companion. His parents wouldn't hear his sports car return till the wee hours. His lifestyle was as expensive as it sounded. His father expended more on Grant than he did on his wife and himself combined. Grant demanded the best of everything: scalped tickets to shows, concerts and sporting events, the finest wines at the finest restaurants, designer clothing fitting to his perceived station in life.

When his father finally finished this tale of woe, I had but one question. Was he looking to adopt another son? If so, I was volunteering. Who wouldn't want to live Grant's lifestyle? Why in the world would Grant ever want a job? No job could ever support him the way his father did.

The father understood. He asked me to call Grant and explain all of this to him. I told him I would be wasting my time and his money. Even if Grant was willing to see me, which was highly unlikely, there was nothing that I was going to say that he would want to hear. My suggestion was to cut Grant off. No country club, no credit cards, no money, period. Give Grant a reason to work.

The father vociferously refused. Grant was angry enough at him already. If he stopped doling out the money, it would mean open warfare. Besides, wasn't Grant depressed? Wasn't I a psychiatrist? Why couldn't I treat his depression and straighten him out?

Yes, Grant was depressed. He had no self-respect for understandable reasons. Even his nightly escapades, the thrill of a lifetime for anyone else, had become mundane for him. In a sense, he was like a chronic alcoholic, getting drunk every night, but no longer enjoying it. Like a chronic alcoholic however, the first prerequisite to treat the depression was to stop the drinking, or in Grant's case, the carte blanche life style. While his father was understandably afraid of the consequences of the withdrawal, he eventually came to accept that it was the only solution. After several half-assed attempts the father turned off the financial pipeline.

Immediately, the father's prediction came true. Peaceful, albeit sullen, coexistence turned into open hostility. Eventually, my prediction came true as well. Grant got a job (appropriately enough, selling luxury cars). Today, a decade later, Grant, charter member of "the lucky sperm club," presides over the empire that his father built.

Why include a 28-year-old in a discussion of adolescence? Because Grant's decade of depression, and his parents' decade of misery, started in adolescence when his parents tried to solve the problem by throwing money at him. The turmoil of adolescence doesn't automatically end when the teen turns twenty. Unless and until the teen is forced to take on the responsibilities of adulthood, the problems worsen.

There are several different definitions of adolescence. The most common, the chronological, is the least useful. The teen years are by that arbitrary definition thirteen to nineteen. If some anonymous lexicographer centuries ago had chosen to call 11 & 12, "oneteen" & "twoteen" instead of "eleven" & "twelve," it would be nine years in duration, instead of seven. If 13 was called "trilve" instead of "thirteen," it would be six. Which is correct? It depends on the individual. How long someone remains an adolescent is determined by how they behave, and how they relate.

Bernie and his parents had had a major battle over the weekend and they came to family therapy to "discuss it," i.e. assign blame. The battle had begun with Bernie announcing that he was going to a dance. The parents asked where. He told them. They were pleased. His parents asked with whom. He told them the girl's name. They didn't recognize it. He described her. They didn't like what they heard. It deteriorated from there. Both Bernie and his parents blamed each other for cruel, deliberate provocations, for starting the fight and spoiling the weekend.

Who was right? As always, both sides were right, and both sides were wrong. As in all family disputes, there were no heroes or villains, only victims. This could have been a quintessential parent-teen argument, but for one fact. Bernie isn't a teen. At the time of this incident, he was 42 years old.

From a chronological perspective, adolescence ends on our twentieth birthday. From a physiological perspective, it ends when our long bones fuse, i.e. we stop growing. From an educational perspective, it ends when we graduate from high school.

None of it is true. As long as our parents are still financially responsible for us, we're still an adolescent. As long as we live in their home, eat their food, drive their car, accept their money, we're not autonomous. As long as they are privy to the details of our romantic lives (like Bernie), we're not independent. Until we become autonomous and independent, we condemn ourselves to continue fighting the "raging battles" of adolescence.

Often it's the child who keeps holding on. More often it's the parent. It's understandable why. No parent wants to relinquish control of a child that they had raised since infancy. Their child growing up is simultaneous with, and, in some cases, causative of, their growing old. While we instinctively realize how critical it is to provide our children roots, sometimes we forget that it is equally important to provide our adolescents wings. What makes it so difficult is, that by their very nature, roots and wings are mutually exclusive. The same doting style that is so reassuring and supportive to the child, becomes suffocating and intrusive to the adolescent. The parental style that is best suited for adolescence is neither open door indulgence nor closed door denial, but a revolving door, which is neither and both. Just as revolving doors were invented[9] to ease the transitional pressure gradient between inside and outside, we as parents have to re-invent ourselves to ease the transitional pressures of our children moving from inside our homes to the outside world.

We can't win. This is a war of independence that we are destined to lose. The wiser choice then is to *give* the teen their independence, rather than making them fight for it. It's not coincidental that America, which had to fight for its independence, is not part of the British Commonwealth, while Canada, which was granted its independence, is.

Independence includes the right to have different taste, different style, and different values. Most frustratingly, it even includes the right to make their own mistakes. Why can't they learn from our mistakes? Why can't they benefit from our experience? Why can't we teach them? Because they'd rather learn on their own. Even if it takes longer, and comes at a higher price, in the end it's their victory, not ours.

For example, the family is going out to a fancy restaurant for a special dinner. The teen comes downstairs wearing a tee-shirt. What are the parents' options? The worst option is, without explanation, to send him upstairs to change. Even if he agrees to, (a very big if), he will resent this perceived put-down, and create a mood of tension that will spoil the entire evening. The better option is to explain that the restaurant requires a tie and jacket, and *suggest*, not demand, that the teen comply. It's still patronizing. The typical wise-ass teen might in turn "suggest" that the family go to a different restaurant. The best option is to merely convey the restaurant's dress code and leave it completely to the teen's discretion. Every teen will greatly appreciate the respect of being treated like an adult.

If the teen still doesn't comply, then at the restaurant he'll be forced to wear that uncomfortable, ill-fitting, unfashionable blue blazer that they keep handy to embarrass non-conformists. There will be no reason for familial tension. In all probability, the mood at the table will be one of bemusement. If the teen feels resentful, it will be at the restaurant, not at the parents.

If parents are embarrassed by their teen's attire, if they feel that it's a reflection upon them, it's the parents' problem, not the teen's. What *is* a reflection upon them is *not* their teen's garb, but their teen's relationship with them. How much the parents choose to complain will be an important factor in determining that. If necessary, parents have to act like patients with Moebius Syndrome[10] who are physically incapable of appearing angry. They have to learn not to take personally their teen's complaints or seeming ingratitude. When he says: "If we had a cool car like Perry's parents, instead of this piece of crap, I wouldn't have trouble getting a date," he's not talking about you, or even Perry. He's talking about himself. He's the "piece of crap." His bravado reflects his own insecurity and poor self-image. Ignore his provocation and everyone will be better off for it.

My medicine professor traditionally had his son come work in his office on school holidays. Both father and son enjoyed these days together. As his son became a teen however, he started sporting a wispy goatee, a scraggly pony-tail, a tie-dyed tee shirt and patched jeans. My professor was concerned about his appearance's impact on his patients. In particular, his most distinguished patient, a famous banker, was scheduled for an appointment.

The key question was, did his office have a dress code? If a patient came in looking like his son, would he be treated? Since the answer was yes, he couldn't legitimately say anything to his son. He could and did attempt however to shunt him off to the lab while the banker was there. As luck would have it, they bumped into each other nevertheless. The banker confronted the professor:

"Isn't that your son?"

"Yes. Yes, it is. I'm sorry. He was supposed to be in the lab . . ."

"How do you do this?"

"Well, you see, he's been coming on vacation. I should have spoken to him, but . . ."

"I don't know how you do this. I've been trying to get my son to come to *my* office for years. What's your secret?"

The postscript should sound familiar from our previous story about Grant. Today my professor is retired. His practice was taken over by his son. (I'll bet he's treating the banker's son.)

Not all parent teen struggles have happy endings. All too often, neither parent nor teen is willing to compromise and the only way for the constant warfare to end is for the two sides to go their separate ways. What a tragedy. The parents lose their child. The child loses his parents. The child's children have been cheated out of grandparents. Can there be any difference of opinion important enough to justify such an outcome?

An even greater tragedy is the suicide rate among adolescents. When James Dean prophetically[11] said to Natalie Wood in *Rebel Without A Cause*: "I thought . . . you better live it up, boy, cause tomorrow you'll be nothing.", he wasn't talking only about himself. Alcohol-related injuries kill almost 1,500 college students every year in the U.S. alone. Over half a million students are injured annually. Over two million drive after drinking at least once a month, and over three million, almost 40% of all college students, ride with a drinking driver.[12]

Five out of every 1000 20-year-old males die in man-made accidents[13], the leading cause of adolescent death. The second leading cause is homicide, and the third is suicide. Three million American teens, more than 13% of every teen 14 to 17, are suicidal[14] every year. Up to 25% of all teens will suffer from a major depressive disorder and half of them will eventually make a suicide attempt.[15]

It doesn't make sense. It makes sense that the suicide rate would be high among the recently widowed. They just lost their life's partner and they don't feel that they have the strength to carry on alone. It makes sense among the terminally ill, a cancer or AIDS diagnosis, for example. They feel that their future is limited to increasing pain and decreasing health. It makes sense among the elderly. They feel that they have nothing to live for.

Adolescents, on the other hand, have yet to lose anything. Their future is unlimited. They have everything to live for. Why would they kill themselves? The reason is obvious. They're angry. The result is obvious. Every large high school has a memorial page in their yearbook.

Summer 1975. I had just started my psychiatric residency. A fellow first year resident came to my office suggesting that we take a break for lunch. We both needed it. As we left the building he was telling me about a frustrating session he had just had with an impossibly angry adolescent patient.

Suddenly we heard his name shouted. It sounded pleasant, but determined. We looked up. His adolescent patient was standing, in her hospital gown, on the ledge of the roof of the hospital. She waved at him flirtaceously and jumped[16]. Her body disintegrated on the pavement a few yards from us.

Summer 2002. David Weissberg, whose family owns and operates the legendary Gramercy Park Hotel[17] in New York City, gets into yet another argument with his wife of two years, Marilyn. Marilyn packs her bags and leaves. David climbs to the roof of the hotel, waits till he sees her leave, and jumps, disintegrating at her feet.

David Weissberg was 46 at the time, but remarkably adolescent nevertheless. His painful life had been one of dysfunction and irresponsibility notable primarily for multiple arrests[18] and hospitalizations. His extreme drug addiction[19] had facilitated his nephew Michael dying of a drug overdose in David's room, on Michael's 19th birthday. David's anger affected anyone who was close to him, of any age.

It seems that every month another teen, in another country, has shot up their high school. The exacerbants are obvious: video games that help overcome their innate, natural reluctance to kill, the internet that helps find kindred homicidal souls and methods, assault weapons that increase their efficiency, but the primary cause remains the same it's always been, their anger.

It is not coincidental that the very last "crime of the century," the Columbine High School massacre of 1999 was perpetrated by two angry teenagers. After all, the very first "crime of the century," the Leopold-Loeb murder, had also been perpetrated by two angry teens. The twentieth century started and ended with angry teens murdering teens. The twenty-first century started the same way. On April 26, 2002 an angry 19-year-old high school student in Erfurt, Germany massacred 17 including students, teachers and himself.

Even when the anger is less obvious, the result is still deadly. Angry teens were found in follow up studies decades later to be five times more likely to suffer a heart attack. Over one third of the angry teens experienced cardiovascular disease, often fatal.[20] It is not coincidental that the word "tragedy" contains within it the word "rage".

Why do teens get charged the highest car insurance premiums? Yes, they're inexperienced, but inexperienced adult drivers don't get charged more. Some of them might still be physically awkward, but most of them are far better coordinated than their grandparents. It takes infinitely more coordination to play a video game or basketball, than to drive a car. The answer lies in the actuarial tables. The teen's vastly increased premium reflects their vastly increased likelihood of wrecking the car, killing themselves and possibly someone else as well.

That's the answer, but it's not the reason. The reason is the driver's seat is the first position of power they've ever had to express their anger. When they get behind the wheel, it's their first opportunity to make an impact, and that impact is often irreversible. Another reason is that teens think they're immortal. Often their competitions consist of who will come closest to disproving that illusion. In South America, the competition is "surfing" on the roofs of speeding trains. In the inner city, it's "long jumping" between the roofs of neighboring buildings. In the suburbs, it's "car racing." Needless to add, alcohol, drugs, and pride, can provide the fuel for all three "sports."

Yet another reason is that a car is the ultimate example of a privilege that they haven't earned, and a responsibility that they can't handle. It would be much healthier if their first car is one that they bought themselves. If they pay for the insurance, the gas and the repairs, they're going to be driving a lot more responsibly than if their parents do. Any building manager will tell you, owners take infinitely better care of their apartments, than renters do. Borrowers are even worse. The only difference between a home and a car is that when you wreck the latter, you invariably damage yourself in the process.

Fortunately in some adolescent phenomena the anger is still obvious, but the results innocuous. As you might have gathered, my adolescent peers' music of protest was folk—Bob Dylan, Peter, Paul and Mary, Phil Ochs, et. al. We found the music that proceeded us, Elvis Presley, Chubby Checker, pointless. We found the music that followed, The Beatles, The Rolling Stones, noisy. Our taste in music reveals not only our place in history, but also in age. Every teen is convinced that "adult" music is boring. Every adult similarly believes that "teen" music is too loud. As a result, teen icons have a short half-life. Today's teens find yesterday's idols, rockers, too sedate. Rocker fans, growing longer in the tooth, predictably find heavy metal noisy. Tomorrow's teens will undoubtedly call heavy metal too sedate. (Having attended many heavy metal concerts, with earplugs, I find that thought unfathomable.)

The unconscious purpose of any teen taste is to disgust, and thus aggravate their parents. What guaranteed both Elvis Presley's and The Beatles' success was not only the caliber of their music, but also how much parents hated them. When teen icons Eminem, Papa Roach, Xzibit and Ludacris toured together they called it the "Anger Management" tour. As

Eminem observed, the worse adults consider him, the more his fans will love him. Lest one imagine that angry music is an inner city phenomenon, listen to Toby Keith's country hit *The Angry American* where he sings "we'll put a boot in your ass." If a parent truly can't stand their teen's new love, the worst thing they can do is to let the teen know it. By expressing their anger, the parent is positively reinforcing the choice. It's true with friends, music, lovers, and everything else.

If a parent really wants to end a practice fast, the best thing they can do is adopt it themselves. In psychiatry this is called "paradoxical intention." It works. For example, when did teens stop growing side-burns? When adults started to. Ditto for sunglasses, long hair, bell-bottoms, and earrings on men. My classmate wore only Nehru jackets throughout his adolescence. He remembers to this day the precise moment that he decided to stop, the night that Johnny Carson came out in a Nehru.

Some teens provoke their parents with more than just music or clothing. They deliberately do the one thing that they know will bother their parents the most. If it's important to the parents that the teen excels in school, the teen will fail. If the parents are very religious, the teen will be agnostic. If the parents are avowed atheists, the teen will become a believer. If a parent is in the military, the teen will be on the protest line. If the parents despise the military, the teen will enlist. Yet, this rebellion, within limits, is a natural, healthy phase of individuation. It is not only a part of a normal adolescence, it defines adolescence.

If one rules with a heavy enough hand, it's sometimes possible to temporarily stifle the rebellion. But not the anger. In the end the price to be paid will be horrendous. The teens who don't rebel, the "perfect" children, often, in the end, either escape or self-destruct.

Every adolescent psychiatrist who hears that expression, a perfect teen, immediately thinks of the same thing,

Anorexia Nervosa. Not coincidentally, Cherry Boone, Pat's daughter, entitled her autobiography on the subject, *The Best Little Girl In The World*. Anorexics are typically perfect, their parents' favorite, their teacher's favorite, the one teen that every adult likes. Not only are they usually attractive and bright, but they're such overachievers, that anorexia is commonly referred to as the "Valedictorian's Disease." Not surprisingly, anorexia and its companion eating disorder, bulimia, tend to be rigid, driven, angry Type A personality types.

What is Anorexia? It is a disease in which a seemingly healthy teen, usually female, slowly, deliberately, methodically, starves herself, possibly to death. She does it ostensibly without anger or rebellion, but always in full torturous view of her parents. In the process, she stops menstruating, loses her breasts and begins to resemble concentration camp survivors, or end stage cancer victims. Can you imagine a worse way for a child to torture a parent?

This is not a rare disease. It affects five to ten percent of the adolescent female population, and its incidence is increasing. Approximately 50,000 people currently suffering from an eating disorder will eventually die from it.[21] Every day another celebrity acknowledges having suffered from it (e.g. Princess Diana), and for some it's fatal, (e.g. Karen Carpenter).

Why is it primarily in girls? There are many reasons, but one is that, in our society, it is often more difficult for a girl to express her anger than for a boy. If she has been unsuccessful in individuating from her parents in any other way, her anorexia is a last resort "Declaration of Independence." With her emaciated skeleton she is saying, "It's my body, not yours!," "It's my life, not yours!," "I'll do with it what I want to, and there's nothing you can do to stop me!"

How do parents typically respond? First with denial—"If it's our daughter, it can't be anorexia.," then with amazement—"What are you, nuts?," and finally, predictably, with anger—"How could you do this to us? You're destroying this family."

How do psychiatrists treat it? The first step is often to hospitalize the girl. Up to 20% of untreated anorexics die prematurely. Anorexia however is the only disease in which a patient is sometimes hospitalized to separate them from their family. In the beginning, the parents aren't even allowed to visit or call, if it is felt that parental power struggle is exacerbating the illness.

The pressure of sex plays an important role as well. Girls invariably receive a great deal more sexual attention and demands than boys do. It's not coincidental that anorexia eliminates both their sexual attractiveness and the possibility of pregnancy. It's also not coincidental that anorexia makes an incipient woman look like a little girl. Just as some teens aren't ready for the responsibilities of a car, other teens aren't ready for the responsibilities of sex. Anorexia solves that problem.[22]

An amazing fact is the progressively decreasing age of menarche. A century ago it was sixteen-year-old girls who had to deal with their bloody introduction into womanhood. Today it's often ten-year-olds. The increasing incidence of anorexia is an emotional consequence of that, as well as a visceral reaction against parents who won't let go.

Eventually all parents do let go. When they do, they find that life becomes so much easier. Their children flourish with their newfound independence. It is not coincidental that when we stop breast-feeding, our babies experience a growth spurt. The same growth phenomenon recurs each succeeding time we cut another umbilical cord[23], including the final one. Our children are no longer our adversaries. They become our friends. Both sides look back at adolescence as an angry rite of passage.

Adolescence is a critical part of our development. It is not coincidental that our nightmares for the rest of our life usually take place in our adolescence. You've probably had them yourself. You're late for a class, or a test, and you can't find the room, or you forgot to study, or you realize you're naked.

Neither is it coincidental that those with the most restricted lifestyle of all, the Amish, allow their teens at the age of 16 to enter "rumspringa," a period of complete freedom devoid of any parental restrictions. While the parents refuse cars, electricity, music, zippers, even insurance, their teenagers are indulging in unlimited sex, drugs, alcohol, hot rods, television, stereo for as many years as they wish. Despite being exposed to every conceivable pleasure, almost 90% of the teens choose to eventually return to the stoic, spartan ways of their tradition.

There is an enigmatic parable in the *Hagaddah*[24] called The Four Sons. The four children are respectively smart, bad, simple, and the child who can't even ask. As well known as the parable is, it makes no sense. A smart child should be paired with a stupid one, a bad child with a good child. What's the point of these four children?

I think they represent the four phases of development.[25] A toddler "can't even ask" a question. As he grows, he acquires language skills, but until adolescence he is "simple." He doesn't question the axioms that his parents and the establishment have laid down. He might occasionally misbehave, but he assumes that he is wrong, and his parents are right. It is only in adolescence that he becomes really "bad." He questions everything. He disagrees with everyone. He is angry at the world.

Just when it seems that this teen is a hopeless cause, he matures. The sapling that was allowed to bend, and therefore didn't break in the winds of adolescent turmoil, is now a mature tree himself taking his rightful place among his family and community. He has become the "smart" son, eager to profit from the wisdom of his elders.

The wittiest observation on adolescence comes from

Mark Twain. He noted that when he was 17, he suddenly realized what ignorant imbeciles his parents were. When he reached 21, he was pleasantly surprised to discover how inordinately much they had learned in just four years.

From the Israelites in Egypt, to Mark Twain in Missouri, to Bob Dylan in Minnesota, adolescents haven't changed. They'll always be different. They'll always disagree. They'll always rebel. They'll always be angry.

> *"Resentment seems to have been given us*
> *by nature for defense,*
> *and for defense only;*
> *it is the safeguard of justice,*
> *and the security of innocence."*
> —Adam Smith (1723-1790)

Notes

---

[1] *Samuel I*, XX: 30

[2] This chapter includes material from *Leave Me Alone! A Teenager's Guide To Adolescence*, a full-length book on dealing with teens.

[3] *Angry Young Man* in 1976 was an early hit for Billy Joel.

[4] Billy Joel's song, *We Didn't Start the Fire*, written in 1989, listed Presidents from Truman to Reagan, as well as sports heroes, movies, celebrities and world events. Among the rebellious adolescent music icons mentioned are Elvis Presley, Chubby Checker, The Beatles and, appropriately enough, Bob Dylan.

[5] Anthropologists, including Dr. Nicholas Blurton Jones of U.C.L.A., explain the prolonged childhood of humans as part of our life history. Comparative life histories of mammalian species indicate that the age of first reproduction is usually proportional to the age of mortality. The longer a species lives, the longer it postpones adulthood. This could explain why child labor was the norm in eras where life expectancy was much shorter. Admittedly this theory is redolent of Lysenko's infamous doctrine that otogeny

recapitulates phylogeny which was ultimately disproven. Nevertheless it seems to make sense that as we, as a species, prolonged our life-span, we naturally, unconsciously prolonged our childhood as well.

Interestingly, even today, poverty stricken countries, with shorter life expectancies, will frequently put children to work at a younger age as well. It is fascinating to speculate if anorexia is a phenomenon of affluence, so might be adolescence as a whole.

[6] *Home Alone,* and its sequel, went a step further, extending to children the adolescent fantasy that the adults have all gone away.

[7] Although George Gershwin is today an establishment icon whose music is featured by philharmonic orchestras, when he wrote *It Ain't Necessarily So* in 1934, that was hardly the case. Indeed, the show for which he wrote it, the all Black *Porgy and Bess,* was as iconoclastic and controversial in its time, as *Hair* or *Rent* were, decades later.

[8] For many years I have known a celebrity whose mantra is: "Honesty is a virtue. Candor is a vice." She had learned the lesson in the public arena.

[9] The revolving door was first patented in 1888. They are particularly necessary in high rise buildings where a temperature gradient between the inside and outside can create a vacuum so strong that a swinging door can only be opened by a weight lifter.

[10] Moebius Syndrome is an unusual congenital palsy of the sixth and seventh cranial nerve that renders its victims unable to produce any facial expression. Even if they're wild with rage, their features remain placid, the ultimate "poker face." This lack of expression, or hypomimia, is seen to a lesser degree in patients with Parkinson's disease or syndrome, like Mohammed Ali, and patients on high doses of typical major tranquilizers.

Ironically, the syndrome was named by the son of August Moebius who created the better known Moebius Strip. The Moebius Strip is a rectangular circular strip that is cut and re-attached after a 180 degree rotation. It can be replicated by closing a belt after turning one end inside out. The irony is that a Moebius Strip, which has no inside or outside, has been called by Francis Schiller in his eponymous book (1982, University of California Press) on the subject: "the perfect symbol of the everlasting riddle of the mind-brain relationship. As the eye or the finger follows the strip's shifting planes, up becomes down, in turns to out, and two merges into one; just as study of mind inevitably leads to pursuit of body and vice versa." The Meobius Strip like the Moebius Syndrome is enigmatically counter-instinctual, yet metaphorically provocative.

[11] By the time movie fans heard James Dean say he'll "be nothing," he was. On September 30, 1955 he drove his silver Porsche over 85 miles an hour and smashed into another vehicle. Both he and his car were mangled beyond recognition. He was 24.

[12] The statistics are all from 1998. They come from *A Call to Action: Changing the Culture of Drinking at U.S. Colleges* created by the National Institute on Alcohol Abuse and Alcoholism's Task Force on College Drinking.

[13] Dr. Steven Woloshin et al, Journal of the National Cancer Institute.

[14] The statistics are for 2000. They come from the U.S. Substance Abuse and Mental Health Services Administration.

[15] Drs. Ann Wagner and Benedetto Vitiello, National Institute of Mental Health Current Psychiatry, July, 2002.

[16] This is in no way intended to attribute blame for the unfortunate incident to the resident, the hospital, or the patient. A thorough psychiatric post mortem analysis revealed how immedicable this particular case was.

[17] The Gramercy Park Hotel is located immediately north of Gramercy Park, New York City's only private, gated park, on Lexington Avenue. Its celebrated patrons included Babe Ruth, Joseph and John F. Kennedy, and Humphrey Bogart who got married there. It housed so many rock-stars in the Seventies that Cameron Crowe filmed *Almost Famous* there.

[18] While David's numerous arrests had been for drug usage, a few months prior to his suicide, his brother had discovered that David had amassed a horde of assault rifles, shotguns and ammunition. The similarity to Columbine cannot be ignored.

[19] David had been addicted to heroin, methadone and at one time

had a $500-a-day speedball habit.—*New York Magazine,* July 8, 2002.

[20] Dr. Patricia Chang et al, Johns Hopkins University, Arch. Intern. Med. 901-06, 2002.

[21] *U.S. News & World Report,* June 10, 2002.

[22] Having lectured on, and treated, eating disorders for thirty years, I have seen firsthand innumerable variations and causes. The psychodynamics, parental reaction and treatment approach that I am describing here is traditional and typical, but hardly universal. It is important to emphasize that not every anorexic, or their family fit this description. Furthermore, the fact that identical twins are more likely to share the disease than fraternal ones strongly suggests a genetic as well as a hormonal aspect, in addition to the better known familial and cultural contributions. Like every life threatening illness, an Eating Disorder is a family tragedy, with no convenient villain to absorb the blame.

[23] Most parents witness a phenomenal physical and emotional growth spurt the first year their child goes away to over-night camp. Admittedly, it is partially the result of the parents not seeing their child on a daily basis for the first time, so the change can be discerned. (Having attended camp for over a decade, I can attest that the growth is not due to the salubrious effects of camp food.)

[24] The *Hagaddah* is the story of the Israelites' exodus from Egypt. It is traditionally read in Jewish homes at the Passover Seder, an elaborate, ritualistic feast that begins the holiday.

[25] As first presented in the fifth annual Jamie Lehmann Memorial Lecture in 1987.

Hell Hath No Fury Like a Lover Scorned

Anger in Divorce and Marriage

"If a man takes a woman for a wife, and she doesn't find favor in his eyes, because he has found something wrong with her, he should write her a divorce, give it to her, and send her from his house."[1]

Nature had never seen two human beings closer than Morris and Max Goldsmith. They were identical twins so identical that no one could tell them apart. They walked alike. They talked alike. They smelled alike. They even had the same distinctive, woodpecker-like laugh. Fortunately, no one ever had to identify them individually, since they were never apart.

The Goldsmiths had had a difficult life. They were Holocaust survivors who had lost their entire family, as well as their wives and children. Still, they managed to endure and prevail. They started second families. They moved to America. They lived in adjacent apartments one floor above my family's. They did everything together. For years I assumed their children were siblings, rather than cousins.

Appropriate to their name, the Goldsmiths operated a jewelry store. Consequently, they worked and commuted together as well. The brothers were together seven days a week. Summers they rented adjoining bungalows. This predictable Doublemint Twins existence continued for over two decades. Their distinctive laughter seemed omnipresent, and in stereo.

One day the laughter stopped. Morris's daughter had

been set up with an eligible young man. She was infatuated with him. He seemed interested in her as well. Appearances can be deceiving. After too few dates, he stopped calling her. She was heartbroken.

Just as she felt that things couldn't get worse, they did. He asked out her cousin, whom he had, of course, met on every date.

At this point in the story the details become controversial. Who said what, to whom, and when, varies, depending on the source. Both cousins however, felt that the way they were treated was unforgivable. Not only did their relationship resemble siblings', but their rivalry did as well.

Eventually, the young man understandably decided to remove himself from this hornet's nest. It only made things worse. Now, *both* cousins blamed the other for destroying their future. They stopped talking. The family meals together became strained. The two mothers tried to intervene. Each however, felt that their daughter was the one who deserved an apology. It turned into an argument. Both cited past incidents where they had been similarly wronged. The argument escalated. Slaps were exchanged.

Morris and Max were at a loss. Over decades they had successfully created one indivisible, happy family. In the space of weeks, it had split into two irreconcilable enemy camps. They tried desperately to prevent the split from effecting their relationship. They couldn't. No one knew exactly how and when it happened, but before long Morris and Max weren't talking either. They dissolved their business. They moved to separate buildings. They vacationed separately. They wouldn't attend the same function together, even at distant tables. You could invite one, or the other, to your celebration, but not both. If you did, neither would attend.

After losing their family together, after surviving the death camps together, after starting over together, the two brothers who were never seen apart, now could never be seen together. When Morris prematurely died, Max didn't attend the funeral.

I can never forget Morris and Max. They taught me two daunting, haunting lessons.

Lesson one—The potential for enmity is directly proportional to the previous closeness.

It seems paradoxical, even counter-instinctual, but it's true. Archenemies in both fact and fiction were invariably once the closest of friends. It is evident in newspapers[2], magazines[3], books[4], movies[5] and comic books[6]. It's as obvious in the historical wars of royal families as it is in a "grudge match" in professional wrestling.

Why? Because there's no anger greater than the anger of betrayal. The closer the betrayer, the greater the betrayal. Hence, the most ubiquitous, and ugliest battles, that only rarely merit media coverage, are those of divorce.

Lesson two—No two people are ever so close that they can't be split apart.

Unfortunately this applies to divorce as well. The most gut-wrenching example is the astronomically increased incidence of divorce in couples that have suffered the loss of a child, a phenomenon we will examine more closely.

Aren't marriage and divorce[7] two separate topics? Shouldn't they be reviewed separately? No. As surely as every divorce starts in marriage, so must every marriage consider the specter of divorce. We should consider divorce before we even think of marriage, as in this chapter's subtitle.

Of course, that does not mean that every couple should contemplate divorce. It *does* mean that the more that we contemplate the consequences of divorce, the more we will work on our marriage. Just as there's nothing that makes us appreciate life more, than the prospect of death[8], there's nothing that makes us appreciate our spouse more, than the prospect of their loss.

Statistics indicate that our chances of getting divorced

approach fifty-fifty. In fact, one out of every three marriages ends before the tenth anniversary.[9] Apparently most of us are simply not very good at marriage. It shouldn't be surprising. We often enter marriage too young[10], too impulsively, too hormonally, in essence, for all the wrong reasons:

> "It's the only way I can escape my house. It'll teach my parents a lesson. Serve them right." "I love her ass/breasts. She's such an incredible turn-on." "He's a doctor/lawyer/ cop/rabbi/etc. I've always wanted to marry one." "She's the best cook I ever dated." "He's the only man big enough to make me come inside." "I always wanted a family like hers." "I'm ripe for marriage, and he's the best available provider." "When I saw how good she was with kids, I knew." "It's Kismet. We like the same music, the same food, everything." "We have the same astrological sign. We were destined to marry." "My mother/father adores him/her."

There are tests and waiting periods for driving, flying model planes and bearing firearms, but for the most awesome responsibility of all, all you need is a few bucks in your pocket and someone to hold your hand. Getting married is the most important decision of one's life, yet it paradoxically requires infinitely more time, money and effort to get divorced, than to get married.

Many even express serious reservations while they're engaged, but get married nevertheless. They don't want to give up the attention and celebration surrounding the wedding. Ironically, they think that breaking the engagement would be more difficult and embarrassing, than getting divorced.

Most states require blood tests before marriage, to decrease the spread of venereal disease. More recently, HIV tests have been added, to curtail AIDS. Every state should require viewing Danny DeVito's film version of Warren Adler's black comedy about divorce and its tragic consequences, *The War of the Roses.* To obtain a driver's license, a driver's education movie is mandatory. By vividly displaying the potential carnage, the film impresses upon the viewer the awesome responsibility of driving. *The War of the Roses* might do the same for marriage.

By witnessing the painful details of Michael Douglas and Kathleen Turner's divorce, or Donald and Ivana's, or Woody and Mia's, people might realize that the superficialities that are so important in wooing become meaningless in marriage. A pretty face, a big bust, a wash-board stomach, well defined muscles, a large paycheck, an impressive resume, an attractive family, are like the spectacular view from a penthouse apartment. It's the first thing anyone notices when they enter. In fact, they usually can't take their eyes off of it. Yet, after you move in and have been living there for two months, you never realize it's there. You might as well be living next to a brick wall.

When you live with someone long enough, their appearance similarly diminishes in importance. Try this experiment. Whose face can you picture more readily, your spouse or Michael Jackson? Your mother or Barbra Streisand? Don't worry. It doesn't reflect your feelings about the respective pair. It reflects the aforementioned phenomenon. The longer you see something, the less important its appearance becomes. What you feel about your spouse is more important that what you see. Their face means less to you than their love.

The enduring qualities in a marriage aren't superficial. They're internal. It's not that important how compatible you are. All differences can be compromised, if both sides care enough. The most important quality in any permanent relationship, be it sibling, parent or spouse, is *not* how much the two people love each other. When people admit to a "love-hate" relationship with someone, usually a "loved one," what they really mean is that they hate someone whom they are supposed to love. Love is not always optional. Like is. The best prognostic indicator is how much you *like* your spouse.

The second most important quality is how much the two people trust each other. Reflecting that, the second best prognostic indicator of a marriage is how much the couple share. You can't share things with someone, if you don't trust them. You have no reason to, if you don't like them.

Sharing is not only a criterion, but more importantly, it also becomes the marriage's greatest ally. The more you share, the closer you are; the more you share, the closer you become. If you want to get closer, share *everything*, the mundane as well as the profound, the trivial as well as the important.

"I should share with my wife that my secretary's boobs turn me on?"

Believe it or not, the answer is yes. Increased sharing means increased trust, which leads to increased security. Besides, if your wife has seen your secretary, and if she knows you, she realizes it already. By acknowledging it, you earn her trust. If she feels secure about your faithfulness, then your appreciating your secretary's breasts becomes no different than appreciating your secretary's coffee. A wife secure in her marriage won't even have a problem pointing out an attractive, buxom woman to her husband. It becomes no different than recommending a poem or a movie that she knows he will like. Needless to add, this has to work both ways. A wife can and should be able to tell her husband that she finds *her* secretary's buns luscious. Similarly, he should be willing to point out a butt-iful hunk to her.

An open discussion of sexual attraction to others is paradoxically a compliment to the marriage. Just as a teen expressing their anger is a compliment to the parents, because they're demonstrating how safe and secure they feel, so is a spouse expressing their sexual attraction to each other. Parents' libidos are as inevitable, and healthy, as teens' anger. Why destroy credibility by denying it? What adolescent isn't angry? What man isn't attracted to this month's centerfold? What woman isn't attracted to "The Sexiest Man Alive"? Better to share, than to lie.

Sharing not only helps avoid anger, but it also helps overcome it. It serves as both vaccine and cure. The difference between successful and unsuccessful marriages is *not* in frequency of anger. If you live with someone full time, you can't help but get annoyed frequently. The question is, how well do you handle those annoyances. Ideally we share everything, especially our anger.

The anger should never be aggressive. If so, the recipient will feel attacked and the conversation will only make things worse. Don't say: "I hate your god-damned snoring!," or even: "Can't you do something about your damn snoring?" Instead, just share what you experienced, and, more importantly, what you felt: "I felt really angry at you last night, when your snoring woke me up again."

The expression of anger need not even be phrased constructively. The mere act of expression is constructive, since it immediately relieves the anger. Otherwise, the anger inevitably builds and eventually explodes, like the Goldsmith wives. By expressing it as soon as it's perceived, it doesn't get a chance to grow. It's a minor thought that, appropriately enough, is quickly disposed of. Unlike EXTAR, or the way we handle anger with anyone else, the expression of anger in marriage should be so frequent as to become casual. The expression of anger outside of marriage is a major production. In marriage, it should be commonplace.

Don't even stop to ponder if your anger is justified before you express it. If you're feeling it, that's justification enough to express it.

"Sweetie, I felt angry at you when I got off the phone with you today."

"I'm sorry, Honey. How come?"

"I felt you were being abrupt with me."

"I'm sorry. I had someone on the other line. I should have told you."

"Maybe you did. I was having a hard day. I should have told you that."

"Why was it a hard day?"

The real life dialogue above illustrates several points. First, though the subject is anger, terms of endearment (Sweetie, Honey) are still used. Second, the anger is expressed subjectively. Saying "I *felt* you were abrupt," instead of, "You were abrupt," focuses on the more important subjective feeling, rather than the less important objective action. Furthermore, it makes them less defensive, since they're not being judged or accused. Within seconds, the real culprit has been identified, not surprisingly, a lack of communication, not sharing enough. Immediately, the anger has been resolved and therapeutic sharing commences, i.e. "Why was it a hard day?"

(Incidentally, which gender did you assume were respectively "Sweetie" and "Honey"? It tells you with whom you identify.)

The famous quote from Erich Segal's *Love Story* was: "Love means never having to say you're sorry." On the contrary. Love means *always* saying you're sorry. The more you love each other, the more you'll say it. If you love someone, you're sorry when they get hurt. It doesn't matter if you hurt them unintentionally. It doesn't even matter if you had no involvement. Love means feeling their pain. Let them know. You'll both feel better.

Most couples are familiar with the **rule**: Don't go to sleep angry. No matter how late you stay up, no matter how tired you are, for the sake of your marriage, relieve the anger before you go to sleep. By sharing the anger immediately, it shouldn't even reach the end of the day.

There's a **second rule**, equally important, that also reaffirms the critical need for sharing: Don't tell me something, if I can't tell my spouse.[11] You tell me that our pastor has been embezzling money, but it's still secret, so I can't tell anybody, including my spouse. This news infuriates me. What can I do with my anger if I can't tell my spouse? Who will invariably be the object of my displaced anger? My spouse.

If someone introduces a secret to you by saying, "you can't tell your spouse," then respond, "then don't tell me." What if, as is common, they reveal first, and only after demand secrecy? Too bad. It's like receiving an unsolicited item with a bill. You keep it and you don't pay for it. Next time they'll know better.

That's easier done when dealing with acquaintances, or even friends. What do you do when it's your own family who has sworn you to secrecy from your spouse? "Mom is going to have a mastectomy, but she doesn't want anyone outside the family to know."

From our wedding day on, our family is the one we live with. Therefore the same rule applies equally, if not moreso, with our originating family. For them to ask you to keep something from your spouse, is at best an insult to your marriage, at worst, an attempt to sabotage it. It's not enough to repeat the secret to your spouse. It's critical to inform the family member that you're going to do so. Let there be no mistake where your loyalties lie.

Of course, it's not unusual for there to be disagreements between "old" and "new" families. Mother In Law jokes[12] are exaggerations, but they come from somewhere. What is crucial is that the anger is confronted by the original member of the family. Call it **marital rule 3.**

> "Sweetheart, we're having all the kids over for our anniversary. We really want the two of you there."
> "Oh, I'd love to. Let me check with my spouse and I'll get back to you."

If the answer is no, the inescapable conclusion that your parents will get is that your spouse was the obstacle. You have unnecessarily caused them to resent your spouse. A far better answer would have been: "Oh, I know we'd both love to. Let me check our schedules and I'll get back to you."

If the answer is then no, don't say: "my spouse can't make it," or worse, "my spouse doesn't really want to come." Say: "*We* can't make it." Is that lying? Not at all. If one of us can't make it, then *we* can't make it, since we are an indivisible couple.

This example also illustrates **marital rule 4**: Never make decisions unilaterally.

No matter how trivial or obvious it seems, if at all humanly possible, and it almost always is, discuss it first. These decisions constantly come up: dinner dates, weekend plans, lending, borrowing, purchasing, selling, inviting, committing, promising, agreeing. The vast majority of the time, you will know your spouse well enough to accurately predict their response. The exceptions however, justify the rule.

> "How could you agree to give her money for that?" "But you like her, and she said it was a charity."
>
> "Yes, I like her. Yes, it's a charity. But it's a reactionary charity. It stands for everything that I despise. Why didn't you discuss it with me first?"

Sometimes the action is reversible. Sometimes it isn't.

> "You sent a non-refundable deposit for a weekend with them? What makes you think we'd enjoy a weekend with them?"
>
> "We enjoy evenings with them. We like them."
>
> "We like them for an evening, *not* a whole weekend. They don't do anything. We'll go stir crazy. I can't believe you did that."

This problem also illustrates **marital rule 5:** The slower person sets the pace.

This rule was true in regard to sex when you were dating. It's true when two people run (or swim, or bike, or ski, etc.) together. It's true when two people go through life together. If one of you likes them, or it, a little, and the other likes them a lot, it makes sense to spend a little time with them, rather than a lot.

There are at least two caveats to this rule: #1 Consideration should be shown by both sides. Otherwise this rule will be used repeatedly by both sides as a passive-aggressive weapon. #2 There will be certain exceptional cases, e.g. parents, employers, etc., where even greater consideration should be shown. "I don't really enjoy their company, but I know how helpful they can be to your career, so I'll suck it up and join you for dinner."

The slower person sets the pace only when both are running. When only one is driving, **marital rule 5A:** The driver decides.

You might prefer to drive faster; I might leave less space between cars. Who's right? No one. The driver decides. If you're driving too fast for my taste, I need to look out the window, or close my eyes, same as you have to if you feel I'm tail-gating. As uncomfortable as I might feel with my eyes closed, the alternative, back seat driving, is simply not a viable option. This principle applies not only to driving, but also to any mutual responsibility: paying bills, balancing checkbooks, decorating a room, cooking a meal, setting the table, washing the dishes, mowing the lawn, putting the kids to bed, etc.

This doesn't mean that there shouldn't be compromise or constructive discussion whenever possible, but even reasonable people will occasionally disagree. When they do, it is unreasonable for one to demand that the other do it their way. Unfortunately, in all of these examples, and the infinitely more unmentioned ones, within reason, there is no right or wrong. We have to respect our spouse's decision.

There *is* a right and wrong in keeping each other's secrets. **Marital rule 6**: Never betray your spouse's confidences.

As we discussed previously, trusting your spouse is second only in importance to liking them. Trusting your spouse includes knowing that they'll always look out for your best interest. It includes knowing that they would never steal from you, cheat on you, or deliberately hurt you. It includes, most importantly, knowing that your secrets are safe with them.

In marriage, at times we assume the respective roles of psychiatrist-therapist, pastor-confessor, and lawyer-client. We are certainly entitled to the same confidentiality that comes with those professions. That's the law. It should be the rule as well. Certain confidences will be obvious. Only a fool, a sadist, or a drunk would reveal their spouse's sexual problems. Other problems however, might seem innocuous, but aren't.

> "You told her about my hernia? How could you?"
>
> "What's wrong with talking about a medical condition? It's nothing to be embarrassed about."
>
> "It's *my* medical condition, and *I* didn't want anyone knowing about it."

The best way to avoid this is, once again, in sharing. The responsibility is bilateral. The proprietor of the secret should inform their spouse, that despite it seeming innocuous, they don't want it revealed. Correspondingly, always check first before revealing anything, no matter how trivial.

An implicit aspect of rule 6 is that we always go to any length necessary to avoid embarrassing our spouse in public. This underlies as well **marital rule 7**: Never argue with, or criticize, your spouse in public.

This rule was discussed in relation to Otto Heinz and criticizing our children in front of others. Needless to say, what applies to our children applies even more so to our equals. While it is important to express our anger to our spouse as soon as we become aware of it, it is more important not to embarrass them in front of others. Even if you feel yourself overwhelmed by your anger, excuse yourself first and retire to a private place. Treat your spouse with the same dignity that you yourself would want. Never wash your family's laundry in public. The issue isn't secrecy; it's common human decency. It's respect.

Is disagreeing with your spouse the same thing as criticizing them? No. Nevertheless, if your spouse is sensitive to that, respect their sensitivity. Of course, in that case, that respect goes both ways. Don't demand that your spouse agree with you in public.

Rule 8: Never use your love as a weapon, or a test. Never start a sentence with, "If you really loved me, you'd . . ." Similarly never conclude with " . . . then you never really loved me." Using love as ammunition in some stupid argument, or power struggle, cheapens it, as well as you.

Rule 9: Don't wait for your spouse to offer, and then get angry when they don't. Incidentally, this rule applies to any relationship.

You want your spouse to do something for you. It can be important or trivial, profound or mundane, social or sexual. Taking out the garbage. Oral sex. A diamond necklace. A surprise party. It doesn't matter. You're too proud to ask. You justify yourself by saying that you'll appreciate it so much more, if you don't have to ask. They should know you well enough by now to offer what your heart desires spontaneously. When they don't, you're disappointed, and angry. When the explosion comes, you finally reveal what upset you. They respond: "If that's what you wanted, why didn't you tell me? I would have been happy to." You reply: "I shouldn't have to."

You're wrong. You should. Asking for something is another healthy form of sharing. By not asking, you're testing them. Your spouse isn't perfect, any more than you are.

Invariably, at times they will fail your test. In reality, it's not their failure, but yours.

Marital rule 10 is not only the final one, but also the most important. When things go wrong, and they will, resist the temptation to blame each other.

The single best thing about marriage is having someone with whom to share the bad times. Sharing the good times is the ultimate luxury. Sharing the bad times is even more valuable. It is a necessity.

How ironically pathetic that the times we need our closest ally the most, we turn them into an adversary. At times the crisis is trivially mundane:

> "If you had been ready to leave on time, we would have avoided this traffic jam."
> "Don't blame me. You were the one who decided to take the Expressway instead of the Parkway."

At other times the crisis is anything but, as with infertility, or as mentioned previously, with the loss of a child.

> "Why didn't you take him to the doctor sooner?!"
> "Why didn't *you*?!"

In theory, we're angry at the injustice of the situation. If we're believers, we're angry at God. We're furious with our fate, and our faith. In practice however, our only available lightning rod is our spouse. We punish them for our loss, and in the process, we punish ourselves.

Our spouse is unfortunately also the displacement when we're angry at sacred mortals as well. So often we feel rage toward our spouse when, we're really furious with our parents, but can't express it. It might sound like the psychoanalytic parody, "it's all your mother's fault," but sometimes the anger towards the parent has never been acknowledged by the grown child.

Johny was always paradoxically delighted when his wife called him at work to complain. He knew that if she was furious with her father, her boss, the children's principal, etc., she would be loving towards him. If her father was sick on the other hand, Johny would suffer. Without a proxy for her anger, he became the inevitable object. Should Johny stay married? What are the wrong reasons to stay married?

#1—For the kids.

There's only one thing worse than coming from a broken home. Living in one.

All children initially dread a divorce because of the uncertainty of their future. Eventually they perceive it as a relief. The fighting has finally stopped. They no longer come home to a house filled with anger. It's poignant to hear a 10-year-old who lives with his mother say: "I wish I was five again, so I'd still have a father." It's more poignant however, to hear a 20-year-old say: "I wish one of my parents had died before I was born, so my childhood wouldn't have been a war zone." Furthermore, if you feel that you're suffering for your children's sake, unconsciously you'll expect them to make it up to you. When they don't, when they misbehave, you'll think of them as ingrates, and be even angrier at them.

#2—To avoid the embarrassment.

Embarrassment fades overnight. No one talks about yesterday's news. Dissatisfaction does not fade.

#3—To avoid hurting your parents.

If your parents love you, they want you to do what makes you happy. No parent ever wants their child to suffer for their sake. Furthermore, as with your children, if you endure misery for your parents' sake, you'll resent your parents.

#4—You can't afford to.

You can't afford not to. If you're married to someone you don't like, or trust, in the long run, it costs you infinitely more to stay married. Both you and your spouse hoard money, hiding it from each other. In the long haul, your only choice is to pay for the divorce now, or pay for it later.

#5—There's no guarantee you'll find someone better.

If you're getting divorced because you've realized that your spouse is not perfect, then you're right. You shouldn't be getting divorced. You won't find anyone perfect. If, on the other hand, you're getting divorced because you're not happy, then just getting out will help relieve that unhappiness. If you find someone new, and the odds are you will, that's gravy. As in baseball, you can't steal second base without taking your foot off of first.

Divorce is major surgery. It's painful. It's debilitating. It's expensive. It leaves a scar that you will have the rest of your life. Most people try to avoid both, if at all possible. Unfortunately, if you avoid it for the wrong reasons, in both cases it will cost you your life.

Growing up, to my friends and me, divorces were like cars. We knew they existed. We saw them everywhere. We just didn't know anyone who had one. In my close-knit, ethnic community, the stigma of divorce was so great that it simply wasn't an option. Undoubtedly there were families who profited from that. Parents who might have taken the easy way out, didn't. Instead they worked on their marriage, to the eventual benefit of all concerned.

Yet, how many marriages, and their families, correspondingly suffered? Living in an over-crowded tenement, we didn't have the luxury of privacy. When Morris Goldsmith wasn't getting lunch, Max's wife had finished preparing his sandwich even before he knocked on the door.

When the Furillos had a fight, we all knew how it started and how it ended. When Mrs. O'Toole went to work in December in sunglasses, we knew exactly why.

In a new millennium, would any of them have gotten divorced? I don't know, but I sure hope so. Maybe then Morris' daughter would have been spared her three divorces. Maybe Nick Furillo, the fastest kid on the block, wouldn't have enlisted in the Marines on his seventeenth birthday and died in Viet Nam. Maybe I wouldn't have come across my old chum Jack O'Toole in Bellevue's detox ward. Jack didn't remember me. He didn't remember much. I wondered if he remembered his parents' fighting. I wondered if he was there because of his trying to forget it.

The worst thing about the unsuccessful marriage is the innocent bystanders. Currently fashionable nomenclature is "the nuclear family." How ironically appropriate. The power of a marriage is like nuclear energy. On the one hand, used correctly, it can solve seemingly insoluble problems. Sometimes it creates miracles. Its power to destroy however, is equally limitless. Divorce lawyers are always comparing their horror stories. They label them "scorched earth."

The anger between the former lovers is so overwhelming, it leaves nothing standing in its path. As irrational as it sounds, the archenemies would sooner dissipate their entire fortune on legal fees, leaving themselves, and their children, bankrupt, than let one penny fall into their adversary's hand. Their anger for each other overwhelms even their love for their children.

Patricia Duff and Ronald Perelman had been divorced five times *before* they married. One would imagine that they would have learned from their previous mistakes. Hardly. Ms. Duff alone went through 20 different lawyers and over three million dollars in legal bills before the judge forbade her from hiring any more lawyers. Their marriage had only lasted 20 months. Ms. Duff apparently needed a different lawyer for each month of marriage. The divorce was twice as long as the marriage and wasted over five million dollars to, in the end, accomplish nothing. In the words of the exasperated presiding judge[13]: "We have two very rich, and two very willful people locked in a dispute which I'm absolutely certain is causing severe damage to (their child). The two have been too focused on attacking, torturing and slandering each other."

"Crazy Eddie" Antar was the first retail electronics giant and marketing genius. Because of his ugly divorce with his first wife Debbie, he felt betrayed by, and became estranged from, his parents, two brothers, one sister and four daughters. To eliminate them from his eponymous company, he sold it. Subsequently, and consequently, he got indicted, went on trial and escaped the country as a fugitive from justice. Eventually recaptured and repatriated he served many years in maximum security federal prison. During his years on the lam, and in jail, he missed his daughters' birthdays, graduations, marriage, hospitalization and, most tragic of all, death. "Crazy Eddie" had it all. To spite his wife, he lost it all.

A man arguing on the phone with his ex-wife picked up a gun and shot his daughter sitting in front of him.[14] He knew the greatest pain he could cause his ex was for her to hear her daughter being murdered. The fact that the victim was also his daughter was secondary.

When, in 1995, celebrated actors Burt Reynolds[15] and Loni Anderson[16] got divorced, both insisted that their son Quinton was their highest priority. Accordingly, both claimed that they would never vilify the other in his presence. Apparently neither of them realized that Quinton could read, since they both published best-selling, mud-slinging exposes of the details of their marriage and divorce.

Similarly, in 2002, equally celebrated John McEnroe and Tatum O'Neal[17] published their own dueling, no-holds-barred versions of their marriage and divorce. Their children, and their children's friends, were thus privy to details of heroin and cocaine addiction, as well as mental and physical abuse. Of course, John and Tatum, like Burt and Loni, also claimed that their children were their greatest concern.

Considering the catastrophic consequences of divorce, some choose not to get married at all. Even if they have a long-term relationship, they maintain separate homes. They never tie the knot. As Oscar winning director Sam Mendes[18] put it: "I don't believe in marriage. People from broken homes just don't buy it."[19]

Though I can understand that point of view, I can't agree with it. Before I met my wife I always felt that there was something missing in my life. When I met my wife, I felt I could conquer the world. After I married her, I no longer needed to.

We teach our children everything else. Within our marriages, we can teach them how to form relationships, how to grow together, how to handle anger as a couple. They can only learn that from our example. In medicine, we often joke that if you want to live long, pick healthy parents. If we want our children to be happily married, we have to show them a happy marriage. Even if it's not within our power, it's no joke.

At a recent wedding I met the son of Morris Goldsmith. He was seated with and joking with his business partner and close friend, the son of Max Goldsmith. For just a moment, I heard their fathers laughing again.

> *"The anger of lovers renews the strength of love."*
> Publius Terentius Afer, (190-159 B.C.E.)

Notes

---

[1] *Deuteronomy* XXIV:1

[2] Ann Landers and Abigail Van Buren, familiarly known as "Dear

Abby," were the most successful advice columnists in the history of the newspapers. As such, they were unavoidably arch-rivals, but they were archenemies as well. Once they were not only the closest of friends, but also the closest of relatives, clones, identical twins. Their falling out came about reportedly over the issue of plastic surgery. Their daughters who continued their columns, continued their enmity as well.

[3] It is virtually impossible to pick up any magazine, of any caliber, and not find a story of betrayal. Former friends, now archenemies include: Eddie Van Halen and David Lee Roth, Bill Clinton and Dick Morris, West Coast Rap and East Coast Rap (which precipitated several homicides), Tracy McGrady and Vince Carter (who were cousins, as well as professional basketball teammates), Woody Allen and Jean Doumanian, Rudy Giuliani and Bill Bratton, Julie and Tricia Nixon, Liza and her sister, Meg Ryan and her mother, Eminem and his mother, Bob Guccione and his son. No industry or relationship is spared.

[4] Sherlock Holmes had as his life-long archenemy, the master of evil, Professor Moriarity. The same Professor Moriarity had once been Holmes' teacher, mentor and idol. Holmes was not only the first prodigiously successful recurrent literary character, but also, according to Guinness World Records, he is the most filmed fictional character of all time, portrayed by 75 actors in 211 movies (as of 2001).

[5] By far the most successful movie series of all time is *Star Wars.* Its emotionally resonant plots contain too many archenemies and betrayals to enumerate, but the most famous is Obi-Wan Kenobi being betrayed and slain by his former student and surrogate son, Darth Vader, who in turn will become the archenemy of his own son, Luke Skywalker.

[6] The archetypical comic book hero Superman has as his archenemy the diabolical Lex Luthor. The same Lex Luthor had been Clark Kent's best friend growing up in Smallville.

[7] This chapter includes material derived from *Marriage 101, A User's Manual to Becoming Happily Married—What Your Marriage Would Tell You if it Could Talk,* a full length book on marriage.

[8] There are many famous quotes about the prospect of death making us appreciate life more. Perhaps the most memorable was Samuel Johnson's observation that: "Nothing concentrates the mind so wonderfully as being at the end of a rope."

[9] From a survey of 11,000 women by the Center for Disease Control and Prevention.

[10] The same Center for Disease Control survey revealed that the younger one marries, the more likely is the prospect of divorce.

[11] The one obvious exception to this rule is proprietary secrets involving our jobs, e.g. judges, spies, shrinks, et al.

[12] Like all jokes, in-law jokes express the anger of the oppressed that can't be expressed otherwise. Two well-known examples:

What is the difference between in-laws and outlaws? Outlaws are wanted.

A man is on safari with his wife and mother-in-law. In the middle of the night he is awoken by his terror stricken wife who has discovered that her mother has left the tent. They search the camp and find her mother in the bottom of a deep pit with a flesh-eating lion.

The wife implores: "You've got to do something!"

Her husband reassures her: "Don't worry. The lion got himself into this. He'll get himself out of it."

[13] Judge Franklin Weissberg.

[14] *Psychiatric News*, July 5, 2002.

[15] A decade prior to his marriage to Loni Anderson, Burt Reynolds had been the most popular movie star in the world for five consecutive years. His movies included *Deliverance*, the *Smokey and the Bandit* series, and *The Cannonball Run* series. His previous wives/relationships included Judy Carne, Dinah Shore and Sally Field.

[16] Loni Anderson is best known for the television series *W.K.R.P. in Cincinnatti*.

[17] Tatum O'Neal is the youngest person to ever win an Oscar. Her movies included *Paper Moon* and *The Bad News Bears*. Her father is the equally volatile actor Ryan O'Neal.

[18] Sam Mendes won an Oscar for directing Best Picture *American Beauty*, a bleak portrait of marriage and family life. He also directed the equally grim *Road to Perdition*, and the foreboding stage productions of *Cabaret* and *The Blue Room*. Did his parents' divorce when he was three contribute to his pessimism, and/or his brilliance?

[19] *People,* July 29, 2002.

PART III

CHAPTER FOUR

"Fuck You!"

Anger In Sex

"If any among you engage in these sexual abominations, your souls will be excised." [1]

In 1993 a young housewife, in a fit of rage attacked her husband with a kitchen knife while he slept. The wound was so minor it barely woke him. His life was in no way threatened. Nevertheless her action became the single most celebrated, and controversial, story of the entire year.

His given name was John Wayne; hers was Lorena; their family name was Bobbitt; the action she had taken was to cut off his penis.

Why did this marital dispute become so important? What earned it the cover of innumerable magazines, the lead of innumerable broadcasts, and the subject of innumerable jokes?

Thousands of unhappy spouses express their anger with violence every week, yet they aren't considered news. Even the phenomenon of a wife severing her husband's penis is not uncommon in other countries. In parts of Southeast Asia, where families live in huts above their livestock on the ground beneath them, the practice is referred to, matter of factly, as "feeding the ducks." The United States has its own history of severed penises. Men have done it frequently to each other, both dead and alive, and even more commonly, to themselves.

What then made John Wayne and Lorena Bobbitt, by all

accounts, a remarkably unremarkable couple, such a newsworthy phenomenon? Why did it capture our imaginations, where far more important stories did not? Why did it provoke discussions and arguments in so many households, many of which had never previously discussed items of a sexual nature?

The answer lies in the power of a potent, indeed combustible, combination, sex and anger. At least six separate factors made the sordid story of the Bobbitts so irresistible:

One: The fact of the severed penis commanded the attention, as well as the sympathy, of most men. **Two**: The fact that Lorena subsequently claimed that John Wayne had raped her similarly caught the attention, as well as the sympathy, of most women. **Three**: The fact that Lorena claimed that her amputation was an act of vengeance resonated with a feminist sense of justice previously expressed in movies such as *Thelma and Louise.* **Four**: The fact that John Wayne claimed that Lorena was upset that he had climaxed while she had not, introduced the issue of fair sex, for the fair sex. **Five**: The microsurgery and medical technology that permitted reattachment was future-shock to many. **Six**: The happy ending, the successful reattachment, was just what the doctor, and Hollywood, ordered.

Absent any one of these factors, it would not have commanded the same attention. Had Lorena cut off his hand instead; had the amputation occurred in self-defense, or in intoxication, or as an accident, or in psychosis; had John concurred that the punishment fit the crime; had reattachment never occurred, it is unlikely that anyone outside the state of Virginia would ever have heard of this unfortunate couple.

Such was not the case. Every subsequent reaction, from the cartoonist who portrayed Thanksgiving at the Bobbitts with men cowering under the table as Lorena prepares to carve, to the comedienne who suggested that Lorena should have disposed of the penis in a Cuisinart rather than on the side of the road, to the columnist who suggested that Lorena be incarcerated in the same cell as Joey Buttafuco, the celebrated statutory rapist, in all cases reflected the particular feelings of the author, rather than the particulars of the incident. The Bobbitts became a national Rorschach Test reflecting our angry feelings about sex.[2]

Roz, a newlywed, was referred by her gynecologist for dyspareunia, pain upon intercourse. He had been unable to find any organic cause and her problem was worsening. Roz had been a virgin at her wedding and, in fact, had expected sex to be painful at first, since that had been the case with her two older sisters. What she hadn't expected was her husband's impatience. Although sexually active when they met, he had been willing to forego premarital sex. Now that they were married however, he had grown tired of this "immature hang-up."

They agreed to a compromise of sex on a weekly basis. It sounded good in theory. In practice however, Roz resented having to do something that her husband knew caused her pain. The more she resented it, the angrier she got, the more she involuntarily contracted her pelvic musculature, the more painful the ordeal became. The angry sex created a vicious cycle.

In the previously mentioned movie *The War of the Roses*, when Kathleen Turner attempts to seduce Danny DeVito, she asks him if he's ever experienced angry sex. He replies, "Is there any other kind?"

Alfred Kinsey had reached the same conclusion in his seminal studies on sex in 1953: "The closest parallel to the picture of sexual response is found in the known physiology of anger."[3]

Psychiatrists, privy to both intimate sexual fantasies, as well as detailed sexual dreams, are invariably struck by the similar themes of dissimilar patients. An investment banker's violent fantasies are no different from an itinerant biker's.

A conventional housewife has the same sado-masochistic sex dream as a siliconized stripper.

A romantic fantasy with a sensitive, loving couple walking off hand in hand into the sunset is fine for a paperback novel. It is not however what either men or women are thinking about while they masturbate. They are imagining domination, power, control, violence, humiliation, even pain. A fantasy is by definition something abnormal, out of the ordinary, that we would never do in real life. It is not exciting to imagine having sex with your spouse in the missionary position in the privacy of your bedroom with the lights off. Rather, the more forbidden an act is, the more arousing it becomes, which is precisely why even highly moral, law abiding citizens will conjure up scenarios including rape and violence.

Ironically, despite the jokes about Lorena Bobbitt never finding another date, precisely because of these fantasies Lorena will attract many men who previously would never have given her a second glance. Even John Wayne himself has made allusions to missing her and wanting to reconcile.

In 1976, a Japanese film by Nagisa Oshima, *In the Realm of the Senses,* climaxed with the heroine providing the hero the "ultimate climax," strangling him to death as he ejaculates. The scene was considered highly erotic by both sexes and the movie consequently did surprisingly strong business for a foreign "art" film. In 1980, an American horror film, *Mother's Day,* climaxed with the heroine amputating the villain's penis with an electric carving knife. In the best selling book and movie *The World According to Garp*[4] a penis is accidentally amputated during fellatio in a fender bender.

Lorena and John Wayne are no different from Laura and Franklin, who didn't need a marital therapist, counselor or mediator. They needed two bodyguards. This long married couple didn't merely harbor resentment. They despised each other. Archenemies have hated each other less. Their antipathy was of Shakespearian proportion. "You wasp . . . you are too angry."[5] "You mad-headed ape! A weasel hath not such . . . spleen as you are toss'd with."[6]

Why did they stay married? They were each independently wealthy and had no children together. When asked together, neither could offer *any* answer, much less a satisfactory one. When asked individually, on the other hand, they confided the identical answer. It was because of the phenomenal sex.

It seemed paradoxical at first. The best sex they ever had was with the person they hated the most. Yet, it wasn't. This was sex, *not* love. Franklin described how with each thrust he would imagine the pain he was causing Laura. Sometimes he would scream "Take that, you bitch!" "Suffer, cunt!" as a punctuation mark. It precipitated a sexual excitement in him that he had never before experienced and could never again replicate. (Both partners had numerous affairs throughout their marriage.)

How could Laura enjoy this sadistic scene? What was *she* thinking of as this was going on? Her sentiments were similar. She would lie back with her eyes open getting off on Franklin's uncontrollable frenzy. She would be thinking, sometimes screaming: "You want me so bad!," "You need me!," "You love my ass!," "You can't live without me!," "I own you!" She wouldn't allow herself to come until Franklin had done so first, but as soon as she felt Franklin's warm ejaculate, as soon as she sensed him writhe, she could no longer resist. Her winning the contest[7] was an irresistible catalyst. Thus they experienced simultaneous orgasm on almost every occasion.

How ironic. The worst married couple ever created were, not coincidentally, the most sexually satisfied. It's not unusual.

After Bonny Lee Bakley was shot in the head on May 4, 2001, her family confided that she had known that her husband, actor Robert Blake of *Baretta* and *In Cold Blood* was going to murder her. She had told her mother: "He told me he had a script written out for me, and he's got a bullet with my name on it." She had even asked her sister what it would feel like to get shot in the head. Why had she remained with him? Her sister explained that Blake's anger ignited Bonny's sexual passion for him. "The more angry he got, the more she liked him."

The primary protagonists of the popular TV sitcom *Northern Exposure* were Joel, a sophisticated New York physician and Maggie, a simple Alaskan bush pilot. Two more opposite people could scarcely be imagined, yet their mutual attraction was obvious to every viewer. After two seasons and too many episodes, they finally consummated their attraction. How? They got into a fight. Not merely a screaming verbal argument, but an actual physical fistfight in which Maggie literally broke Joel's nose. Their battle continued for several days until they both lost control again. This time they engaged in a wrestling match. During this second altercation simultaneously, inexplicably, their antagonism turned into ardor. By mutual, wordless consent, their struggle climaxed in sex.

Maybe that's what made *Northern Exposure* such a different, quirky show. Could that kind of atypical behavior occur on a more typical sitcom?

Cheers was one of the most popular sitcoms in the history of television. Its stars were the bartender Sam Malone, portrayed by Ted Danson, and his barmaid Diane Chambers, portrayed by Shelley Long. Diane was an erudite, cultured, feminist scholar. Sam was a crude, ignorant, womanizing ex-jock. They were as ill-suited for each other as Joel and Maggie, or as Laura and Franklin. They were also as attracted. How did they finally consummate their attraction?

Sam and Diane were typically arguing with each other in Sam's office. The argument escalated into insults. The insults escalated into mutual threats of physical violence. The tension escalated as they belligerently approached each other. As they were about to strike each other, Sam suddenly said: "Are you as turned on as I am?" Diane replied: "More!" Their first sexual encounter ensued.

Shelley Long left *Cheers*, but the angry sex did not. A new romance ensued between the tart tongued, insulting waitress Carla portrayed by Rhea Perlman, (not surprisingly Danny DeVito's wife) and the arrogant, insulting restaurant owner portrayed by Keene Curtis. Once again, sexual foreplay consisted of humiliating put-downs of escalating proportions.

Movies, even by celebrated writer-directors, recapitulate the identical theme. In Woody Allen's *Curse of the Jade Scorpion*, the protagonists, portrayed by Allen and Helen Hunt, spend the entire movie insulting each other and wishing each other a horrific death. Yet, at the very end they fall in love and marry. As Allen writes in the movie: "You can't hate somebody that much without there being at least a little bit of attraction underneath it all."

It should not be surprising that one can be simultaneously attractive sexually and unattractive emotionally. Throughout history nice and sexy have been mutually exclusive: Doris Day was nice. Raquel Welch was sexy. Pat Boone was nice. Marlon Brando was sexy. Perry Como was nice. Elvis Presley was sexy. June Allyson was nice. Jane Russell was sexy. Meg Ryan was nice. Pam Anderson was sexy. Tom Hanks was nice. Russell Crowe was sexy. Sandra Bullock was nice. Madonna[8] was sexy.

Long before records, television or movies, long before *Like A Virgin*, there was already the Madonna-whore dichotomy. It postulated that the woman who made a good wife and mother could never be the woman who enjoyed, or was enjoyable at, sex. Good women and good sex were mutually exclusive. The former, the Madonna, was a sweet, innocent, seemingly virginal saint. The latter, the whore, was an assertive, foul-mouthed, selfish slut. The lucky man who could afford it would keep both, a wife and a mistress. The former was for show; the latter was for blow.

As far as arousal is concerned, the actual physical attractiveness is less important than the image. Mistresses aren't necessarily better looking than wives. Their attitude however, exudes sex. Wives are wholesome. Mistresses are whore-some. Never can the twain co-exist. When Donna Reed for example, won an Oscar for portraying a prostitute in *From Here To Eternity*, she was described by the media as an incredibly sexy woman. When shortly thereafter, the same Donna Reed, same face, same body, became the perfect wife and mother on *The Donna Reed Show*, she instantaneously lost her erotic allure.

Our most important sexual organ is not between our legs, but between our ears. Contrary to the attention bestowed on the Bobbitts, both the penis and the vagina, are from both an anatomical as well as a physiological perspective incredibly unimpressive organs. Their extraordinary importance in our minds, comes from our minds.

The vagina itself is barely an organ. It is nothing more than a potential space. Absent something inside, it remains collapsed. When necessity demands, it can expand prodigiously, like a snake's jaws, to accommodate a baby's head. Reflecting its relative simplicity, it is the only organ that human technology can easily replicate. Even before the Bronze Age, man discovered that the penis could be effectively replaced with but a hand.

How effective is the vagina at stimulating a penis? At best, it's satisfactory, providing the two requirements, friction and lubrication. At worst, if the woman isn't herself aroused, and therefore not providing lubrication, or if she previously underwent a stretching delivery, thus reducing friction, the stimulation of the penis can be less than ideal.

Compare it to the man's own hand. Friction is always perfect by hand, given the many, finely tuned, voluntary muscles. Furthermore, unlike the vagina, there is an instantaneous, instinctual feedback system between hand and penis. Pressure can be increased or decreased as needed, and even applied strategically, none of which a vagina can do. Lubrication is guaranteed, providing a few drops of lanolized lotion are available. Bottles of lotion never have headaches, inhibitions or angry feelings. As Woody Allen said to Diane Keaton in *Annie Hall*[9]: "Hey, don't knock masturbation. It's sex with someone I love."

If, in fact, a man's hand is functionally more effective at stimulating a penis than a woman's vagina, then why, given a choice, do men usually prefer the latter? Because a woman consists of more than just a vagina. There are other parts, to see, feel, hear, touch and smell. It is the gestalt of those parts, the total woman, that arouses the man, not merely the vagina. Furthermore, as with Laura and Franklin, Joel and Maggie, and Sam and Diane, sometimes the friction of the genders is more stimulating than the friction of the genitals.

The penis is, in a sense, an evaginated version of the vagina. Unlike any other appendage or organ, it contains no bone, cartilage, muscle or working parts. It is nothing more than a thin hose surrounded by a sponge. When that sponge fills with blood, it becomes erect and potent. When, as most of the time, the sponge is empty, the organ is largely worthless. If the vagina is nothing more than a potential space, then the penis is basically a potential organ.

In fact, there are circumstances, both accidental and deliberate, when the penis can disappear. It doesn't dematerialize of course, but rather it invaginates into the body cavity. It can result from blunt force, for example, jumping, instead of diving, off the high board. It has been used by transvestites for centuries to create the illusion of a vagina. A famous example was the Chinese opera singer/ actor in "M. Butterfly" who successfully deceived his French Diplomat husband for years.

For the purpose of stimulating a woman, a finger or a dildo, an artificial replica of a penis, is infinitely more effective. Unlike the real thing, a dildo can be controlled, size selected, made to vibrate, applied directly to the clitoris, and remain hard as long as the woman desires. Dildos, whether plastic, metal or vegetable, never get drunk, selfish, insecure or angry.

Yet, women rhapsodize about particular penises as if they were God's gift to their gender. Despite that, women's obsession with the penis still pales in comparison to men's. Indeed, when men, or women, speak of "the organ," it is so self-evident, it need not be specified further. A soldier wounded in the chest or abdomen, even critically, will fight to his last breath. The same soldier wounded, even superficially, in his genitalia will immediately become incapacitated.[10] This is not cowardice, but rather the fact that the soldier would sooner die than live without his self-perceived manhood.

Even in peacetime, many men are phobic of surgery proximal to the penis. They wear trusses and carry their testicles around in a wheelbarrow, rather than submit to hernioraphies. With frequently fatal consequences, they postpone and avoid prostatectomies. They would sooner defy and deny prostate cancer, which strikes one in eight men, than have a urologist painlessly stick a needle through their penis to remove it.

In Malaysia, men afflicted with a psychiatric malady called "Koro" become convinced that their penises are disappearing, invaginating into their bodies. They panic, convinced that if their penis disappears entirely, they will consequently die. To avoid this, they tie strings around their penises and even enclose them in a locked box for safekeeping.

Although rare, Koro has been seen in non-Asian men in the United States as well. Daniel, a 23-year-old virgin had always felt insecure about the size of his penis despite repeated reassurances from his physicians. When his fiancée Stacy broke their engagement, he became convinced that his penis was shrinking into his abdomen, and the results would be fatal. His delusion persisted despite medical reassurances and psychiatric intervention. It resolved only when Stacy returned to him.[11]

It is ironic that the penis has come to represent the male, both positively and negatively, because in reality, the penis is nothing more than a front. The media continually referred to Lorena having emasculated and castrated John Wayne. Nonsense. True emasculation, removal of the testicles is not only far more painful, but its consequences are infinitely more dire.

A man with a severed penis has a serious transmission problem, but his libido, potency and masculinity are in tact. A man without testicles on the other hand, not only loses his sexual desire and his ability to procreate, but also, endocrinologically speaking, he is no longer a man. His penis becomes a largely vestigial organ, like an appendix. Its only utility is urination accuracy.

Any homeowner can attest that it is infinitely easier, and less expensive, to replace a peripheral hose than the central pump. When transsexual operations were more common, patients would report that the key change was *not* the removal of the penis, or even the surgical creation of the vagina, but rather the removal of the testicles and its physiological sequelae, e.g. changes in facial and body hair, muscle mass, pitch of voice, etc.

Had Lorena sought to express her anger effectively rather than symbolically, she would have removed John Wayne's testicles instead of his penis. She didn't, because in her mind a man is fundamentally a penis. Of course, she probably wouldn't have used the word "penis." She would have used instead its synonym, "prick" [12].

Why is the word "prick," or its female equivalent "cunt," universally considered to be such a contumely affront? For that matter, why is "Fuck you!," the title of this chapter, considered the ultimate invective?

Even among adults, the "F" word—Fuck, carries far more weight, than the "S" word—Shit, the "H" word—Hell, or any other word. A professional basketball referee or baseball umpire, for example, will tolerate insults including the "S" and "H" words, but mention "Fuck" in any of its many permutations, and you're out of the game. What does "Fuck" mean? It literally means having sex. How can a term for making love be insulting? Because it reflects the anger inherent in sex. "Fuck you!" says "I will fuck you!" "I will dominate you!" "I will penetrate you involuntarily!" "I will rape you!"

Yet, it's not only said by men to women. It's most frequently said by heterosexual men to each other. It's said by women to each other, and even by women to men. It's the first words that immigrant taxi drivers can express fluently[13], long before they even understand what it means. Its variation, "Go fuck yourself!" means at best, "Go masturbate!," at worst, "Go penetrate yourself with a dildo!" In effect you're inviting the object of your scorn to have an enjoyable, sexual experience. No matter how nonsensical or inappropriate the sexual meaning becomes, the anger component retains its impact.

Not coincidentally, most of our other vicious insults use the same sexual metaphors. "Up yours!" means "I will stick my penis up your ass!" When someone tells you to "Stick it in your ear!," "it" refers to someone's penis, although it's unclear if it's yours or theirs. "Jerk off" whether as a noun, or as an imperative, refers to masturbation. "Cock sucker," "Twat licker," "mother fucker" are all self explanatory.

The rage of sexual jealousy[14] is self-explanatory as well. It is arguably the single most common cause of homicide. Famous examples can be found in the Bible—King David sending Bathsheba's husband off to die on the front lines; in Greek tragedy—Euripides' *Medea*, abandoned by Jason, kills everyone she can, including her own sons; in Shakespeare—Iago inciting Othello to murder Desdemona; and in every era's headlines.

On February 27, 1859, U.S. Congressman from New York, Daniel Sickles[15] shot to death Phillip Barton Key, U.S. district attorney for the District of Columbia, and son of Francis Scott Key, composer of the national anthem. The murder took place in broad daylight, in Washington's Lafayette Square, in front of many witnesses. When finally dragged away, Sickles said: "Is the scoundrel dead yet? Good. One less wretch in the world." Sickles' lawyers argued at his trial that Sickles, a notorious womanizer, was nevertheless justified in his actions because Key was having an affair with Sickles' wife. It was the first time that temporary insanity was used as a defense. The jury acquitted Sickles in less than 70 minutes. The courtroom exploded in cheers.

On June 25, 1906 Stanford White, the most influential and successful architect of his era, was shot to death at a gala in Madison Square Garden[16], one of the many buildings he had designed. He was murdered by Harry Thaw, jealous husband of White's "friend," showgirl Evelyn Nesbit. Thaw successfully used the insanity defense as well.

Two famous, jealous murders of the late twentieth century occurred but months and miles apart. Richard Herrin, a Mexican-American high school valedictorian and Yale scholarship student was informed by his girlfriend, Bonnie Garland, daughter of a prestigious Scarsdale lawyer, that though she loved him, she was going to see other men. He hit her with a hammer until, in his own words, "her head split open like a watermelon."

Nearby and even more infamously, Jean Harris, head mistress of the prestigious Madeira School for Girls, shot to death Dr. Herman Tarnover, the celebrated Scarsdale Diet Doctor, when it became clear that he was leaving her for another woman.

Studies of sadism and depraved murders[17] indicate that their victims are frequently prostitutes. Serial killers in particular, from Jack The Ripper on, often specialize in street-walkers. There are practical reasons for this to be sure. These women are easy to meet privately and their disappearance isn't quickly noticed, if at all. There are emotional reasons as well. Whores represent the essence of sex and therefore become the object of the ire it arouses.

Our sexual frustrations are also reflected in our jokes:

A man walking on a beach finds a bottle and picks it up. Instantaneously a giant genie appears and announces: "I will grant you one wish, anything you've ever wanted."

The man pulls a map out of his pocket. "See these twelve countries. There are currently wars in each one of them. I want you to stop all the fighting. I want world peace."

"Listen pal, I'm a genie, not a miracle worker. How about something more reasonable?"

The man sighs and puts away the map. "O.K. Can you have my wife give me a blow job when I get home?"

"Let me see the map again."

Misandryst jokes are no less funny, or less vicious:

As the groom takes off his shoes and socks, the bride, who hadn't previously seen him undressed, is shocked.

"What's the matter with your toes? They're tiny and mis-shapen."

He jokes reassuringly: "That's because I had Toe-lio!"

He removes his pants.

"Your knees. They're also tiny and mis-shapen."

He jokes again: "And that's because I had Kneesles!"

As he doffs his underpants, she exclaims: "I can see you had Small-Cocks too!"

Sometimes it's not the content that's funny, but the context:

"Former Governor Ann Richards, of Texas, attended a dinner party during which a male friend

started to describe, in pointillist detail, the breasts
of a young lady he'd just seen. The women at the
table stared carefully into space, feigning deafness.
A brief silence followed. Then Richards spoke: 'Well,
girls,' she boomed. 'Have you seen any good dicks
lately?[18] '"

Some jokes insult both sexes simultaneously:

The President attends a Washington Redskins
game and in the locker room afterwards notices the
enormous organ of their tackle, Hog Hogan.

"Hog. I got to tell you. I've never seen one that
big."

"Mr. President it's easy. Every night, before you
go to bed, whack it against the bedpost. You'll be
amazed how quickly it grows."

The President returns to the White House, goes
upstairs to tell the First Lady about his new discovery,
but she's already fast asleep with the lights off. He
quietly undresses and starts whacking his organ
against the bedpost. The distinctive noise awakens
the First Lady.

"Hurry up, Hog. Tiny will be home soon."

Professional comedians observe that the most successful
material is invariably off color, i.e. sexual in nature.
Consequently all comedians are much funnier uncensored
in nightclubs than they are restricted on television. If humor
is the sublimation of anger, then how funny we find a joke is
directly proportional to how much of our anger it expresses.
Does this mean that nothing angers us as much as sex does?

It's possible. It's more likely however, that since sex is
still a forbidden subject, it remains the largest reservoir of
unexpressed anger. Most of us would sooner complain about
our living conditions, our rotten luck, or our spouse's

selfishness, then about our not being sexually satisfied. Hence the need to express it in humor.

Though sex retains the mystique of the forbidden fruit, it should be treated no differently than any other aspect of a relationship. The key is communicating. If you're still hungry, it's your responsibility to inform your spouse of that. Don't blame them, if they didn't read your mind. Extending the metaphor, if it's impolite to leave the table before your spouse is done in the dining room, no less should apply in the bedroom. If it's healthy to share with your spouse your tastes in other areas, why not in sex as well? Discussing your sexual fantasies with each other is neither an insult nor a threat. On the contrary, as with any sharing, it can't help but bring the couple closer.[19]

Once the excitement of the incipient infatuation is over, what makes a great lover is no different from what makes a great roommate. Consideration and sensitivity are infinitely more important than the size of one's penis or tightness of one's vagina. If differing tastes in other areas can be compromised, then why not differing tastes in sex as well? If we can alternate between French and Italian food, why can't we alternate between oral and missionary sex as easily? Another option would be an appetizer of one and an entree of the other. Variety, the spice of life, should apply no less to our greatest pleasure, than to our other tastes.

Another variable guaranteed to improve our sensual pleasure is time. The more time you take, the more pleasurable the experience. A tasting menu is an extraordinary, expensive experience only available in the finest of restaurants. What is it? A series of appetizer sized portions served sequentially. The individual presentation gives you the time to savor each. What if they were all served simultaneously? Then you're eating the combination platter, redolent of a cafeteria, or an "All you can eat" buffet. Removing the luxury of time converts the most expensive culinary experience into the cheapest. The same is true with sex.

I once consulted with The Sexiest Man Alive. He had understandably experienced innumerable sexual liaisons with many of the sexiest women on the planet. I asked him which had been the most pleasurable. His answer surprised me at the time. In retrospect, it shouldn't have. It was early in his career, before he had achieved any fame. He had picked up a girl hitchhiking. She was hardly beautiful, but it became explicitly clear soon after they met that they would be having sex as soon as they reached home. Home was three hours away. What made the sex so unforgettable was not the act, or the person, but the fact that they had spent three hours talking about it beforehand.

Imagine you had purchased at auction a French vintner's fifty-year-old masterpiece. Would you appreciate it more if you just uncorked it and drank it straight out of the bottle, or if you had an oenophile with you to slowly decant it and point out the wine's incredible color, bouquet and viscosity before you even had that first precious sip? Would you drink it impulsively, or would you plan an evening around it? In sex, as in food, and wine, the presentation is as important as the product.

Our sex life is limited only by our imagination, but should not be by our inhibitions and ignorance. Furthermore, if it's our mind that creates the excitement in the first place, we need not relinquish that excitement when we limit ourselves to a single partner. We can revitalize our sex life by role playing or pretending. The scenarios can be as innocuous as picking each other up in a singles bar, or as intense as rape.

Is rape a healthy scenario, even as a pretense? If it's consensual and mutually enjoyable, it's no different from pretending to be an Empress and her slave. In both cases, the play-acting allows us to do safely what we normally can't.

Rape has always been the tip of the iceberg of sexual

anger. It's the most salient manifestation of male anger, and simultaneously the greatest precipitant of female outrage. Sadly the vast majority of rapes perpetrated throughout history have gone unreported and certainly unpunished. Until recently the fact of marriage was mutually exclusive to rape, i.e. if your husband did it, it wasn't rape. (Lorena's defenders cite this to justify her behavior as her only recourse against John Wayne.) Even a date could be considered a form of marriage. You couldn't claim rape if you invited him into your room.

Where rape was concerned, the victim was more on trial than the accused. In several notorious cases, unabashed rapists were acquitted because juries felt that the victim's dress had been too provocative, and therefore a contributing factor. Women contemplating pursuing a rape charge had to accept the likelihood that their entire sexual and non-sexual history could become the focus of the trial and the media coverage. A member of America's "royalty," the Kennedy family[20], was charged with date rape. The heavyweight boxing champion of the world, Mike Tyson, was convicted of it, and went to jail.

July, 2002. Pakistan. The 12-year-old brother of Mukhtar Mai was accused of wooing a 22-year-old woman above his social status. He denied it. A tribal court found him guilty nevertheless. Their sentence? His 18-year-old sister Mukhtar Mai would be gang raped. Four men carried out the court's punishment, apparently still common in Pakistan.

In the U.S. however, the pendulum has begun to swing, some say too far, others say not far enough. Some say that accusations of rape have become the modern day equivalent of McCarthy's accusations of Communism. Others say, despite progress, most rapes still go unpunished.

The very definition of what constitutes rape has been brought into question. At one time it was thought to be obvious. When sexual penetration was physically forced upon an unwilling individual, that was rape. Now it's not so simple.

Some claim that *any* sexual intercourse without explicit, valid consent is by definition rape. If a valid consent cannot be given while intoxicated, it means that even if a woman, or a man for that matter, agreed to have sex, but had been drinking, they could subsequently claim to have been raped.

At least one college instituted a complex code of behavior regarding all sexual matters. Male students were instructed they needed to get an explicit, sober, verbal consent before each specific, increasing step of foreplay. May I kiss you on the cheek? May I kiss you on the lips? May I introduce my tongue into your mouth? May I touch your breast through your sweater? May I touch it beneath your sweater, but above your shirt? How about beneath your shirt, but with your bra still on?

Reflecting the legal definition of sex, we have witnessed a President of the United States deny that he had "sex" with his intern since he had only had his penis in her mouth. Reflecting the legal definition of rape, we now have condoms that can be date stamped with the woman's fingerprints to prove the consensuality of the encounter. Even consensual sober sex under false pretenses can be considered rape. In one case a woman slept with a man pretending to be a movie producer who would give her a big role. When she discovered his ruse, she charged him with rape[21].

Other angry sexual controversies include pornography, whose definition varies both by era and location. Some claim that beauty contests (like Miss America), girlie magazines (like *Playboy*) and titillating television or movies (like *Baywatch* and *Basic Instinct*) are all sexually demeaning to women, despite the fact that the women who participate do so voluntarily and for profit.

Beauty contests do not begin and end with corporate sponsors. Adolescent boys of any age commonly indulge in the sport of rating their female contemporaries as to their attractiveness. A "ten" was a well-understood compliment long before Bo Derek's movie of that name was released.

Women are not without recourse, or for that matter, any less cruel. Some years ago coeds at an Ivy League college published and distributed a circular, rating and mocking the sexual practices of various men on campus. As with rape, and all other expressions of sexual anger, one can only imagine the consequences on the victims' future sexual functioning.

Though we lack comprehensive studies for comparison, most sex therapists believe that the incidence of sexual dysfunctions has increased. While the causes vary, anger remains a common denominator.

A Brooklyn Chassid consulted for an erectile dysfunction. When asked what he fantasized about as he was trying to become aroused, he said that he thought about his Rabbi's latest sermon. He was advised to instead focus on the most erotic, stimulating fantasy he could imagine. He returned to report that it hadn't worked. When asked about his fantasy, he replied that he had focused on the Biblical verse: "Be fruitful and multiply." His erotic imagination left much to be desired.

With much trepidation I suggested that he purchase an issue of *Playboy*. He was, as I expected, outraged. I suggested that we discuss it with his Rabbi. To my relief and my patient's dismay, the Rabbi ruled that, since this was for the express purpose of procreation, under these circumstances, it was not only permitted, but indeed imperative. My patient was bothered by the ruling, but being utterly devoted to his Rabbi, he agreed to comply.

When he returned, he was enraged. He slammed the door on his way in, pounded on my desk and informed me that no matter what I said, no matter even what his revered Rabbi said, he would never purchase that magazine again. He acknowledged that he had finally consummated his marriage, but *that* wasn't the point. The point was, that for a recognizable Chassid as himself to purchase a *Playboy* was a personal humiliation. As he stalked out of the office, he declared again that nothing could make him buy such a magazine again. Under his breath however, he noted that he had purchased a two-year subscription.

Not only do we assume that we know everything there is to know about sex, but also, we get angry if that proves not to be the case. A devout Christian couple had eschewed sexual relations prior to marriage. After marriage they had immediately achieved erection and penetration, but ejaculation continued to elude them.

I was struck by how totally the husband dominated the relationship. Not only did he answer every question posed to the two of them, but he also answered questions addressed to his wife directly. It seemed ludicrous for him to be answering a question as intimate as her ability to lubricate or her pleasure at penetration, but she didn't make an issue of it, so neither did I. If she hadn't said "Thank you" when I took her coat, I would have wondered if she was mute.

I asked if he ever varied the frequency of his pumping after penetration. He didn't understand the question. I explained that by "pumping," I meant his moving up and down, in and out. He still didn't understand. I asked, if he didn't move, what did he do after penetrating? It was a stupid question on my part, since he immediately became very defensive. How was he supposed to know? He wasn't the type to read dirty books, or go to X-rated movies. "It wasn't written in Scriptures." No one had ever told him.

Suddenly I heard a low murmur. His wife was uncharacteristically muttering something. At first I couldn't hear her distinctly, but she quickly increased both her volume and her intensity. "No one ever told you? No one ever told you?! *I* told you! Every night I begged you! Move! Do something! No, you said! It's unseemly, you said! All you do is lie there like a flounder! You thought you knew better! You always think you know better!" The following week they reported that their problem had been solved. This time however, the wife did all the talking.

Another quiet lady, a mousy librarian, frightened her next-door neighbors. Through the porous walls of their high rise, they heard her screaming "Oh God! Please! Help! God! Oh my God!" Since, in the decade they had lived together, they had never heard a peep from her even when they met in the elevator or the corridor, much less through the walls, they became alarmed. They phoned her, rang her doorbell, called the doorman, all to no avail. It was only when the police arrived and threatened to break down her door that she finally opened it. She was wearing a crimson blanket and a matching face. Standing behind her, wearing another blanket, was a man looking equally meek and equally embarrassed. She never referred to the incident to her neighbors or the doorman, but moved out soon thereafter. She never said goodbye.

On the subject of inadvertent eavesdropping, all parents fear their children chancing upon them "in flagrante delicto." Child psychiatric literature indicates that witnessing this "primal scene" can have traumatic effects. When these children are finally willing to discuss what they saw, what do they describe? Not sex. Not even love. Invariably they resort to terms of violence: "Mommy and Daddy were wrestling, naked." "Daddy was peeing in Mommy's mouth." "They were fighting. He was hurting her. She was screaming." "She was sitting on him, pooping on his face and chewing on his penee as I came in." "He was on top of her, beating her up again and again. It was only after she prayed to God that he stopped. When she saw me, she made believe that they were joking, but she couldn't fool me. "

On the one hand, these children, like the librarian's neighbors, are clearly misinterpreting the sounds they are hearing and the sights they are seeing. On the other hand, the feelings that they are sensing might not be that much of a misinterpretation after all.

Some claim that sex has replaced the purse string as the controlling factor in the competition of marriage. Others claim that behind closed doors, sex was always the controlling variable. Overlooked is the fact that control is as often relinquished as it is usurped.

Jerry had an unusual erectile dysfunction, since he had been sexually active without incident for two decades prior. A secondary erectile dysfunction like this is far less common than the primary erectile dysfunction of the Chassid, for example. Fortunately, Jerry's problem was idiosyncratic, limited to one particular individual. He was able to have sex with any other woman without problem. The solution seemed as obvious as the old punchline. If it hurts when you move your arm that way, don't move it that way. Avoid that particular woman.

The solution wasn't satisfactory. Jerry was smitten, indeed obsessed, with this woman. Sex with any other woman didn't satisfy him. In his mind it was no different from masturbation. Lana, the object of Jerry's desire, was a cocky, bisexual, statuesque Amazonian beauty who was Jerry's partner in a successful new restaurant. According to the trendy columns, the hostess Lana's flirtatiousness was as critical in attracting customers as the cook Jerry's food.

It wasn't as if Lana was demanding sexual favors from Jerry. On the contrary, her exact challenge to Jerry prior to their first liaison was: "I don't think you're man enough to fuck me." Her words were a self-fulfilling prophecy. His failure amused her no end, but humiliated him. He was determined to make amends. Just as a watched kettle never boils, a watched penis never rises. The harder Jerry tried, the more inevitable his failure.

The problem was not guilt. Neither Jerry nor Lana were in another relationship. The problem was not the adolescent fear of a vagina dentata, a vagina with teeth. Jerry was far from adolescence. The problem was not physical. Jerry was functioning fine with other women. The problem was simply that Jerry was trying too hard. The solution was equally simple. Stop trying. Focus on other aspects of sex, kissing, hugging, foreplay, instead of Jerry's raison d'être, fucking her brains out.

Jerry agreed to the game plan in the doctor's office, but when he stepped into Lana's bedroom, and she sadistically teased him, he couldn't help himself. In the end, the man who boasted of a thousand sexual conquests, had become effectively castrated. When he left my office for the last time, frustrated and angry, he confided: "I would have been better off with Lorena Bobbitt." He was right.

Lana's anger was no less cutting than Lorena's. Nevertheless, Lana and Jerry, Laura and Franklin, Sam and Diane, Lorena and John Wayne, and sex and anger, will continue to find each other.

> *"If your life at night is good,*
> *you think you have everything,*
> *but, if in that quarter, things go wrong,*
> *you will consider your (life) most hateful."*
> -Euripides (480–405 B.C.E.)

Notes

---

[1] *Leviticus* XVIII:29.

[2] This chapter includes material derived from *Marriage 101, A User's Manual to Becoming Happily Married—What Your Marriage Would Tell You if it Could Talk*, a full length book on marriage.

[3] *Sexual Behaviour in the Human Female* (1953), Alfred Kinsey, Saunders.

[4] *The World According to Garp* (1982), John Irving, Modern Library.

[5] Petruchio to Kate. *Taming of the Shrew*, II, i. William Shakespeare.

[6] Lady Percy to Hotspur. *King Henry IV*, Part I, II, iii, William Shakespeare.

[7] The most famous episode of the most successful sitcom of all time, *Seinfeld*, was similarly titled *The Contest*. Originally televised on November 18, 1992, and written by Larry David, the show's creator, "the contest" was to determine who could refrain from

masturbating the longest, though the word masturbation was never used.

[8] In Madonna's exorbitant, yet successful, eponymous book on sex, she poses with crucifixes, as she does with whips and chains. Simulating crucifixion alternates with simulating rape and bestiality. *Sex* (1992), Madonna, Warner Books, Inc.

[9] *Annie Hall* is Woody Allen's greatest movie. It won Oscars in 1977 for Best Picture, Best Director, Best Actress—Diane Keaton, and Best Original Screenplay. Its focus is relationships in general, and sex in particular. In one humorous, yet revealing, scene Woody and Diane are simultaneously complaining to their respective shrinks about too little and too much sex between them.

[10] When I worked at Tel Hashomer, an army hospital in Israel, the front line medics reported that there were only two injuries that would emotionally incapacitate a soldier in the heat of battle, an injury to his genitalia, or his eyes. More serious thoracic or abdominal wounds would be ignored.

[11] "A Case of Koro" Carol Berman, M.D., CNS News, May 2002.

[12] William F. Buckley once received an insulting letter from a Dr. Prickman. In his reply Buckley noted that his friends referred to him as "Buck." How did the Doctor's friends refer to him, Buckley inquired.

[13] Many city dwellers have experienced immigrant cabbies who don't understand even rudimentary English. Nevertheless, when angered by another driver they become anomalously voluble. "Turn left in two blocks," they don't understand, but they can say "Fuck you, you mother fucking son of a bitch" effortlessly.

[14] Readers interested in jealousy might want to review Nancy Friday's eponymous book on the subject. *Jealousy* (1985) Nancy Friday, Perigord Press.

[15] Readers interested in this now forgotten, seminal moment in American legal history should consult Thomas Keneally's biography of Daniel Sickles, *American Scoundrel: The Life of the Notorious Civil War General Dan Sickles* (2002) Thomas Keneally, Nan A. Talese/Doubleday.

[16] The murder of Stanford White is described in E.L. Doctorow's best

seller, musical and movie, *Ragtime*. *Ragtime* (1975) E.L. Doctorow, Modern Library.

[17] Michael Welner, M.D. of the N.Y.U. School of Medicine has attempted to create a Depravity Scale to objectively measure the sadistic component of these crimes. He points out, as have many others, that the most accurate harbinger of future criminal sadism is children who torture animals. Earlier studies had indicated a diagnostic triad of animal torture, fire-setting, and bed-wetting.

[18] *New York Magazine*, August 5, 2002, Jennifer Senior.

[19] A more extensive discussion of spouses sharing sexual fantasies about others is provided in the previous chapter on marriage.

[20] William Kennedy Smith was not convicted of rape. The verdict, and the trial, were controversial nevertheless and included testimony by the defendant's uncle, Senator Ted Kennedy who had accompanied the defendant on the night in question.

[21] After a publicized trial, the faux movie producer was acquitted of the rape charge.

CHAPTER FIVE

Do Not Go Quietly into the Night

Anger in Old Age

"Human carcasses fall like dung on an open field." [1]

I wish I could use her real name. Some of you would recognize it. She would have liked that. Legally, it wouldn't be a problem, since when she died, she left no heirs, or estate. Ethically, I'm not sure.

Let's call her Frances Flame, in honor of her trademark, fire-engine red hair of which she was so proud. One of the many headlines in her scrapbook described her as "the drawing red dame, Frances Flame."

Frances had been an artist. Future art historians will determine how talented she had really been. (Occasionally I read of her work being sold, but I never know if the price has gone up or down.) In her time, she had certainly been well known. It was for more than just her art. (Isn't that the case with most artists?) She was beautiful. She was flamboyant. She was outspoken. She was brazen in her single lifestyle, which even hinted of bi-sexuality, unspoken of in her time.

I met her after her time. I had just graduated medical school. I was starting my psychiatric residency at Mt. Sinai Hospital in New York City. She was the first patient assigned to me. The fact that she was assigned to a resident meant that she was a "service" patient, as opposed to most patients who had their own private physicians. It meant that she had no resources left.

I think she was in her late 70's at the time, but I couldn't be sure, since she perpetually lied about her age. She could have been 80, or even 90. She was suffering from advanced arthritis and glaucoma. This was particularly devastating, since her reduced manual dexterity and vision prevented her from both producing art and appreciating it, depriving her of her two sources of income, painting and reviewing. The years had not been kind to her appearance either. She was still spry, but she no longer possessed the face and figure that drove both sexes wild. She still had her flaming red hair. It was no longer a natural wonder.

She had been brought to the hospital by the police because she had been causing a scene. They thought she was crazy. They were right. The admitting psychiatrist labeled her a "Paranoid Schizophrenic," a fairly common diagnosis.

By the time I saw her, like any Monday morning quarterback, with the benefit of her history, and scrapbook, I questioned the diagnosis. Schizophrenics are usually dysfunctional from early adulthood. Frances had been not only functional, but also very successful, for most of her life. As she continually reminded me, she had been famous. She didn't phrase it in quite those words. She put it in the present tense. Nevertheless Frances was paranoid. She had a firm, fixed delusion that everyone was out to get her.

It had all started years earlier with her next-door neighbor, not coincidentally, a handsome, young man. He had been entertaining a lady friend one night and had been making the kind of noises associated with that kind of activity. The music, and especially the sounds, bothered Frances no end. She banged on his door to complain. Needless to say, when he answered, (clad only in a towel, Frances took pains to point out), he was not pleased.

From that moment on, Frances realized that he was out to get her. The next thing she noticed, (from her peephole), was that weeks later he had a large box delivered. It was labeled a television. She knew better. It was an x-ray machine. He was using it to look into her apartment to see her when she was naked. How dare he! Years earlier Frances had repeatedly refused rich socialites and girlie magazine publishers who had offered her large sums of money to take nude pictures.

Frances stopped getting undressed in her bedroom. (She had once lived in a penthouse duplex, but she was now reduced to a studio apartment.) When she had to change her clothing, she would go into her bathroom and lock the door. He would not be deterred. He was obsessed with her. He turned the x-ray power even higher, so he could now see her even in her bathroom. The increased voltage had side effects. *It* was the cause of both her arthritis and glaucoma. She knocked on his door to explain to him the damage that he was creating. He laughed. He already knew. In case anyone was eavesdropping, he acted as if she was crazy.

He eventually moved out. Nevertheless, Frances knew that he couldn't let go of her. Sure enough, the next tenant was also an attractive young man, obviously a henchman for her former neighbor, who had obviously moved out to better coordinate the spying, safely away from Frances.

Frances was right. Within days, she began to notice that she was being followed. They were good. They would each follow her just a short way, before they would transfer the tail to a cohort. She was on to them however. She had cracked their code. To identify each other, they each wore, somewhere on their person, appropriately enough, the color red. No matter where she went, no matter what she did, there was always someone around wearing the telltale color. Her obsessed neighbor needed to know her whereabouts all the time. Because of this, there were hundreds, perhaps thousands of people watching her. As with all delusions, Frances' observations were 100% correct. It was her conclusions that were out of touch with reality.

The treatment of paranoia includes reality testing, what's real, and what isn't. What should I tell Frances? That no one was looking at her? That no one was interested in her? That the very idea of a young man being sexually obsessed with her was a pathetically preposterous joke? That her delusion was the only way that she could once again make herself feel important? That her deteriorating health was an act of God, not of man, and therefore it would never improve, since there was no x-ray machine to turn off? Should I tell her the unvarnished truth[2], that she really wasn't important at all?

Frances liked me. Maybe it was because I was interested in her. Maybe it was because I was the first person to pay any attention to her in years. Maybe it was because I was too drab a dresser to ever wear red. If I told her the truth forcefully enough, maybe she would have believed it. Maybe we could have "cured" her paranoia. But her paranoia was only a symptom. The underlying cause was her depression. If we eliminated her symptom, we would have worsened her disease.

On the other hand, I couldn't say that her delusion was real. I could say that she had nothing to fear. I assured her that no one was going to harm her. I assured her, even more strongly, that no one was angry at her. I did something else as well. I had noticed one day that one of the other patients' visitors, (Frances never had any herself), had recognized Frances. Far from being embarrassed, Frances couldn't have been more gracious. She even showed her scrapbook. For the rest of that day, Frances never mentioned her delusion.

In hospitals in general, psychiatric wards in particular, we preserve patients' anonymity. We avoid listing famous names. Sometimes we deliberately falsify them. Nevertheless, I suggested that Frances leave her scrapbook in the community room, where all the patients, and their visitors, spent most of the day. It worked. The more people looked thru her scrapbook, the more attention she got. Some people remembered her. Some people claimed they did. It didn't matter. Frances flourished. We discharged her to a nursing home, rather than back to her lonely, isolated existence.

She thought that a clever move, but she warned me: "You know he'll eventually find me there. He won't stop trying until he does." I replied: "I can understand why he would." I gave her only one prescription on discharge. Her scrapbook should remain on public display.

> "When I was young and miserable
>   and pretty
> And poor, I'd wish
> What all girls wish: to have a
>   husband,
> A house and children. Now that I'm
>   old, my wish
> Is womanish;
> That the boy putting groceries in
>   my car
> See me. It bewilders me that he
> doesn't see me."
>
> —"Next Day" by Randell Jarrell[3]

Frances had been attracted to her young neighbor. She had gone out of her way to get his attention. She did what she had always done. She flirted shamelessly. When he showed no interest in her, she was furious. Worse, he had the audacity to have a sex life, where she had none. Hearing the sounds of his lovemaking incensed her. She couldn't control herself. She interrupted him. When he, understandably enough, expressed his annoyance, Frances' anger turned to fear.

An x-ray machine is a common delusion of old age because it serves many functions. It explains the undeniably salient manifestations of decrepitude. Moreover, just as Frances desired to visually spy on her attractive neighbor, the x-ray machine was her projection of her desire onto him. She wanted him to see her naked body, and desire it as much as she desired his.

While this anger-fear cycle occurs in all ages, it is most pronounced at the extremities. The very young and the very old perceive themselves, accurately, to be the most helpless. As such, they also feel the most vulnerable to any retribution, real or imagined.

One evening chauffeuring an elderly lady we came across a roller blader. I was fortunate to see him, because he wore no reflectors. I was able to swerve at the last second and avoid him. As we passed him, the lady impulsively yelled out of her open window: "Get off the road, you moron!" At first, she was proud of her accurate, albeit intemperate, outburst. When we arrived at her destination a few blocks away however, she seemed reluctant to step out of the car. When no one answered the door right away, she became frantic. She kept on looking back into the pitch black to see if the blader was coming. When the door finally opened, her fear disappeared, but was replaced by embarrassment. After a few uncomfortable moments, she offered by way of both apology and explanation: "It's not easy getting old."

Depression in the elderly has always been ubiquitous in the psychiatric literature. The name has changed. No one calls it "Involutional Melancholia" any more, but the problem remains. It's easy to understand why. As mentioned previously, depression is anger turned inward. No one has more justification to be angry than the elderly. Though the contrast isn't always as great as it was with Frances, most aspects of every elder's life have gone downhill. They need not have glaucoma for their eyesight to deteriorate. A certain degree of hearing loss is inevitable with aging. Often, the most frustrating loss is the cognitive one.

Senior citizens can impress you that they can remember what they ate at their wedding 60 years ago. You don't realize, (but they do), that they can't remember what they had for breakfast 60 minutes ago. They can tell you the history of every knick-knack in the room, but they can't remember why they entered the room in the first place. They can find their childhood fishing hole, but frighteningly, sometimes they can't find their way home.[4] In retaining memory, our brains are like union shops, first in, last out.

All bodily functions become more difficult. Things we always took for granted—breathing, eating, chewing, defecating, urinating, are suddenly problematic. Things we never gave a second thought to, now become critical. At bedtime, we worry if we'll have a good night's sleep. Upon awakening, we worry if we'll have a good bowel movement. If either is missing, the day is shot.

In view of the many concerns of the elderly, it should not be surprising that they are prone to anxiety as well as depression. Over half of the depressed aged[5], and almost one in every five seniors, "suffers from significant anxiety symptoms." Moreover, "medical illness, which is present in 86% of the elderly, is commonly comorbid with anxiety."[6]

To make matters worse, treating both depression and anxiety in the aged is far more difficult than in the general population. The aged can be prohibitively sensitive to the side effects and drug interactions of commonly used psychotropic medications. As a result, every drug manufacturer has started to produce their medication in reduced strength "geriatric dose."[7] Unfortunately even the geriatric dose is often too problematic.

Even the placebo effect often turns into a nocebo effect with the aged. A placebo, an inert substance that has a positive effect because the patient expects that it will, is powerful in all areas of medicine, but most powerful in psychiatry. Up to 40% of depressed patients improve on placebos. Some assert that 80% of Prozac's efficacy is due to the placebo effect.[8] In the elderly, however, a negative expectation produces a self-fulfilling prophecy.

A depressed, anxious 85-year-old woman feared that any medication would exacerbate her irritable bowel and produce uncontrollable diarrhea. Sure enough, every drug her psychiatrist prescribed her, including a sugar pill, had the same unacceptable result. The sugar pill was thus a nocebo, an inert substance that had a negative effect because of the patient's expectation. As the lady said: "I have enough to worry about without the pills."

The worry list includes the seemingly most important body function of all, sex. Bob Hope, then in his 80's, joked about his sex life: "I still enjoy it. In fact, last spring's was particularly enjoyable." When George Burns[9], then in his 90's appeared on the Oscars with his co-star, then 18-year-old Brooke Shields, he joked: "The studio is spreading rumors about a romantic affair between us to sell tickets. They're smart. I'd pay to see it."

Those jokes were told by two successful, functional, universally beloved elders. They reflect it. Compare it to the bitter joke told by the hoary man who would not describe himself as any of the above: "The nurse needed a stool sample, a urine sample, a sperm sample and some blood. I gave her my underpants."

Humor is the **first**, and best, weapon against the anger of aging. Self referential jokes are effective for anyone, of any age, to cope with adversity. The jokes can even confront the elephant in the living room that few want to notice, our imminent deaths. The following jest was selected in a global on-line survey as the most popular joke in Australia:

> A man on vacation in the tropics, e-mailed his wife who was arriving the next day. Unfortunately he mis-typed the e-mail address and his note went to an elderly woman whose preacher husband had just died. It read: "Dearest wife, just checked in. Everything prepared for your arrival tomorrow. Your Loving Husband. P.S. You can't imagine how hot it is down here."

Formulaic, vaudeville one-liners are less helpful than a

sense of irony. The ability to make fun of ourselves keeps everything else in perspective.

The **second** weapon is precisely that perspective. Perspective always requires examining things from a distance. There are two ways we can look back at our glory days. We can be negative and say, look what I can no longer do. Far better to be positive and say, look at what I accomplished. A scrapbook, like Frances Flame's, is never as valuable when it's being assembled, as it is when it's being reviewed. Prepare for the future now. There is nothing immodest about preserving mementoes of our achievements. We do it for our children without hesitation. Why deny ourselves?

If you appear in a newspaper, save the clipping. Copy it now, so it doesn't yellow. Make several in fact, so you don't worry about losing it. If you appear on television, tape it. If you're being honored, bring a camcorder. If you throw a surprise party for your spouse, hire a photographer and a videographer, the same way you would for your child's wedding. Just as your child will only get married once, your spouse will only turn fifty once. Even if that picture of you with the President, or the pneumatic actress, or the future Hall of Famer, doesn't seem impressive right now, frame it anyway. In time it will become priceless. Don't be concerned with what others think. You're not doing it for them. You're doing it for yourself, not for now, but for later.

A **third** tool is to find alternatives. My classmate, the best basketball player in the history of my high school league, went on to be drafted by the (then) Baltimore Bullets. By the time he graduated law school he had stopped playing basketball. Some of the reasons for stopping were familiar. As we age our bodies are less able to absorb the physical trauma of a physical game. We no longer have the time to play regularly enough to be competitive. The game no longer consumes us. At least one of his reasons was different. He could no longer be the best. He switched to tennis, where he wasn't competing against his own legend.

Certain sports are more forgiving of age. A. E. Hotchner, the author, biographer, playwright, and Paul Newman's philanthropic partner, then in his eighties, beat me, then in my forties, at tennis, six-love. Octogenerians complete 26 mile marathons. Hulda Crooks climbed 97 mountains between ages 65 and 91, the most recent Mt. Fuji in Japan.[10] Bob Hope remained a talented golfer in his nineties. If you can no longer walk the course, use a cart. If tennis is too stressful, play table tennis. If running is difficult, walk. If walking is painful, swim. If you can no longer paint, sketch. If you can no longer sketch, draw. If you can't draw, write. If you can't write, photograph. Don't look for obstacles to prevent you. Look for ways to overcome them. If your arthritis prevents you from writing long hand, type, two fingers at a time, if you have to. If you can't do that, dictate into a computer.

That leads to a **fourth** suggestion. Stay active. Keep yourself occupied. Give yourself a reason to get up every morning. It's not important whether you're getting paid. It's important whether or not you have someplace to go. Nothing makes a person feel more important than being missed. That holds true at any age, but most of all for the elderly. If you have some activity to perform on a regular basis, you will be missed. The more peoples' lives you impact on, the more important you'll feel. Being needed adds years to your life, and life to your years.

The **fifth** approach is not to deny your anger, but use it constructively. After a cursory physical exam a physician announces to his 90-year-old patient that he can't find anything wrong with his knee. He then tells the patient that he doesn't think any radiological tests are warranted. "After all your knee *is* 90 years old." The patient gets up and asks for his records. As he leaves, he says: "So is my other knee, and *it* doesn't hurt!"

An excellent example of the constructive use of anger is special interest groups, like the A.A.R.P.[11], representing the elderly. Using their collective powers they fight discrimination or "ageism," and in addition, frequently obtain special privileges. In the Orient, the elderly are treated with special reverence by tradition, rather than by law. In the new world, money and votes speak louder than tradition.

A **sixth** approach is taking pride in our age. There are privileges that come with seniority. Take advantage of them. Whether they are pragmatic, like senior discounts, social security, and pensions, or emotional, like community deference, you've earned it.[12] You might as well enjoy it.

We shouldn't take our longevity for granted. Too many of our contemporaries are no longer alive. We should relish the extra time we've been given. If we're going to lie about our age, we should hyperbolize rather than diminish it. It's more impressive that we're this vital at the age of 82, rather than 79.

More and more, movies have senior citizens saving the day. In 1977 Art Carney starred in *The Late Show* as an elderly, overweight, wheezing, deaf, detective who solves the mystery, kills the bad guys and gets the girl. At the time a geriatric action movie was an aberration. Not any more. In 1986 Burt Lancaster and Kirk Douglas were heroic retired hoodlums in *Tough Guys*. In 1998 Paul Newman[13] was a heroic elderly detective in the aptly named *Twilight*. Two years later he was a seemingly decrepit ancient bank robber who winds up with the money and the girl in *Where The Money Is*. In 1996 Clint Eastwood was a card carrying A.A.R.P. safe-cracker who single handedly terminates a corrupt U.S. President in *Absolute Power*. Finally, in 2000 Clint Eastwood, Tommy Lee Jones, Donald Sutherland, and James Garner do nothing less than save the entire planet in *Space Cowboys*. Apparently there's nothing the elderly can't accomplish.

The **seventh** and final approach to fighting age is the most controversial, literally erasing its signs. Anti-aging procedures are performed by plastic surgeons, Ear, Nose and Throat doctors[14] (ENT's), ophthalmologists, dermatologists, gynecologists, radiologists, dentists, podiatrists, cosmeticians, hairdressers and beauty consultants. Their services are described euphemistically as plastic surgery, rejuvenating procedures, spa medicine, aesthetic surgery and beauty operations.

When over 100,000 doctors[15] were asked if they would be interested in expanding their practice to include these procedures, 70% said yes. Their reasoning is reminiscent of Willie Sutton[16]. In an era when H.M.O.s severely limit patients' medical treatments and their physicians to its reimbursement, elective procedures have become a gold-mine to their suppliers. "Why should (you) remove someone's gallbladder for $500 when (you) can get $500 for giving a shot of Botox?"[17] The suppliers' motives are obvious, but so are the patients'. Who wouldn't want to look younger?

Procedures include Ablative laser skin resurfacing, Botox injections, Chemical peels and Dermabrasion. The alphabet of possibilities doesn't stop with the face. You can lift your arms, breasts, butt, thighs, chin, cheeks, brow, face and wrinkles. Alternately, or simultaneously, you can reduce your ears, eyelids, nose, tummy, love-handles, knees and varicose veins. You can lighten or darken, reduce or augment, your breasts, teeth, hair and face.

Celebrities as diverse as Michael Jackson, Demi Moore, and Greta Van Susteren have famously used these procedures to enhance their careers. Layman use them to reverse aging. The well-off and the well-known have other options to disguise aging as well. Michael Douglas, Cher, Dr. Benjamin Spock, Joan Collins, Senator Strom Thurmond, Tony Curtis, Donna Karen, Larry King and innumerable others have all married, and in some cases had children with, spouses young enough to be their own children. Having children younger than your grandchildren can be thought of as defying your geriatric status, or denying it.

Even with all these approaches, anger will persist in some. There are those bitter elders whose primary goal in life seems to be to inflict as much pain as possible onto others. Their misery not only loves company. It demands it.

Paul's grandmother wasn't pleased when he married out of faith. As she got older, she hid her displeasure less. Whenever he returned home, she would insult his wife's religion. The rest of the family was all apologetic, but what could they do? They would make believe she was joking. They would try to change the subject. Behind her back they would explain she was senile. Paul empathized with his wife, but what can you do if someone is senile?

If his grandmother was so senile that she had lost bowel control, would she still be eating at the table? Would the family be forced to smell her feces as they ate? In effect, Paul's wife was experiencing the same thing. At Paul's insistence, the family banned his grandmother unless she behaved herself. Medical literature indicates that senility is irreversible. His grandmother's recovery was miraculous.

My five-year-old daughters were riding with my wife on a city bus, singing together. My wife noticed that the elderly lady next to her wouldn't take her eyes off of them. She didn't seem pleased. My wife thought of asking them to be quiet, but then realized that they were making less noise than many other people on the bus. The lady glared: "Why don't they shut up!"

My children didn't hear her. My wife did, but didn't know what to say. She finally replied in a low voice: "Is it that you had an unhappy childhood, or is it that you never had any children?" The lady didn't answer. She seemed subdued. My wife sensed her sadness and felt guilty. "I'm sorry." The lady shook her head. She now had tears in her eyes. So did my wife. The lady got off in a few stops without saying another word. As she got off, she gave the kids some after dinner mints from her purse.

In the movies no matter how bitter the elderly are, they all have a sentimental side that responds to expressions of affection, as in *Home Alone* or its sequel. Real life is different.

In temple one morning J.J., sixteen at the time, heard that Mr. Mole was in the hospital. Mole, an elderly curmudgeon, never had a kind word to say to anyone. "The Mad Mole," as the kids called him, also didn't have any family. J.J. realized that Mole wouldn't be getting any visitors at a time that he needed them the most. J.J. decided to do a "mitzvah." He was a Sabbath observer. The hospital was across town. He had to walk in the 90 degree sun. At the time, he was still quite husky, so he was sweating bullets by the time he arrived at the hospital to discover that Mole was on the top floor of the only pavilion that wasn't air-conditioned. He couldn't take an elevator on the Sabbath, so he arrived at Mole's door short of breath and soaked.

As J.J. walked in, Mole's eyes bulged in amazement. When Mole didn't say a word, J.J. started speaking. He told a white lie, saying the whole temple was concerned about Mole. He made polite conversation for twenty minutes. Mole remained silent. Finally J.J. announced he had to go. Mole motioned J.J. to come closer. He needed to tell J.J. something. J.J. wasn't good at accepting thanks. He tried to decline. Mole insisted. When he finally got within arm's length, Mole grabbed his tie and pulled his head down until J.J.'s ear was inches from Mole's mouth. With great effort Mole finally whispered. "There's something I have to tell you."

J.J. tried to be gracious. "It's really not necessary." "No. I have to tell you this. You're fat. You're really fat. That's why you sweat so much. You're the fattest kid I've ever seen." Still grasping J.J.'s tie, Mole promptly fell asleep.

Sometimes the elderly can be as narcissistic as they are insensitive. Molly was having a dinner party for one of her clients, a famous author. As a treat for her retired, increasingly withdrawn father, Molly invited him to join them. She even gave her father the seat of honor, next to the author. The conversation understandably revolved around the author's current bestseller. Her father interrupted: "You know, they wanted *me* to write a book."

The author couldn't have been more solicitous. "Oh really. About what?" "I can't talk about it."

The conversation quickly returned to the bestseller. After a few minutes, her father abruptly interrupted again: "I was in the army, during the war." The author again responded politely. "What was that like?" "I can't talk about it."

Molly could feel everyone looking at her. Not only were her father's interruptions rude, but they were non-sequitors, as well. Molly understood what her father was doing. She sympathized with him. Her father *had* been a war hero, and when she was growing up, his experiences were commonly the focus of their dinner conversation. When her father said "I can't talk about it," he expected to be pressed for more information, the way his children did in the past. Her father hadn't read the author's book, probably wasn't interested in it, and possibly couldn't understand it. His attempts to focus attention back on himself were clumsy, yet poignant.

Molly's father, like Mr. Mole, had lost touch with etiquette. As many get older, they regress to childhood and lose the veneer of politeness that camouflages the congenital narcissism that we each possess. Without the protective ozone layer that we call manners, our inherent selfishness, like the sun, becomes unbearable.

There are two mutually exclusive pieces of folk wisdom on the mind-set of the elderly. The first one states that the elderly become caricatures of themselves as they age. Someone who was friendly in their prime, becomes even friendlier in old age, but someone who was angry becomes even angrier. The second theory, more pessimistic, says that most people become more irritable when they start to deteriorate. While we would all prefer to believe the former, the truth of the latter is hard to deny. Not surprisingly, the more that the individual loses their mobility, their power and, above all, their independence, the more depressed and angrier they become.

There is no blood test to calibrate our anger, but there is

an exercise that, although subjective, is surprisingly revealing. Imagine an anger spectrum ranging from 0 to 100. 0 is someone totally devoid of anger, a practical impossibility of course. In theory, a 0 would be a cross between a saint like Mother Teresa, and the comedian-philosopher Will Rogers[18] who famously said, "I never met a man I didn't like." 100, unfortunately, is easier to find in real life. It represents the human equivalent of a rabid dog who will viciously snap at anybody. The character Don Logan[19], portrayed by Sir Ben Kingsley in the movie *Sexy Beast,* is an excellent cinematic example.

Pick the least angry person you've ever known in your whole life and assign them a number on the scale. They'll probably rate somewhere between 2 and 15. Conversely, pick the angriest person you've ever met and assign them a number, probably between 85 and 98. Repeat the exercise with the angriest and least angry people you *currently* know. The numbers should be less extreme. Write the names and numbers down as you do it, or you'll start to forget them. Rate friends, acquaintances and figures in your current life, the more, the better. Do it instinctively. Don't agonize over each one. There are no repercussions to your choices. Save the most important people, your spouse, parents, siblings, children, for last. After you've rated everyone, and *only* after you've rated everyone, rate yourself. Your rating is valid only if it's based on a comparison to many others. If you take the obvious short cut and rate yourself first, the number is less valuable. It will reflect more your wishful thinking, than reality.

Most find this exercise fascinating. They discover that the number that they finally assign themselves is significantly different, 5 to 10 points or more, from the number that they would have originally imagined. It becomes even more valuable if you retain your evaluations, and then much time later, *without* first consulting your original notes, you repeat the exercise.

The latter aging theory would suggest that as we age, our rating should go up, i.e. we've gotten angrier. In fact, that has been the case with many elderly with whom I've conducted this exercise. It's particularly pronounced, predictably enough, in isolation, like Molly's father, and in hospitalization, like Mr. Mole.

There are however many exceptions. They can occur at any age. But only if we want them to. Whether we're in a hospital bed, a bus seat, a nursing home or living securely with our family, in the end we must accept that each stage of life has both its inherent advantages and disadvantages. The last stage is no different. Satchel Paige used to say: "Age is a question of mind over matter. If you don't mind, it doesn't matter." George Bernard Shaw once said: "It's a shame that youth is wasted on the young." He could have just as easily have said: "It's a shame that wisdom is wasted on the aged." If however, we take advantage of that wisdom, it's not wasted. Growing old becomes a very attractive option, especially when you consider the alternative.

An Indonesian fable tells of a father and adolescent son returning home from toiling in the fields. Father turns to son and says: "Tomorrow, instead of coming to work with me in the fields, go into the forest and chop down a tree."

"Why, father?" "Use the wood to build a litter."

"For what, father?" "Your grandfather has become too old to work in the field. He can no longer help our family. He is making our life more difficult."

"I don't understand, father." "Tomorrow night bring home the litter. Your grandfather will drink wine and sleep soundly. We will put him in the litter. We will carry him out and leave him deep in the woods. We will return home by morning."

"But what will happen to grandfather?" "That is for God to decide."

The son, obviously distressed, cannot disobey, or even disagree. The next morning he dutifully sets out for the forest. By the time the father returns home, the son is still not yet back. Finally, long after dusk, the son enters the cabin. The father notices that he has made not one, but two litters.

"I only said one. Why did you make two?" "The first is for grandfather, as you instructed me."

"Then what is the second for?" "The second is for you, when you reach grandfather's age."

That night the father and grandfather drink wine together. When the grandfather falls soundly asleep, the father destroys both sleds.

I wish I had told that story to Frances Flame. She would have liked it. She would have liked it a lot.

"There is no old age for a man's anger, only death."
—Sophocles (496–406 B.C.E.)

Notes

1 *Jeremiah* IX:21.

2 25 years later a psychiatrist portrayed by Jeff Bridges in the movie *K Pax* faced a dilemma similar to mine. His patient Kevin Spacey claimed to be a visitor from outer space. Should Bridges tell him the truth, that, in reality, he's trying to forget the fact that his wife and daughter were raped and brutally murdered? As with Frances, the truth isn't always therapeutic.

3 *The Lost World* (1965) Randall Jarrell, MacMillan.

4 In a poignant scene in *On Golden Pond*, Henry Fonda confides to his wife Katherine Hepburn that he couldn't find his way home. The 1981 film, adapted by Ernest Thompson from his play, is a powerful portrait of aging, warts and all. Fonda, Hepburn and Thompson all received Oscars for their efforts.

5 Dr. Alistair Flint, Univ. of Toronto, 2002 American Association for Geriatric Psychiatry annual meeting.

6 Daniel Christenson, M.D., Neuropsychiatric Institute, Univ. of Utah

School of Medicine, 2002 National Conference of the Anxiety Disorders Association of America.

7 As but one example of "geriatric dosing," when Eli Lilly and Co. first produced Prozac, the most popular of all psychotropic drugs, $2.5 billion in sales in 2001, it was in a "one size fits all" version. One 20 mg tablet daily was the right prescription for everyone. This was designed, and succeeded, to make the drug popular with internists and general practitioners who found it "fool-proof" to prescribe. Many years later, 20 mg daily is still the recommended starting dose, but now there is a 10 mg version recommended as the "elderly starting dose."

8 Irving Kirsch, "The Emperor's New Drugs", *Prevention and Treatment*, July 2002.

9 George Burns is probably the best-known example of someone whose greatest success was as a senior citizen. He and his wife Gracie Allen, who predeceased him by 32 years, were a comedy pair in vaudeville, radio and television in the 1930's, 40's and 50's. At the age of 80 he won an Oscar for *The Sunshine Boys*, his first film in 36 years, (which he only got because his best friend Jack Benny died.) For the next 20 years he became the toast of Hollywood and Broadway. He starred in a dozen movies including the title role in the hugely successful *Oh, God!* and its two sequels, and innumerable profitable concert performances. Though he claimed: "I can't die, I'm booked!", the man born Nathan Birnbaum in 1896, finally passed away soon after turning 100.

10 *Time*, February 22, 1988.

11 The A.A.R.P., American Association for Retired People, has become an incredibly powerful lobby acting as an advocate for the aging population. No pragmatic politician can ignore them or the people they represent.

12 The idea of "earning" our extra years of life was powerfully dramatized by Steven Spielberg in the World War II movie *Saving Private Ryan*.

13 Paul Newman has joked for years that he's ready to retire from acting, but that people prevent him by continuing to write (elderly) roles for him.

14 Ear Nose and Throat doctors who perform cosmetic surgery refer to themselves as "facial plastic surgeons." Plastic surgeons take exception to this practice.

15 The *Physician's Medical Law Letter* polled its subscribers nationwide irrespective of specialty.

16 Willie Sutton was probably the world's most famous bank robber. He is best known for his reason for robbing banks: "That's where the money is." This reference in no way implies that cosmetic medicine is illegal or immoral.

17 Alan Matarasso, M.D. "One of N.Y.'s top plastic surgeons." *New York Magazine,* May 27, 2002

18 In his time, Will Rogers was the most popular man in the country. Presidential candidates would beg him to campaign with them. His quote was so well known that the ultimate insult was to tell someone: "Obviously, Will Rogers never met you!"

19 Sir Ben Kingsley's portrayal of Don Logan was so outstanding that it won several awards, and was nominated for an Oscar. Amazingly enough, the same actor had equally convincingly portrayed Gandhi, Don Logan's antipode.

PART III

CHAPTER SIX

Demanding to be Number One

Anger In Business

"Beware your neighbor; don't trust your brother; though they do it with guile, they are out to sabotage you."[1]

L et's say that George sold widgets. If you knew what he really sold, his identity would be too obvious.

George sold widgets extremely well. He had gotten into the field as a young man and, with a combination of innovative ideas and inexhaustible hustle, he had revolutionized the industry. For many years his privately owned company had been the world's leading supplier of widgets. Although his sales never declined, as with all successes, his ideas were imitated. Eventually, a conglomerate exceeded his company in market share and became number one in the field.

I met George when he was starting his "comeback." What an inappropriate word. One "comes back" from failure. Neither George nor his company had ever failed. On the contrary, they had always been a highly profitable venture. I asked George why he spoke of a "comeback." He responded: "I *was* number one, and, Goddammit, I'll *be* number one again!"

George's ambitious plans, as all ambitious plans, involved borrowing huge sums of money. If his calculations proved correct, his expansion would once again make him number one. If his calculations proved to be incorrect? George smiled: "You can't be number one, if you don't think positively."

George was in his sixties. He lacked nothing in life. He had eight cars and four homes in three countries. He could buy whatever his heart desired. He vacationed wherever and whenever he wanted to. He had delegated day-to-day operations of his company to his son, who was now President. He became Chairman. He had attained both a life and lifestyle of which most of us can only dream. He had wealth, prestige, respect and that most precious of all commodities, time. Why was he willing to sacrifice the latter and jeopardize the former, just for the sake of being number one again? He smiled: "This country wasn't built by people who were satisfied to be number two. You don't succeed unless you demand to be number one."

George's explanations were so hackneyed, it was as if he wasn't saying anything. I felt like I was back with my Bar Mitzvah boy who wanted to go to Disneyland. We both understood perfectly well what he was determined to do. Neither of us however, understood why.

Eventually, the right question came to me. George's company hadn't been number one for a decade. Why, only after ten years, did that situation suddenly become intolerable? When had he realized that he couldn't accept his company being runner up? George smiled. He actually *did* remember the precise moment. He was being honored by a prestigious charity. The giants of many industries, including his own, had flown in to salute him. In what seemed to be a particularly appropriate show of respect, the chairman of the conglomerate that was now number one had been selected to present George with his medal.

His name was Tom. Although he and George were, of course, familiar with each other, they had only rarely come into personal contact. Tom's presentation was appropriately laudatory. He enumerated George's many achievements. He spoke of how he felt honored to be in the industry that

George had revolutionized. At the end however, Tom couldn't help but put in a little plug for himself. A year later, George could still remember his words verbatim: "When people ask me how my company could have moved ahead of George's, I remind them what Einstein said of Galileo: 'If I can see further than he, it's only because I'm standing on his shoulders'."

George was livid when he heard that. No one knew it. He kept smiling. He gave Tom a warm handshake. He kept to his prepared text until the very end. As he thanked Tom for his remarks, he couldn't help but add: "You better watch out Tom, or one of these days you might find *me* standing on *your* shoulders." George smiled when he said it. Tom smiled in response. The audience laughed and applauded.

George was angry at Tom. He had never cared about him before, but that one remark was inexcusable. He was determined to pay him back. There was only one way he knew how. He was going to become number one again.

Because of one remark, George was prepared to go to war. Because of his anger, he was determined to risk not only his own future, but his company's, and his family's, as well.

By the time the dust settled years later, George had succeeded in vanquishing Tom. Not only was Tom's company no longer number one, but Tom was no longer Chairman. Their companies had engaged in what the media had labeled "The Battle of the Titans." Each company had been so resolute to gain market dominance that their competition escalated into a nuclear price war. As with all nuclear wars, both sides had been devastated. Tom's company had fallen from number one to number three. Tom had been forced into early retirement by his board of directors. George's company had gone into bankruptcy. Its remaining assets had been sold off by its creditors. George himself was forced to sell whatever he owned that wasn't in his wife's name.

In the end, millions of dollars were lost, thousands of jobs were gone, and a strong company ceased to exist, all to assuage one man's anger over an intemperate remark. George and Tom's battle of wills destroyed both of them. George lost. His family lost. His company lost. His employees lost. The only winners were the bankruptcy lawyers and the scavenging companies who replaced George and Tom at the top of a still profitable industry.

George and Tom were renown in their industry in particular, and fairly recognizable in the business world in general. Al and Frank were renowned world-wide, two of the most recognizable names of their era. Al, like George, had been number one. Al, like George, had retired successfully and had lacked nothing as he approached his "golden years." Al returned to fight Frank because he felt slighted by him, as George felt slighted by Tom. Al, like George, lost. He died a bitter failure.

Al was Al Smith, the governor of New York, the Democratic candidate for President of the United States in 1928, the most popular politician of his era, the universally admired "Happy Warrior."

Frank was Franklin Delano Roosevelt, Al's friend, protégé and hand-picked successor as New York State Governor. An unschooled, albeit brilliant, man, Al rarely wrote personal letters. He made an exception to write to Frank: "I know of no man I have met in my whole public career who I have any stronger affection for than yourself . . . I will not get into a fight with you for anything or anybody."

Four years later he contradicted himself. He was angered by Frank ignoring his advice. Ill advisedly he challenged Frank for the 1932 Democratic nomination for President. He lost decisively and ignominiously. He was never again "The Happy Warrior." Frank went on to cure "The Great Depression," defeat Hitler and Tojo, and win World War II. He became the most popular President in American history, the only one to be elected four times. Nevertheless he never forgave his mentor. He continued to ignore Al, unless he had the opportunity to further humiliate him.

Who had named Al Smith "The Happy Warrior"? The man who had nominated him for President in 1928, Franklin Delano Roosevelt. Frank had made Al "Happy," and angry, and then unhappy.[2]

George & Tom, like Al & Frank are old news. In a new century, nothing has changed. On July 21, 2000 *The Wall Street Journal* published a front page story on the business rivalry of Myron Hochman and Arnold Spirtas, the demolition kings of St. Louis. Their conflict has continued over five decades. It included innumerable anonymous accusatory letters, dozens of government inquiries and investigations, civil suits, six figure government fines, six figure legal fees, and physical confrontations. Myron and Arnold's fathers had been the best of friends. They became the worst of enemies. As Arnold says: "When someone has such a hate or jealousy for someone, he won't stop. I hope it's over. It's debilitating to a person's business."

Indeed it is. Years ago the retail giants of New York City were Macy's and Gimbel's. They were archenemies located next door to each other who freely acknowledged that they weren't concerned with anyone, but their nemesis. Their competition towards each other was so legendary, in the movie *Miracle on 34th Street*, (where they were both located), it took Santa Claus to perform the eponymous miracle of momentarily quelling their rivalry. If you walk down 34th Street today, you'll discover that Macy's went bankrupt, and Gimbel's is nowhere to be found. They should have listened to Santa.

The automotive giants of our country, and the world, for most of the last century were General Motors and Ford. Like Macy's and Gimbel's, they were legendary sworn enemies. Like Macy's and Gimbel's, they were each concerned only with the other, determined to be number one. Like George and Tom, they were so obsessed with each other, that they noticed only too late the influx of cheaper, better-made imports. When they finally realized, they tried to shift the anger of competition into the anger of nationalism. Before, they had advertised that it was stylish to buy their cars. Now, it became patriotic to do so. It didn't help.

Business school students discover that most industries, both large and small, are at one point dominated by a rival pair. The examples are endless: Hertz and Avis, McDonald's and Burger King, Remington and Norelco, Kodak and Polaroid, Nike and Reebok, Hershey's and Nestle, CBS and NBC, Coke and Pepsi, Microsoft and Apple, GM and Ford, Macy's and Gimbel's, Myron and Arnold.

When management's focus shifts from the bottom line to the adversary, their decisions become jaundiced. When the adversary is demonized, the results can be devilish. Witness Michael Jordan, Charles Barkley, et. al. refusing to receive their gold medal at the 1992 Olympics because they would be wearing a warm-up suit made by their competitor, Reebok, instead of their sponsor, Nike.

While, as we described in "The Fear of God," I—3, schadenfreude is natural and inevitable, traditionally it was condemned. A 19th century British archbishop, R. C. Trench, wrote that the very fact that the word existed was undeniable evidence of our damnable corruption.[3] Schopenhauer wrote that its presence in any individual was a clear sign of evil.[4] It is only in the business arena that schadenfreude is promoted and even advertised.

There was once an unwritten rule in advertising. Never give your competitor free publicity by mentioning them in your ads. That rule disappeared with black and white television. One result was the debacle of New Coke. New Coke was a response to Pepsi's "taste test," wherein Pepsi advertised that more consumers preferred the taste of Pepsi to Coke. Despite being number one at the time, Coke designed a new formula to win Pepsi's "taste test." Coke's foolish decision was comparable to a boxer, well ahead on points, overconfidently attempting to knock out his opponent.[5] By focusing on our competitor, instead of our goal, we wind up playing his game. As a result, we lose the game and miss our goal.

This loss of perspective was first described by Dr. Leon Festinger in the 1950's in his Social Comparison Theory, wherein we only compare ourselves to our neighbors, rather than to society as a whole, or objective standards. If I run a race focused only on besting my adversary, even if I beat him, I've still lost the race to all the other runners who weren't distracted by my obsession.[6]

This prideful competition leads to foolish battles of attrition. As mentioned earlier, many lawsuits are perpetuated solely by the litigants' anger toward each other. In oft-repeated words, they sue "to teach the bastard a lesson." They hire lawyers for the exclusive purpose of vicariously expressing their anger. The angrier the lawyer is, the more the client likes him. The fact that an angry cross-examination alienates a jury, and snatches defeat from the jaws of victory, doesn't matter. The sight of the adversary sitting helplessly on the stand, being mercilessly attacked is too pleasurable to give up. That transient thrill is more important to the client than the ultimate triumph. In business as in divorce, the cost of the lawsuit eclipses any eventual possible gain, yet the parties persist.

Witness an interesting demonstration. An auctioneer offers a twenty-dollar bill to the highest bidder. The results are predictable. The first bid is for ten dollars. Within two bids the final price is reached, twenty dollars.

He then auctions a second twenty dollar bill with one significant difference. Any bid has to be paid, whether it wins, or not. If you bid ten, and someone else bids fifteen and wins, you still have to pay ten dollars. (All the money goes to charity). This time the first bid is for one dollar, instead of ten. The increments are five cents each, instead of five dollars. The bidding lasts over half an hour, instead of half a minute. The most significant difference is that the bidding doesn't stop at twenty dollars. The winning bid is over a hundred dollars.

In both the lawsuits and the auction we get caught up in the process. We can't step back and objectively view our dilemma. All we can think of is the money that we've already spent that will have been wasted if we withdraw now. We violate a cardinal rule of economics, Gresham's Law. We throw away good money after bad. In the words of the auction "winner": "I'll be damned if I was going to let him, (a "friendly" rival), walk away with that twenty dollar bill." In the heat of battle, anger overwhelms reason.

Call it anger. Call it pride. Call it competitiveness. Call it macho, although it occurs equally among women. Call it an inability to lose. In the end, it can only be called a fact of business. "One of the more puzzling mysteries of television: How could the cost of broadcast rights for the Olympic Games climb so high when the networks keep losing so much money? The answer lies in the fierce rivalry among the Big Three Networks."[7]

Eighteen months after the Olympic bidding war the same scenario recurred. This time the prize was the NFL football broadcast. The rivals had been expanded from "the Big Three" to include a fourth, the Fox television network. The self-destructive competition had been exacerbated further by a new kid on the block.

Coincidentally there was another entertainment battle to the death transpiring simultaneously. Marvin Davis and his former employee Barry Diller were in a protracted war of attrition over Paramount. Many industry observers pointed out that their struggle had less to do with the corporation's worth, than with their preexistent enmity. An almost identical episode, albeit even more expensive, occurred ironically enough in the very place that our Bar Mitzvah boy Barry had imagined that no one was angry, The Magic Kingdom of Walt Disney.

In a move that would cost Disney hundreds of millions of dollars, its CEO, Michael Eisner, refused to pay his former protégé, Jeffrey Katzenberg, what he was owed because of his "personal animus." Eisner acknowledged that he had been "so aggravated" by his protégé that he had gone "to the dark side." He admitted that "in anger" he had said: " . . . I hate the little midget." Katzenberg in turn admitted that he was so "furious . . . I couldn't possibly stay another day." A national magazine headlined their story: "Two Angry Men." I couldn't help but wonder what a grown up Barry now thought of Disneyland.

As any high school student can attest, intra-mural competition, like the sophomoric one between Eisner and Katzenberg, can be more vicious than inter-mural. It's easier to hate someone whom you see every day, than someone you only see twice a year.

Two interns, Lester and Chester, head and shoulders above their contemporaries, were assigned to the most prestigious hospital ward. They each had been valedictorian of their respective medical school. There was a mutual respect between Lester and Chester, as well as an intense competition. As time wore on, the competition became aggressive. Lester interrupted Chester. Chester corrected Lester. Lester looked at Chester's charts over his shoulder. Chester examined Lester's patients behind his back. Even as an occasional observer, I became concerned. The chief resident assured me that competition breeds excellence.

It also takes its toll. Within weeks Lester and Chester had ceased talking to each other and could no longer maintain the illusion of collegiality. The tension between them was felt by the entire ward, staff and patients alike. Within months Chester could no longer keep up. On morning rounds he was having trouble finding his lab results. There are few mistakes in medicine more critical than not maintaining current blood values. Not being aware of an abnormal result can be a fatal oversight. The chief resident called Chester in demanding an explanation for these lapses. Chester had none. Chester was placed on probation, the first blemish on a previously perfect record.

Several weeks later Lester's beeper went off in his briefcase. A nurse opened his briefcase to find out who was paging him. In his briefcase she found a collection of lab slips on Chester's patients. Lester had been stealing Chester's lab results.

That wasn't the first time I had seen competition breed sabotage. I remember the Drosophila (fruit fly) breeding experiment which encompassed several months and counted for the majority of our Genetics grade back in college. By the penultimate week it became obvious whose experiments would be successful and whose wouldn't. Then, someone sprayed the entire incubator with Lysol. All the experiments were destroyed.

Viva got into Harvard Law School. Her acceptance letter stated that she should contact the school within a specified period of time, or they would offer her place to someone on the waiting list. Unfortunately she hadn't seen her letter. Her suite mate had taken it. If someone hadn't chanced upon it, Viva's career would be significantly different today.

I was consulted by a manufacturer who was experiencing an astronomical increase in the percentage of "seconds," goods that were subsequently rejected by their own quality control. Management was panicked.

I spent hours at the factory trying to discover the cause of the problem, but got nowhere. The workers were tight-lipped, claiming to know nothing. The managers were willing to answer anything I asked, but genuinely knew nothing. In desperation I took the foreman out for drinks. He was cooperative, but defensive. He claimed, truthfully I thought, that no one in the company was as bothered as much by the seconds as he was. He had been with the company all of his working life. His father had held his position before him. He took every "second" as a personal failure. When quality control rejected an item produced on his watch, it bothered him no end. In fact, several months ago he had become so frustrated that he had taken extreme action. He had announced to the entire production floor that the worker who produced the largest number of "seconds" in the coming season would be fired.

Bingo! I saw a fruit fly.

I checked the dates. The increased percentage of "seconds" had coincided with his announcement. The foreman's threat had had a paradoxical effect. It had precipitated fear, but also anger. The increased percentage of "seconds" had been so high, there had to be more than one factor accounting for it. There was:

A—The constant pressure of this dire threat, (because of the recession, it was unlikely that the fired worker would get another job) increased the workers' anxiety, deleteriously affecting their efficiency.

B—The workers, to a man, resented this heavy-handed punishment. They expressed that resentment by subconsciously sabotaging their own work.

C—These men weren't stupid. They each realized that their own percentage of "seconds" was increasing. They understood that their job was in jeopardy. The easiest way to save it was to increase their co-worker's percentage of "seconds," i.e. deliberately sabotage his work.[8]

D—Sabotaging someone else's work was also the perfect way to passive-aggressively screw the company without having to take responsibility for one's actions.

E—If there was a particular co-worker that one didn't like, (and who doesn't have one), sabotaging his work was the perfect way to get rid of him.

After discussion, the foreman rescinded his threat. In addition, the management offered a bonus, to *every* worker on the production floor, inversely proportional to the *whole* floor's reduction of "seconds." Within days there were dramatic results. The increased money was a motivational factor, but so was the decreased anger.

A variation of this approach is used in military training.[9] When one recruit fails a task, the entire platoon is punished. Not only does this motivate the individual recruit better than any individual punishment, it also encourages the platoon to help its weakest link, promoting cohesiveness.

The very word "sabotage" originates from an act of anger. "Sabo" is the French word for the protective wooden clog that factory workers commonly wore years ago. When a worker got fired or laid off, in an act of revenge, he would "accidentally" drop his shoe, clogging the machinery. The result was devastating. The machinery would grind to a halt incurring expensive damage. The factory lost significant time, and money, removing the "sabo." Like any effective practice, it became so widespread that a term was created to describe it.

While the "sabo" has disappeared, the practice has not. A contemporary equivalent would be "tossing a wrench in the machinery." It can be changing the codes, stripping the gears, or crashing the computer. It can be Clinton-Gore staffers removing every "W" from White House keyboards before George W. Bush assumed the presidency.[10] It can be superintendents taking the key to the service elevator when they go on strike. A theatrical example is portrayed in the musical, *The Pajama Game.* A front page *New York Times* story headlined "Layoff Rage" describes a former employee causing $20 million in computer damage sabotaging a long planned public stock offering.[11]

Revealingly, sabotage isn't limited to our species. Researchers in Japan and Britain discovered that wasps secrete a chemical that make ant colonies aggressive. The ants turn on each other and, thus distracted, cannot defend themselves against the wasps.[12] The wasps are duplicating what publicists do when they sow negative disinformation about a rival's upcoming project. These disinformation campaigns strike gold if they manage to create dissension among the competitor ants .

Competition brings out the best or worst in us depending if we respond to others' achievements with envy or with jealousy. Although the two words are used synonymously, there is a critical difference between them.

If I am envious of you, it means that I want what you have. It doesn't mean that you can't have it too. It doesn't mean that I resent you for having it. It doesn't mean that I'm angry at you. Envy is a healthy emotion that makes me want to emulate the achiever and repeat or exceed the achievement. As such, the chief resident was right. Envy combined with drive can lead to excellence. As necessity is the mother of invention, so is envy the mother of competition.

Jealousy, on the other hand, shifts my focus from the achievement to the achiever, from what you accomplished, to you. I am jealous of you, not of your achievement. I resent you for achieving it. Jealousy makes me want to destroy you. It doesn't lead to excellence. It leads to revenge and mutual destruction, as with Othello, or George and Tom. Jealousy is the mother of schadenfreude.[13]

What can be done to avoid the destructive effects of anger in business?

1—The single most important rule is, don't take business personally. Business is business. It's not personal. At least, it shouldn't be.

If someone gives you a giant order, it doesn't mean that they're your best friend. It only means that your merchandise satisfies their needs. It means that this transaction is to your mutual business benefit. Conversely, if someone cancels a large order, it is not a betrayal. It is not a reflection on you, or on your relationship with them. It reflects only their company's needs at that moment in time.

The minute we start taking business personally, (like George did), we lose our objectivity. We start making decisions based on factors other than the market. We express our feelings thru our decisions. Invariably, our decisions are poorer.

2—Business should be conducted in a business-like manner. If business shouldn't be taken personally, it shouldn't be conducted personally either. If you expend your energy yelling, you're not going to be thinking as efficiently as you can. It won't be too long before you burn out. Charles Bludhorn, the head of Gulf and Western, was notorious for publicly humiliating his executives by pitting them against each other. He screamed at them to "kill" one another in order to get ahead. Not surprisingly, Bludhorn died of a heart attack on the company plane.[14]

This rule is implicitly understood. Assume you had a choice between buying two companies, both of which look identical on paper. You visit both companies, one of which is conducted professionally, the other like a madhouse. Which would you sooner buy? You're sitting in a reception room waiting to see your accountant, (lawyer, chiropractor, doctor, tattooist). You can't help but notice that everyone on the staff, including the professional is howling and cursing at each other. How quickly will you make another appointment?

Civility derives from civilized. Civilization is the most advanced stage of human development that allows us to congestedly co-exist and perform at peak efficiency. Absent the courtesy and politeness that comprise civility, we expend our energy shouting and our attention defending ourselves. As we discussed in "A Bitter Price To Pay"—I, 2, the price of constant vigilance is pain, illness and death. As Lucy observed in *Peanuts* in 1972: "It's hard being bitter."

There are, unfortunately, certain businesses in which yelling is the norm, (trading in the pits, for example). Not coincidentally, these professions have very short half-lives. Ten to fifteen years is the maximum that someone can work in that capacity. You retire at 35, instead of 65.

It is unfortunate that politeness is commonly mocked as insincere. As David Letterman joked: "There was a recent poll about the behavior in this country, and it's stunning: 79% said they felt Americans were extremely rude. The other 21% told the poll taker to take his clipboard and shove it up his ass."[15] The ideal business operates like the ideal family. Everyone can express their feelings, but in a constructive, respectful fashion.

3—Business should not be your life. If your best friend is a business associate, you're in trouble. If your only friends are your business associates, you're in worse trouble. Business should only be a way to make a living. It should not be your be-all and end-all. If it is, how can you not take it personally?

Your personal satisfactions, pleasures and love, your raison d'être, must come from outside the office. Otherwise, business will come to mean too much to you. A workaholic is as unhealthy as an alcoholic. In both cases, their addiction reflects the vacuum in their outside life. In both cases, it's a manifestation, as well as a cause, of depression. In both cases, it's an unconscious plea for help, and inevitably leads to a conscious, often explosive, expression of anger.

4—Anger should not be a business tool.

A popular needlepoint in many supervisors' lounges says simply: "Anger + Authority = Attention." A minor variation is the poster that hangs in air marshals' offices: "Dominate + Intimidate = Control.[16]" The difference of course is that air marshals deal with terrorists. Supervisors deal with the terrified. Figures of authority who immediately resort to anger to obtain our attention are like policemen drawing their guns for an expired meter. What's left for a real crisis?

We see it in our parents, unfortunately. We see it in our teachers. We see it in our camp counselors. We see it in our drill sergeants, and as the needlepoint stated, we see it in our supervisors. We see it because it works. But it only works at first. We become inured to it, and eventually it only serves to provoke our contempt.

5—Try to be fair.

Be fair with your customers, your suppliers, your competition and especially, with your co-workers and employees. No one likes it when things don't go their way, and in business, things don't always go your way. People get downright angry however, if they feel that they were cheated. They will find a way to express their anger, sooner or later. You can't be sure how. You can't be sure when. You can be sure that it will cost you dearly.

The worst thing about our foreman's threat, was that it was unfair. It was the equivalent of a teacher announcing that they were going to fail a student with the lowest grade on a test, even if that grade is a 90. It was an unfortunate example of the aforementioned Social Comparison Theory. Fair means rewarding loyalty. Fair means not taking unfair advantage. Fair means honest. Fair is fair.

No one likes losing, but no one resents the winner if the game was played on an even field. The extra profit you can unfairly extract in the short run isn't worth the damage to your reputation in the long run.

Fascinatingly there are only three instances in the Bible where a specific behavior will guarantee long life. One of them is conducting business in an equitable manner.[17] (The other two are being respectful to one's parents[18] and kind to animals.[19]) This triad of honesty, respect and kindness is a fine formula for any life, of any length, and should be a sine qua non for any business. It is not coincidental that the corporations with the best reputations for fairness usually stay successful the longest. In the animal world, it is only the survival of the fittest. In the human world, it is also the survival of the fairest.

6—Positive reinforcement is preferable to negative reinforcement.

It's true that a combination of the two, the proverbial carrot and the stick, is most effective. All too often however, we neglect the carrot and we frustratingly find that the donkey becomes more stubborn, even in the face of increasing pain. Negative reinforcement, or more precisely adversive conditioning, especially if it's unfair, inevitably increases the anger of the person whose behavior you're trying to change. Angry people don't always respond rationally. The result might be that, as with the "seconds," the problem gets worse rather than better.

7—Eliminate the causes of divisiveness.

7A—If an issue, or an incident, has created acrimony, don't assume it will resolve itself. Don't think you can sweep it under the carpet. Confront it and rectify it. Ignoring it is like ignoring a tumor. It will spread and grow until it has poisoned the entire operation.

The 1989 Buffalo Bills were arguably the most talented team in the NFL. They not only had Hall of Fame coach Marv Levy, they had Hall of Fame Quarterback Jim Kelly, Halfback Thurman Thomas and Defensive End Bruce Smith. The three players were All-Pro, the very best in the league at their respective positions, each a candidate for the league's MVP.

Unfortunately they also had dissension. Kelly suffered a sack against the Colts, separated his shoulder, and blamed Offensive Tackle Howard Ballard, the team's most popular player. This led to a Kelly-Thomas feud, public accusations, and two assistant coaches engaging in a fist fight. They became known as "The Bickering Bills" and performed abysmally.

The following year they made a concerted effort to confront the resentments and grow closer. Receiver Steve Tasker said: "We became one huge extended family." They then achieved an unparalleled four straight Super Bowl appearances. The personnel remained the same, but the issue had been eliminated.[20]

The Bickering Bills' issue was trivial, but only in retrospect. Not all are. The Denzel Washington film *Remember The Titans* tells the true story of a Southern high school football team that was able to overcome its racial discord to win the state championship. Ever since it was released it has been repeatedly shown to teams of every sport before a big game.

It has replaced the Gene Hackman film *Hoosiers* as the inspirational movie of choice because racial acrimony is a much more consequential issue than simply being an underdog.

7B—If a particular employee is irreversibly disgruntled, eliminate them. No matter how talented or profitable they are, the company as a whole will be enriched by their departure.

In 1996 the New York Yankees won the World Series for the first time in almost two decades. Nevertheless they knew they had a problem. They were alternating two talented third basemen, but both were unhappy campers. Wade Boggs was not only a future Hall of Famer, but was also arguably the greatest hitter of his era. Charlie Hayes could field and hit for power and, in fact, had caught the last out clinching the world championship.

Defying their success, the Yankees chose to eliminate both discontented stars and signed instead Scott Brosius, heretofore a journeyman third basemen, albeit with a cooperative attitude. Brosius flourished, becoming a .300 hitter for the first time in his career, and so did the Yankees, becoming the most dominant team in the history of baseball.

Most, but not all, employees have the capacity to be Sancho Panza or Dr. Watson, the obedient loyal assistant. A few have the capacity to be Don Quixote or Sherlock Holmes, the brilliant leader. The best employees have the capacity to be both, depending on the needs of the moment.

8—Good morale is as contagious as resentment. Plan assiduously to promote it.

On January 30, 1962 three young schoolgirls in a small village near Lake Victoria, in what is now Tanzania, got the giggles. In retrospect, they got the Giggles. They couldn't stop laughing. Their laughter was so contagious it affected almost half of their school. These laughing fits were so pertinacious, lasting weeks at a time, that within months the exasperated administration had no choice but to shut down the entire boarding school. Since the affected students were then dispersed to their various villages, the contagion spread. By the time the epidemic relented over two years later, 14 schools had been shut down.[21]

Laughter clubs[22] are one example of an extra-curricular activity designed to enhance a company's morale, albeit more popular in India than in America. Common examples here are company teams, holiday parties, summer picnics, team dinners, charity drives and even betting pools. Anything that enhances the sense of belonging to a family, or a team, is effective.

The psychology of belonging to a larger group is incredibly powerful. It is seen in families, athletic teams, cities, countries, and even religions. I can criticize my sibling, but I'll be furious if anyone else does. Similarly I can insult my president, but I will be patriotically livid if a foreigner does. Perhaps most viscerally *I* can mock my religion ("Hebe," "Kike"), my culture ("Mick," "Dago"), or my race ("Nigger," "Spic"), but if an outsider repeats my exact words, a fistfight will ensue.

Although former manager Tommy Lasorda has often said that if you cut him, he would bleed Dodger blue, that kind of loyalty to a company is more distinctive in Japan, than America. In a healthy sense employees are following the first rule mentioned, business is business, not personal. They know that if times get tough, the company will lay them off. A company's loyalty to its employees, once emblematic of I.B.M., no longer exists. Consequently the 1960's lyric: "I'm a company man" from *How To Succeed In Business Without Really Trying* is sadly anachronistic. When Aaron Feuerstein, in the late 1990's, chose to continue paying his employees at Malden Mills after the factory burnt down, it was front page news, and he sat next to the First Lady at the State of the Union address, precisely because it was such an aberration. Nevertheless, if a company can invest the time, money and effort to convince its employees that the company sincerely cares about them, the rewards are immeasurable.

9—Focus on cooperation rather than competition.

For any species to succeed cooperation has to be hard-wired into its psyche. In fact, it is. Researchers in Belgium, France and Spain discovered that ants, without any communication, will spend many hours cooperatively moving corpses of their brethren into orderly, equally spaced plots. The final dispersal is as neat and efficient as the most meticulously planned human cemetery.[23] No individual ant stops to ask "Why do I have to break my back doing this?," or "What's in it for me?" Even if the corpses are unknown to them, they cooperatively work without hesitation.

Fortunately humans are no different. As *The New York Times* proclaimed in their headline: "We're Wired to Cooperate."[24] Researchers from Emory University, using magnetic resonance imaging, discovered that the very act of cooperation "makes the brain light up with quiet joy."[25] Evolutionary theorist Professor Peter Richardson points out that "the depth and breath of human altruism far exceeds" any other species.[26] Dr. Ernst Fehr of the University of Zurich presented findings of how willing people are to take risks to insure cooperation.[27] Dr. Elinor Ostrom of Indiana University found that all communities have some form of monitoring to insure equitable sharing.[28]

If cooperation is so innate, then why are there so many exceptions? Perhaps Rodgers and Hammerstein had the answer when they wrote in *South Pacific,* "You've got to be taught to hate." Children learn to steal and be selfish from their parents. Employees learn it from their supervisors in the incipient stage of their employment. If a company's leitmotif is positively rewarding cooperation, that lesson will be quickly learned as well. Not only will the enterprise be more efficient, but its employees will prefer to work there since they are experiencing less cognitive dissonance from their congenital tendencies. Everyone prospers.

10—Don't mix business and pleasure.

This had been more earthily expressed as, don't defecate where you eat. The reason should be obvious. If you have a personal relationship with your business associates, it becomes impossible not to take business issues personally. There are two subdivisions to this rule.

10A—Don't allow intra-office romances.

Many will argue that intra-office romances are instinctual and inevitable. It's true. So are romances between high school teachers and their students. Neither are healthy however, and neither should be tolerated. At best, an intra-office romance means that business will become a secondary concern to these two people, and possibly others, if anyone else in the office was attracted to either of them. No one can reasonably expect that business will be a higher priority to two lovers than their romance. At worst, the sad reality is that most romances don't end successfully. If hell hath no fury like a lover scorned, how will that affect the business relationship between these two people, and their respective performances?

I was sitting in the chart room when Dr. Winner walked in and politely said to Nurse MacIntyre: "Could you please take an EKG on Mrs. Leslie." Nurse MacIntyre crisply replied: "Take your own fucking EKG."

At that moment I immediately understood three things: One—Dr. Winner had been dating Nurse MacIntyre. Two— Dr. Winner had stopped dating her. Three—she was angry and was going to pay Dr. Winner back. As they stepped outside to argue, I also realized who was going to be the biggest loser of all. Mrs. Leslie. When an office romance breaks up, the office suffers.

10B—Don't allow nepotism.

With each succeeding person from the same family, the potential for business disaster increases geometrically. How can you not take business personally when you're dealing with your brother or sister, your father or mother, or your daughter or son? All the issues discussed previously, sibling rivalry, rebellion against parents, role reversal, become expressed in terms of business.

This is even worse than an intra office romance, since the relationships are longer and stronger. Romantic relationships come and go. Familial relationships don't. Can anyone even pretend to be objective when dealing with their own family? No physician would ever treat a member of their own family. No lawyer would ever defend their own blood relative. It's no different supervising a member of your own family.

It's foolish from every conceivable perspective. Not only do we wind up losing our objectivity, we also decrease our efficiency, we lessen the respect of our employees and their motivation to improve, since they've learned that promotions are based on blood lines, not performance. Meritocracy is dead. We also violate a cardinal rule of investing. We put all our eggs in one basket.

Would George have been so obsessed to initiate his ill-advised venture if his own son hadn't been his second in command? I'm not sure. I am sure that someone more objective than his son, someone who wasn't concerned with avenging his father's honor, would have argued against the idea, and possibly prevented it.

At the very least, if George didn't have all his children working for him, he would only have bankrupted one generation of his family, not two. Knowing George, I suspect that it hurt him more to see the financial ruin visited upon his children by his actions, than upon himself.

No one ever said on their death bed, "I wish I had spent more time at the office." As we get older, we realize that our passion belongs in our home with our families, not in our office with our businesses. Sometimes we reach that conclusion by realizing what we've missed at home. Sometimes we realize it by seeing what went wrong at home as a result. Sometimes we realize it by confronting what went wrong at the office as a result, like George.

Avis used to advertise that Number Two tries harder.

Sometimes we try too hard. Demanding to be Number One isn't necessarily a virtue.

A religious aphorism states "Who is the wealthy person? The person who is happy with what he has." For all his homes, cars, and money, in retrospect, George had never been wealthy. He had however been angry. It cost him dearly.

> *"Toil is the lot of all, and bitter woe the fate of many."*
> —Homer (circa 1000 B.C.)

Notes

---

1 *Jeremiah* IX:3.

2 Readers interested in Al Smith, Franklin Delano Roosevelt, and New York State politics should consult Robert Caro's masterful biography of Robert Moses: *The Power Broker* (1974) Robert Caro, Knopf, from whence this vignette derives.

3 *The New York Times*, Warren St. John, August 24, 2002.

4 Arthur Schopenhauer (1788-1860) had an uncharitable view of life in general. His other observations included: "To desire immortality is to desire the eternal perpetuation of a great mistake." and "Ignorance is degrading only when found in the company with riches."

5 In 1946 Billy Conn fought Joe Louis for the heavyweight championship. Conn, congenitally a light heavyweight, was much quicker than Louis and had the fight won handily on points. Unfortunately, in the end, he went for the knockout, and was instead knocked out himself by the more powerful Louis. Had he been content to merely win, the championship would have been his.

6 The most famous example of two running adversaries obsessed with each other occurred in the 1984 Olympic women's 3000 meter final. It was the most anticipated showdown of the Olympiad

finally pitting world record holder Mary Decker against teen prodigy Zola Budd who had broken her record. Everyone knew they would finish first and second, But in which order? All eyes were only on them. Their eyes were only on each other. On the fifth of 7 ½ laps they collided. Budd finished seventh. Decker didn't finish the race.

7 *The Wall Street Journal*, August 7, 1992.

8 Increasing a colleague's seconds to save your own job is reminiscent of the widely known joke of two friends encountering a grizzly bear. When one starts to run, his friend admonishes him: "You can't outrun a grizzly!" He replies: "I don't have to. I only have to outrun you."

9 Cinematic portraits of boot camp training can be seen in: *Full Metal Jacket, An Officer and A Gentleman*, and *We Were Soldiers*. In the first film, written and directed by Stanley Kubrick, when Drill Sergent Lee Ermey catches Vince D'Onofrio with a forbidden doughnut, it is his platoon that is punished with push-ups while D'Onofrio finishes the doughnut. Ermey and D'Onofrio's power struggle climaxes in a fatal confrontation.

10 The General Accounting office estimated the cost of the Clinton-Gore sabotage to be $19,000. It included sadistic references to the incoming Vice-President's cardiac condition and sophomoric caricatures of the incoming President as a chimpanzee. Similar sabotage had occurred in the two previous administration changes as well. (*U.S. News & World Report*, June 24, 2002.)

11 *The New York Times*, Eve Tahmincioglu, August 1, 2001.

12 *The New York Times*, Henry Fountain, June 4, 2002.

13 The general population's jealousy, and schadenfreude, is partially satisfied by tabloids, gossip columnists and paparazzi. All three are designed to deprecate celebrities, be they business, political or show business.

The tabloids reveal the most embarrassing details of a celebrity's life, no matter how tangential, or ancient. In terms of gossip, as Bertrand Russell said: "No one gossips about other people's secret virtues." The paparazzi (the term derives from a feral pack of photographers in Fellini's *La Dolce Vita*) are the most satisfying, since their photos are the most undeniable.

TIME (July 1, 2002) wrote that Ron Galella, "the godfather of paparazzi," and Andy Warhol, the artist of paparazzi, "had in common their anger." Paparazzi stalk and torture their prey. Robin Williams pointed out in *One Hour Photo* that the very term "snapshot" was derived from hunting. Susan Sontag observed: "To photograph someone is a sublimated murder."

14 *Jealousy* (1985) Nancy Friday, Perigord Press.

15 *Entertainment Weekly*, April 15, 2002.

16 *The New York Times*, Matthew L. Wald, May 25, 2002.

17 *Deuteronomy* XXV:15.

18 *Exodus* XX:12, *Deuteronomy* V:16.

19 *Deuteronomy* XXII:6-7.

20 New York *Daily News*, August 2, 2002.

21 *The New York Times*, Eric Trump, July 27, 2002.

22 Since laughter is considered healthy, today over 1000 laughter clubs exist all over the world. These are not comedy clubs where laughter is precipitated by (hopefully) funny material. In laughter clubs people assemble and laugh, facilitated only by the infectious nature of laughter itself.

23 *The New York Times*, Henry Fountain, July 23, 2002

24 *The New York Times*, Natalie Angier, July 23, 2002

25 *Ibid.*

26 *Ibid.*

27 *Ibid.*

28 *Ibid.*

PART III

CHAPTER SEVEN

The Raging Mob

Anger In Groups

"And Aaron said: 'You know the masses; they are evil.'
And Moses saw that [indeed] they had broken loose."[1]

"Why'd you shut down the elevator?"

He was a little, old, wizened Black man. He was sitting in a folding aluminum chair more appropriate for a beach at noon than for a Harlem sidewalk at midnight. But for two things he would have been an eccentric, perhaps even amusing, character. Number one, he was angry. Number two, he was talking to me.

It was a hot summer Saturday night. My med school classmate was moonlighting weekends for the Medical Examiner's office. He was responsible for examining any unnatural death on the island of Manhattan. I was tagging along. He was upstairs inspecting a corpse with a bullet hole through its left ear. He needed an otoscope. I retrieved it from the car when the old man in the chair addressed me.

"I'm talking to you! Why'd you shut down the elevator?!"

I offered my friendliest smile. "I really don't know anything about your elevator. I think you might be mistaking me for someone else."

"Ain't no mistake! You think you can sneak in here middle of the night and no one will notice?"

With his voice raised, the old man was attracting a crowd. Two young men came over. "Who is he?" they inquired.

"This here's the landlord."

They walked up to me and got in my face. "You the goddamned landlord?"

"No, I'm not. I'm a doctor. I'm here with the medical examiner's office."

Several other men seemed to appear out of nowhere. "Who is he?"

"Landlord."

"Son of a bitch. *Now* he comes!"

I was surrounded. They were all men. They were all Black. They were all angry. They were all yelling at me.

"How come you never call me back?"

"When you going to fix that leak? Don't you tell me next month again!"

"What are you gonna do about all them rats?"

The old man, still in his chair, was simultaneously playing narrator and cheerleader: "He tried to sneak in like a thief. Don't let him sneak off! Don't let him get away again! Thinks we're all goddamned fools! Thinks he's too smart for us. You show him!"

The confrontation was escalating. Since they were all yelling simultaneously, they had to yell even louder to be heard. One of them started jabbing me in the chest with his finger for emphasis. I had given up trying to respond. There was nothing I could say. Besides, I knew my voice would advertise my panic. A second man started jabbing me, with two fingers, harder. It was only a matter of seconds before the fingers would clench into fists.

Suddenly, a lady screamed out of the second story window directly above us: "Why you all making such a goddamned racket at this hour?"

Someone responded. "We caught the landlord. He was trying to sneak in."

"Are you blind as well as dumb? Landlord's twenty years older, twenty pounds heavier. Landlord ain't got no beard. What did the good Lord give you eyes for?"

Just like that, it was over. No one asked me to corroborate her testimony. No one apologized. No one said good-bye. As suddenly as they had gathered, they had dispersed.

I stood there alone, massively relieved, but still feeling the aftereffects of my confrontation. My heart was pounding. My mouth was bone dry. My clothing was drenched in sweat. It wasn't from the heat.

I was holding the otoscope for which I had returned. I started back into the building. The old man was still sitting there. As I walked past him, he glared at me and muttered: "Elevator don't work."

Though it seemed like an eternity to me, the whole episode probably took less than three minutes. Though they seemed like an army, the mob was probably six men, give or take. Can six people even qualify for a "mob"? The word "mob" is an abbreviation of the original Latin phrase "mobile[2] vulgus," meaning "the excitable populace." By that definition, my Harlem hextet certainly qualified as a mob.[3]

In Latin, the word "vulgus" (or "vulgar"), has two distinct meanings. On the one hand, it means "popular" or "common," referring to the masses. On the other hand, in its more contemporary, contemptuous usage, it means "obscene" or "indecent." In ancient Rome, the masses were considered obscene. In 13 B.C.E. Horace wrote, "The people are a many-headed beast." In contemporary society, the masses are angry. Mobs are still obscene, and angry.

I was touring Europe when I chanced upon a demonstration. I was attracted by the excitement and the television cameras. Though I had no idea what the protest was all about, I decided to stop to watch. It almost cost me my life.

Before I knew it, the noisy, albeit controlled, demonstration turned into an uncontrolled riot. Previously, I had been wedged into the crowd. Suddenly, the crowd turned into a mob and, willy-nilly, I was part of it. Wherever the mob surged, whether I wanted to or not, I went. I couldn't stop.[4] I couldn't change direction. I couldn't escape. I couldn't understand what I was hearing. Unfortunately, I understood all too well what I was seeing.

People were being attacked. I didn't understand why or whom, but even as a medical student, I understood what. I saw blood flow. I saw savage, merciless trauma. I saw at least one man die. Eventually with the belated, seemingly begrudging intervention of the authorities, the mob fragmented. Many bodies and much blood were left behind.

When I made it back to my hostel, I learned that the demonstration was by the labor unions protesting the influx of foreign workers. I learned that the mob had attacked anyone they had deemed to be foreign. I learned that several people had died and many more had been hospitalized. I had received only inadvertent bruises. Several observers remarked that they were surprised that the mob hadn't attacked me, a swarthy foreigner. They weren't joking. I wasn't laughing.

A mob decides on the objects of its collective anger instantaneously. There's no due process, grace period or opportunity for appeal. There's no chance to argue or persuade. Judgement and sentence are both immediate. An unfortunate example was the bearded Italian who made the mistake of driving through Crown Heights while a Black mob was gunning for Hasidic Jews during the infamous riots. His beard proved fatal. No one stopped to ask him his religion before murdering him.

Had there been a European equivalent of the old man from Harlem, another embittered, confused denizen, I would have been one of the casualties. Ironically, in both cases I was endangered by the color of my skin. In Harlem, it was too light. In Europe, it was too dark. As Sartre put it: "Hell is other people."

The reaction to these two incidents is often the same. Fellow Americans conclude from the latter incident that foreigners are volatile. From the former incident, fellow Caucasians conclude the same about Blacks. Mob violence, like venereal disease[5], is always thought to be someone else's problem.

The reality is that mobs transcend all geographical, cultural, racial and religious boundaries. Mobs know *all* languages, colors and Gods. Even sadder, they transcend all temporal boundaries as well. Thomas Jefferson observed: "Man is the only animal which devours his own kind." There have been mobs since the dawn of recorded history, and there is no sign that they're ebbing. If anything, the opposite might be true. Why?

A raging mob is so much more than just a salient manifestation of group anger. Incredibly diverse factors empower it. Like most phenomena of this magnitude, it is multi-determined. Its causes include:

1—Heroism of the Masses

In ancient Rome, any cause embraced by the masses was automatically suspect. As mentioned, any popular idea was consequently deemed vulgar. The philosophers and, more importantly, the rulers, dismissed and, if necessary, suppressed the desires of the masses.[6] Thucydides, in *The Peloponnesian War*, ascribed the fall of democratic Athens to the irrational anarchy of the unchecked masses.

Today we live in a democratic era. The masses no longer merely obey. They in fact rule, through their elected leaders. Any ruler who wishes to stay in power must constantly take the pulse of the population. The masses, and even the mobs, are no longer viewed as rabble needing to be suppressed. They are often legitimized, sometimes even deified.

The 15,000 Indians who demonstrated at Amritsar, and were subsequently fired upon by British troops, are today considered the heroes of India's independence. Gandhi harnessed the strength of the unarmed masses through civil disobedience and emancipated his country without a weapon being raised.[7] The Iron Curtain of Communism, ("the evil empire" in the words of Ronald Reagan), was *not* brought down by the collective armed might of the Western World. It was destroyed by mobs of its own citizens. The riots in Red Square proved more potent than the billion dollar "Star Wars" technology. The Palestinian mob that celebrated the *September 11* attack on America did not perceive itself to be glorifying terrorists. As they fired their rifles in the air they were celebrating their victory over their American oppressors. In their minds, *they* were the good guys.

Today, every mob sees itself as heroic. Demonstrators, and even rioters, as they are arrested, imagine themselves on the side of the angels. In a previous era, a record of an arrest could be an irreversible stigma. In our time, it is often perceived of as an idealistic rite of passage, or even a badge of courage. The more heroic we perceive mobs, the more ubiquitous they inevitably become.

2—Intolerance of Injustice

In discussing temper tantrums, we saw that the fuel for the fire, the sine qua non, was the perception of injustice. In a very real sense a riot is a mass temper tantrum. As in a temper tantrum, there is a perception of having been cheated. As in a temper tantrum, there is a need to express that rage, the consequences be damned. The sense of outrage comes *less* from the thought that someone did something wrong. It comes *more* from the realization that they got away with it. Remember, the Rodney King riots were *not* precipitated by his assault. They only started months later when the accused policemen were found not guilty.

What precipitates a ghetto riot is not the fact of a Black man being murdered. It's not even the fact that he was murdered by a White man, a drug deal gone bad, for example. Rather, it's the fact that the shooter was a policeman, as in New York City's Washington Heights, and consequently will not be punished. An injustice is far more frustrating than a transgression. A movie audience can tolerate the hero dying,[8] but it cannot tolerate the villain going unpunished.[9]

My high school phys ed teacher, an Israeli émigré, was an Olympic addict. His life was a predictable cycle. For forty-seven months he eagerly anticipated the Olympiad, meticulously following new prospects. On the forty-eight month he reveled in the Games. When I chanced upon him recently I brought up his favorite topic. He soberly informed me that since 1972 he no longer had any interest in the Olympics. I wasn't surprised. 1972 was the infamous Munich Olympiad with the barbaric murder of the Israeli athletes by Arab terrorists. I commiserated. "It was obscene the way Avery Brundage[10] continued the Games without a pause."

He shook his head. Apparently I missed the point. "What was obscene was the basketball finals. We[11] won that game not once, but twice! It was goddamned highway robbery! Those (blanking) cheaters! I'll *never* forgive that! Never!"

3—Forces of Nature

In physical science there is a critical concept called entropy. It refers to the innate, spontaneous tendency of any system to disintegrate. To oppose this force of entropy we expend energy to maintain the integrity of the whole. Absent that energy, disintegration ensues. It holds true of a house that is not being lived in. It holds true of a car that is not being maintained. It holds true of a body that's no longer alive.

It also holds true of a body that is alive. Any parent can attest to an infant's innate desire to destroy. While that desire becomes suppressed as we get older, by both our superego and society, it never really disappears. Given the unsupervised autonomy of their own room, what's the first thing that every teen does? Create havoc. Who doesn't enjoy collapsing an elaborate house of cards, destroying an intricate sand castle at dusk, or taking a sledgehammer to a luxury car?[12]

The *Lethal Weapon* films all have as a major scene the complete destruction of a huge, expensive building or home. The audience spontaneously responds by laughing and applauding. Between the four films there are 19 separate explosions, 31 cars wrecked, and 81 people killed. The series is a phenomenal success.[13]

A riot gives its participants the opportunity to indulge that destructive force of nature. Finally, they can destroy a police car, wreck havoc on a business establishment, or burn down a building. This force works in the absence of the previous factors of heroism and injustice.

Several weeks after the Rodney King riots in Los Angeles there were similar riots in Chicago. Over 100 people were hospitalized, over 1000 people were arrested, businesses were looted and buildings were burnt to the ground causing over $10 million in damage. What precipitated this major destruction? The hometown Bulls had won their second consecutive basketball championship.

One year later the Bulls won again. This time the victory didn't even take place in Chicago, but across the country in Phoenix. The result in Chicago? Even worse. This time, in addition to the hospitalizations, burglary, arrests and monetary damage, there were three celebratory murders in the "victory riot."

Shouldn't the city have been prepared? It was. The police presence that night was increased by 400%. Prison vans and armored trucks had been mobilized for mass arrests. Firemen, judges, prosecutors and public defenders were all standing by. The city spent three million dollars in vain to prevent a recurrence. The death and destruction were as inevitable as Michael Jordan's victory.

This is hardly a "Windy City" phenomenon. A few days earlier there had been an identical riot in Montreal to celebrate the Canadians winning the Stanley Cup. Professional rioters came prepared carrying steel bars to break windows and garbage bags to carry their loot. In some cases, to increase efficiency, trucks backed up to the storefronts. A few months earlier there had been a riot in Dallas celebrating the Cowboys winning the Super Bowl. In addition to the familiar trauma and damage, there had been the irony of rioters destroying the very busses that the city had provided gratis to transport the rioters to the festivities.

The king of the American victory riots (for now) remains Detroit. Not only did they have the first one (in 1968 when the Tigers won the Series), but they've had the most (four—1968, 1984, 1989, 1990), and the worst. In the guise of celebration, Detroit revelers have raped, stabbed, run over and shot at least eight separate fatalities. These murders weren't accidental or inadvertent, like a stray bullet. Innocent people were pulled out of cars and deliberately stabbed or shot to death for no explicable reason.

There have been similar, albeit thankfully less deadly, riots in Pittsburgh (1971), New York (1977) and San Francisco (1985). The ubiquitousness of the victory riot has created the anomaly of a city's police force, fire fighters and hospital personnel rooting for their home team to lose the championship game. Better a loss of pride, than property, limb and life.

Unfortunately the riot can often be a win-lose inevitability. In 2001 the University of Maryland basketball team lost in the Final Four. Result? A riot with over a half million dollars of destruction. The following year, for the very first time in their university's history, they went all the way and won the national championship. Result? Another riot.

Unfortunately the sports riot is hardly an American phenomenon. International soccer riots make our riots pale in comparison, both in terms of frequency and intensity. In one soccer riot alone in Lima, Peru, in 1964, 500 people were severely injured and another 293 were murdered. On a smaller, simultaneously more pathetic scale, over 20 people were seriously injured in a remote Bangladeshi village when fans of Brazil and Argentina's soccer teams fought with iron rods and large rocks over which flag would be raised on the village's tallest coconut tree.[14] None of the fans who fought had ever actually stepped foot in Brazil or Argentina, on the other side of the planet.

The riots that erupted in Moscow in 1993 when President Boris Yeltsin ordered tanks to depose Parliament were understandable. A decade later they were eclipsed by over 8,000 rioters rampaging through Red Square. Their cause? Russia had lost to Japan in soccer. The mobs attacked anyone who looked vaguely oriental, injuring many, murdering one.[15]

Sports Illustrated noted that a sign that the apocalypse was upon us was the fact that local California police needed reinforcements with "pepper spray and batons to contain a melee involving 300 spectators that erupted at a girl's flag football game."[16]

In the violence that is committed in the name of Nike, the goddess of victory, there is no heroism being displayed. There is no injustice being avenged. There is only entropy.

4—Mass Hysteria

One lovely spring afternoon in fifth grade, Varda Klughaupt threw up in the middle of class. Someone, somewhere, concluded that the fish cakes that we had for lunch had been spoiled. Suddenly Vivian, Sol and Bookie all threw up. Within minutes, dozens of kids needed to go to the bathroom and/or the nurse's office. Within the hour, the entire school was dismissed early and sent home.

Were the fishcakes really spoiled? Of course not. I had eaten more of them than anyone, and I felt fine. Vivian, Sol and Bookie threw up *not* because of what was in their stomach, but because of what was in their head.

In the aftermath of the Rodney King riots in Los Angeles, there was a planned massive demonstration in New York. It was called for Friday. By noon the news had spread like wildfire. A sales clerk had been shot at Bloomingdale's. Three people were murdered outside Madison Square Garden. Businesses were let out. People fled home and locked their doors behind them. Streetfront stores were closed and shuttered. By 3 P.M., downtown New York City was a ghost town. In the end, it turned out that none of it was true. The city had been as blameless as the fishcakes. It didn't matter.

Less than a month after *September 11* there was a rash of rashes throughout the U.S. Large scale outbreaks occurred in Indiana, Virginia, Oregon, Massachusetts, California and Pennsylvania. The etiology was thought to be anthrax or poisoned books on Islam, or chemicals from infected airplanes, or AIDS, or diseased frogs, or mad-cow disease, or an allergy to old math textbooks, or biological warfare.[17] Interestingly it only occurred in school-girls[18] and it only occurred on school property during classes.

Were these girls feigning illness to avoid class? No. You can't fake a rash. You can however create it unconsciously when the symptom is suggested to you by someone else experiencing it, particularly during a highly anxious period. There were over 70 reports of mass hysteria in medical journals between 1973 and 1993. There were undoubtedly ten times as many incidents not reported, like my fishcakes, since the diagnosis is considered insulting by the victims, though there's no reason it should be perceived that way.

Any psychosomatic manifestation, including mass hysteria, is a salient manifestation of the power of the brain, *not* of the weakness of the mind. It is fueled by uncertainty and catalyzed by rumor.

Rumors are both the catalyst *and* the fuel for riots. Like children playing telephone, the outrageous facts grow with each re-telling. No one ever knows how it started, but it takes on a life of its own. Revenge is taken for outrages that never occurred. By the time the rumor has been killed, it's too late. The damage has been done.

5—The Cloak of Anonymity

Being part of a mob gives us permission to do things that we would never do on our own. The infamous gang "wilding" of the Central Park jogger included teens who had never before been arrested. Somehow, the fact that everyone else was doing it, made it permissible in their minds. Often referred to as mob psychology, the participation of many others liberates us from our internal restraints. The phenomenon can result in evangelical fervor, a mass orgy, a "wilding," or a riot.

Afterwards, we might feel guilt, or even amazement, at our actions. At the time however, we have lost our identity to the collective will of the mob. As long as the mob exists, we as individuals do not. In some ways being part of a mob provides the same intoxicating, heady, uninhibiting feeling that alcohol does. Needless to say, adding the influence of alcohol, or drugs, to the influence of a mob is even more potent. The infamous N.Y.C. Puerto Rican Parade molestation mobs were but one unfortunate example.

6—Opportunity and Greed

This is of course the ugliest aspect of mobs. Yet, it is undeniable. In every mob there is a certain percentage of scavengers who see the disruption as an opportunity. Rioters who come equipped with crowbars, wire-cutters and pickup trucks, as in Montreal, are not spontaneous. The stores that are looted, the televisions that are carried off, are not expressions of outrage. They are expressions of greed.

No matter how catastrophic the event, there will still be vultures looking to take advantage. Witness the fake rescue workers who subsequent to *September 11, 2001* walked off with souvenirs, loot and donations. Bill Cosby maintains that the looting of the Rodney King riots in Los Angeles would have been replicated on Fifth Avenue, if the steel doors to Tiffany were suddenly removed. He's probably right.

Sometimes a temporary state of anarchy is used as an opportunity to settle a personal vendetta. History records the murder as an inadvertent, anonymous, riot statistic, when in reality it wasn't anonymous and it wasn't inadvertent. Many of the murders of supposed Palestinian collaborators fall into this category,[19] as did sadly some American casualties in Viet Nam.[20]

7—Rebelling against the Establishment

Gay Talese has theorized that one cause of inner city riots is the absence of strong father figures. Statistics support him. Seventy percent of all juvenile criminals in state reform institutions have no fathers.

As we discussed in adolescence, it is both normal and healthy to rebel. What happens when there's no one to rebel against? Society, the establishment, becomes the surrogate parent. The reality is that society does take on certain parental obligations. In the absence of a parent, the government will provide the physical necessities such as food and shelter. Ambitious programs will even try to provide recreation and guidance. Despite that, absent a parent, a great deal will inevitably still be missing.

It makes sense then that the rebellion should be directed against the society that tried but failed to meet this frustrated young individual's needs. From the inner city youth's perspective, by trying, the establishment was saying: "We owe you." By failing, society precipitated the youth's overwhelming frustration. Worst of all, unlike a healthy adolescence, this is not a rage that disappears with adulthood. The adult might be more discreet in expressing his anger, but he's no less convinced that he got a bum deal from society.

When football legend Jim Brown was convicted of destroying his wife's car, he was offered anger management classes in lieu of prison. He refused. While imprisoned he went on a starvation diet to show society who was the boss. Jim Brown[21] was in his sixties at the time. Rebellion has no age limit.

8—Positive Reinforcement

John Hinkley shot President Reagan and permanently maimed James Brady for one reason, in his mind. He was trying to impress the actress Jodie Foster.[22] He calculated correctly that his crime would be front-page news all over the world. He knew that he would become an instant celebrity with his picture on the cover of all the magazines.

It is an unfortunate reality that the more extreme that the crime is, the more famous the criminal becomes. By murdering the right person, a failure can become inextricably linked with his victim in the annals of history. Four decades later, more people remember the name of President Kennedy's assassin than what President Kennedy accomplished. More people remember President Lincoln's assassin[23] than his vice-president who succeeded him.[24]

Despite the anonymity that the mob provides, the same positive reinforcement occurs in riots. Due to our modern technology, when on April 29, 1992, under the pretext of the Rodney King riots, "Damian Williams, the young Black thug, crushed white trucker Reginald Denny's head into a near-fatal pulp,"[25] he then turned to prance and preen for the television camera as if he was dancing in the end zone after a touchdown, so he could see "highlights" of himself endlessly repeated on the subsequent news reports.

Because of these videos, a decade later, the names of Damian Williams, the Black thug, and Reginald Denny, the White victim, are still remembered. No one remembers the Black heroes, Lei Yuille, Titus Murphy, Terri Barnett and Bobby Green who came to Denny's aid. No one remembers Bennie Newton, a Black ex-con turned reverend, who threw himself on the body of Fidel Lopez after a Black mob ripped him from his truck, robbed him, busted his head open, sliced his ear off, stripped him and spray painted his chest, torso and genitals black. No one remembers Reverend Newton waving a Bible and defiantly yelling: "Kill him and you have to kill me, too!,"[26] because no television camera was present to publicize it.

At a certain point the media collectively decided to publicize assassins less. At a certain point television decided not to show "fans" who run out on the field disrupting the game. It's an idea worth considering for rioters, who disrupt life, as well.

9—When the Cat's Away

A practical factor in how far a mob will go is the instantaneous calculation of what the immediate consequences will be. It is not coincidental that the worst riots tend to occur when there is a perceived withdrawal by the forces maintaining order. Even as a foreigner, it was obvious to me that the police were reluctant to intervene with the union mob, many of whom were probably their friends and neighbors. I'm sure it was more obvious to the mob.

When, in 1969, the Montreal police went on strike, six banks were robbed and 100 stores were looted before the Mounties restored order. When the Los Angeles police department, which had unfortunately been identified as the cause, chose to withdraw initially from the Rodney King riots, it gave the mob their proverbial second wind. The anarchy that ensued was predictable. Similarly catastrophic consequences resulted from police inertia in Montreal in 1993, and most notoriously, in Brooklyn's Crown Heights in 1991. When Third World mobs storm U.S. Embassies, it is clearly with the collusion of the governing authority. The militia lets the mob know what is encouraged, and what is forbidden. The mob complies.

Is our society so uncivilized, that in the momentary absence of authority, we will always immediately unravel? No. It is a reaction to particular circumstances.

Take fifteen children and leave them alone in a playground. What usually happens? They occupy themselves. They make friends. They form teams and start a game. More often than not, they're completely successful in organizing themselves.

Take those same fifteen kids and put them in a classroom with a strict disciplinarian as their teacher. Of necessity, they behave beautifully. What happens however, if that teacher suddenly, inexplicably disappears? Bedlam. They had come to rely on that teacher to provide their discipline. They didn't have to develop it on their own. When they started to misbehave in the teacher's absence, and saw they were getting away with it, invariably their misbehavior escalated.

What would have happened in my Harlem confrontation, if I had a gun that I was willing to use? Two possibilities. If my adversaries also had a gun, I'd probably be dead. If no one else did, they would probably have left me alone, even if they righteously believed that I was the landlord who had done them wrong.

Woody Allen says in *Annie Hall* that, when dealing with Nazis, sticks and stones are much more effective than clever words. The same is true when dealing with a mob.

10—Boredom and Excitement

Why did I become, albeit inadvertently, part of that European mob? Because I was bored and looking for excitement. As mundane as that sounds, it remains an important factor in many mobs and riots.

Researchers at Eotros University in Budapest studied "the wave," the phenomenon of a "sweeping mass of spectators rising in sequence around a stadium," commonly seen at athletic events.[27] They discovered that it obeyed many of the same laws of physics as an ocean wave, a forest fire, the P-Q-R-S wave of a heart beat,[28] or for that matter a riot. In particular, the more bored the crowd is, the easier it is to start the wave. When the game is exciting, there is no wave.

For eight years Bill Buford, an American author, lived and partied with English soccer hooligans. In his book, *Among the Thugs*, he concludes that the vast majority of these mobs weren't interested in the sport, in their team, or even their country. They were excited by the opportunity to run amok. They rioted every chance they had. They stole; they vandalized; they murdered with little or no justification for the sheer thrill of it all. In one riot alone in 1985, 39 people died. Over the years, tens of thousands have died in soccer riots. The realization is unnerving. Soccer is a child's game. There's no injustice, no oppression, no poverty. There are however some bored, amoral on-lookers who are really looking for excitement.

11—Displacement

Despite the fact that his technique was far from perfect, Dan Gable was the greatest wrestler in history. In high school he won 64 of 64 matches. In college he won 117 of 118 matches including 25 straight pins. Though he weighed 140 lbs., he beat every other wrestler on his team including the heavyweights 1 ½ times larger than him. In the 1972

Olympics he won the gold medal by winning six matches without letting any opponent score a single point. That is comparable to winning the World Series without allowing your opponent to get a single hit. Before Gable it simply wasn't conceivable. Even as a coach his teams won an unprecedented 15 national championships.

What motivated Dan Gable?

When Gable was 15, his only sibling, his sister Diane was raped and murdered by a neighbor, Tom Kyle. After the murder a distraught Gable confided to his father that Kyle had once told him that he was attracted to Diane, but if she wasn't interested, he might have to hurt her. Gable's father responded by beating Dan up, accusing him of being responsible for his sister's murder.[29]

Consciously, Gable thought that his single-minded devotion to his sport, and resultant success, would in some way compensate his parents for their loss. Unconsciously, when Gable mercilessly beat up opponent after opponent, is it possible there were two adversaries in particular that were the object of his anger?

Many people similarly carry with them an insatiable anger. They can't express it at the objects of their wrath because those people are unavailable or unassailable. They can't sublimate it and displace it as successfully as a Dan Gable, or to a far lesser degree, a Mike Tyson. Instead they are like a bolt of lightning looking for an available lightning rod onto which they can discharge their fury. A riot provides them that opportunity.

12—Humiliation

An often repeated question is, how could Germany, arguably the apex of human culture, the birthplace of Mozart, Goethe, Beethoven, Mann, Hesse, Dietrich, Strauss, et al also have executed the most inhumane butchery in the history of mankind? It is a complex question with many answers, but one of them is the fact of Germany's humiliation after World War I. Humiliation is an incredibly powerful motivator.

As a liaison psychiatrist I was once paged to the Coronary Care Unit to see a Munchausen patient. Munchausen patients who pretend to be sick for primary gain can be incredibly deceitful as well as frustrating. This one was apparently violent as well. As I entered the C.C.U. he was on top of someone, flailing away at him. I grabbed him from behind, pulled him off his victim and wrestled him to the floor. He was berserk, but fortunately I was stronger and had the superior position. I tried to immobilize him until security came or he calmed down. After a few minutes the latter occurred and I gingerly released him to discover to my shock that, in fact, he was the cardiologist who had paged me in the first place. I had dragged him off the Munchausen patient who by now had scurried away.

My colleague had become violent because he had felt humiliated by this patient. He had admitted him to the hospital in the first place. He had given him a scarce, valuable bed in the C.C.U. He had held his hand both literally and figuratively when the patient's pain exacerbated inexplicably. When he realized that his trust had been betrayed, that he had been made into a laughing stock, he lost it.

One reason for the implacable Arab enmity towards America is the humiliation they feel having lost three wars to Israel, supported by the U.S. Would the United States itself ever have revolted against Britain if it didn't feel so humiliated by the incredible contempt with which King George III treated his colony? The unemployed workers who rioted in Europe were as humiliated as the thousands of Russians who rampaged in Red Square after losing the World Cup match to Japan.

The mob is empowering. Suddenly an emasculated, helpless, impotent man becomes omnipotent. A rioter who gleefully stomps a victim lying helplessly on the ground is in his mind celebrating a victory. For once in his life he is a winner, not a loser. For once in his life he doesn't feel humiliated.

13—De-humanization

The single most uncomfortable moment of my life occurred the day we buried my father. His body had not been properly identified, so before the funeral could begin, the casket had to be opened and I had to verify that the three-day-old cadaver was indeed my father. As the lid was being lifted and the smell of death wafted into my nostrils, I suddenly felt like an actor playing a part. My response had been scripted. I knew exactly how I was supposed to appear, and what I was supposed to say.

I was experiencing the phenomenon of de-personalization, a defense mechanism we invoke when confronted with moments of overwhelming emotional intensity. Simultaneously, I underwent de-realization. Both then and now I recall the event from the perspective of a fly on the ceiling looking down. Not only wasn't this happening to me, it wasn't really happening at all. It was like a scene from a movie being filmed from a crane. Movies can be intense, but they aren't personally threatening.

When I at last had to look at my father's corpse, his face discolored, his nose mashed off to the side, I perceived it not as his body, but rather as a Tussaud-like wax mannequin of him that apparently had been damaged in transit. This was de-humanization. While all three, de-personalization, de-realization and de-humanization, are experienced by rioters, the last is the most significant. It is also another answer to our question about Nazi Germany.

The Einsatzgruppen were the German army corps responsible for efficiently turning Jews into landfill. They logistically engineered the process of sardine-packing, wherein Jews were forced to lie on top of each other in the cavernous pits they had dug, and then machine-gunned one layer at a time. This method enormously reduced the wasted space between the bodies when they were shot at the edge of the pit, as had been done hitherto.[30]

How did the Einsatzgruppen live with themselves? One method they used was the same utilized by town-wide lynching parties of Blacks. These weren't people. They weren't human. This isn't murder. It's extermination, an unpleasant but necessary chore anytime human beings are discomfited by a vermin epidemic. Only with this rationalization can one comprehend the photographs of White children gleefully pointing to the Black bodies hanging behind them, or the sight of a German soldier humming as he walked along with a dying infant still crying weakly, impaled on his bayonet.[31]

De-humanization isn't reserved for heinous purposes. Surgeons utilize it when they gown every part of the body but their operating field. They need to focus on the task at hand and not be distracted by the humanity, similar to first year medical students, or medical examiners, as they dissect a cadaver.

It was not coincidental that Daniel Pearl, *The Wall Street Journal* reporter, was forced to recite: "My mother was a Jew. My father was a Jew. I am a Jew." as Arab terrorists cut his throat with a butcher knife. Whether in an abduction, a lynching, a massacre, or a riot, it is easier to butcher someone if you can convince yourself that they're less than human because of the color of their skin, their language, or their religion. If they aren't human, it isn't homicide.

14—An Innate Dissatisfaction

I save this reason for penultimate because in many ways it's the most important. Just as a forest fire can't be ignited from wet trees, a mob can't be formed from a happy, content populace. An unhappy, dissatisfied population is as potentially incendiary as a parched forest. All both need is a spark.

Was the European union demonstrating and ultimately rioting because of their stated reason, the unfairness of importing labor? No. Their anger came from the fact that they were out of work. Their explosiveness reflected the fact that they were frustrated that they couldn't provide for their families.

The haves point out that it's always the have-nots who riot. They're right. It's not because the have-nots are morally inferior or less civilized. It's precisely because they're the have-nots.

How else can the masses express their collective anger? They can throw the rascals out. Witness our quadrennial presidential elections. After many months of bitter, expensive campaigning, the loyal opposition finally chooses a candidate to challenge the incumbent. The newspaper publishes the latest national poll. If the election was held today which candidate would win? The answer is usually neither of the above.

More people would vote for a third candidate, whom they freely admit they know nothing about, than for the establishment candidates. Why? For the same reason that in terms of reputation, being a congressional incumbent is more of a handicap than an advantage. *The New York Times*[32] headlined a column on the phenomenon of third party candidacy, "The Angry People." Accordingly, more congressional incumbents are choosing to retire from politics than ever before.

When the country is doing poorly, in any way, the electorate is understandably angry. Some of them will express their resentment by rioting. More of them will express their anger by protesting. Fortunately, most of them will express their frustration by voting, which ultimately is the most effective way.

Usually, by the time the election is held, the anger has been sufficiently expressed so that one of the safer establishment candidates is chosen. The Eugene McCarthys,

George Wallaces, Jesse Jacksons, Ralph Naders, Jean-Marie Le Pens and Ross Perots serve their purpose, but are rarely elected. Every now and then however, we witness the phenomenon of Governor Jesse "The Body" Ventura or Mayor Sonny "and Cher" Bono. When it happens, it's like a joke, or a suicidal gesture that went too far. It's eventually rectified but the dissatisfaction has been duly noted.

With a joke like Jesse "The Body" Ventura, the long-term consequences are minimal. They have to watch their elected leader moonlight as an announcer for "extreme football," or listen to him at a press conference express his desire to be reincarnated as a size 38-DD brassiere, but one short term later, the prank is over. When they elect a demagogue, like Adolf Hitler[33], the unforeseen consequences are catastrophic.

15—An Unseen Spark

I had been treating Pamela for years. She had never called me at home before. She had to see me immediately. It couldn't wait till tomorrow. I took her at her word. I met her at my office at midnight.

She explained in angry tears that if she hadn't been able to see me, she would have thrown her husband Ervin out of the house that night. I was shocked. I had never met Ervin, but after all this time, I had some sense of the man. He seemed like an O.K. guy. We *had* been discussing her dissatisfactions with him, but by the end of the session she always felt more positively towards him.

Being surprised in therapy usually means I've done something wrong. How could I have been so out of touch here? I inquired as to the cause of the explosion. What had Ervin done today? She responded, nothing in particular, just more of the same. It was all rather vague. He was insensitive. He was patronizing. He was unappreciative.

I was confused. It would have sounded reasonable at our

normal appointment, but in the context of an emergency session, it didn't make sense. Why the urgency? When did she realize that she could no longer tolerate her husband? This was no small decision. They had been married for 18 years. They had four children together. She said she had come to her conclusion over dinner. I asked if Ervin had done anything in particular over dinner. She said that Ervin hadn't been home for dinner. He had to work late. Pamela had eaten dinner with her neighbor, Mindy.

Bingo.

Mindy had moved in a few months earlier. Because of their proximity, shared interests and contemporaneous children, they had quickly become friends. In retrospect, not coincidentally, Pamela had simultaneously become increasingly dissatisfied with Ervin. Mindy was unhappily married. She made no bones about it. She complained bitterly about her husband, as well as about husbands in general. She encouraged Pamela to talk about Ervin and sarcastically pointed out his imperfections. On this evening in particular they had shared a bottle of wine and discussed their respective sex lives. Mindy was outraged at Ervin's behavior and by the end of dinner, (and the bottle), Pamela was as well. Mindy was shocked that Pamela was willing to tolerate Ervin. No one else would, she informed Pamela.

In the end, Pamela never got divorced. She never even entered marital therapy, as I had suggested. She did stop discussing Ervin with Mindy. When she did, she discovered two things. Number one, there was nothing else that Mindy wanted to discuss. Number two, she wasn't that dissatisfied with Ervin, after all.

It might sound like Mindy was the true villain here. In reality, she wasn't. Mindy wasn't playing Iago to Pamela's Othello. She had no malice. Mindy was simply unhappy. Misery always loves company. In this case, misery, and Mindy, demanded company. Mindy's equivalent wasn't Iago, but Lieutenant Keefer in Herman Wouk's play *The Caine Mutiny Court Martial.* Keefer, a glib, clever college graduate, constantly pointed out to Lieutenant Maryk, a well-intentioned, uneducated second in command, how incompetent the commander, Captain Queeg was. Keefer's observations, like Mindy's, were grounded in reality. Neither of them lied. They merely emphasized. They let their less savvy friend reach an erroneous conclusion.

Keefer, like Mindy, wanted to have his cake and eat it too. He despised Queeg, but wasn't prepared to accept the consequences of mutiny. He let his friend Maryk hold the bag for that. By inciting Maryk, he was able to vicariously express his anger towards Queeg through Maryk's actions. Best of all, he bore no responsibility. Similarly, Mindy wasn't prepared to divorce her husband. By inciting Pamela however, she could vicariously express her own anger without suffering any consequences.

What does this have to do with a mob? Why save it for last?

Remember my nightmare in Harlem? Let's assume a worst-case scenario. What would have happened if I had been murdered by that mob? Possibly the person who struck the fatal blow would have been arrested and, if so, probably plea-bargained his way down to a lesser charge. It's unlikely that the others in the mob would have been arrested at all, (like the members of the mob who murdered Yankel Rosenbaum in the Crown Heights riots).

Would the police have even spoken to that little old man in the aluminum chair? If they did, it would have been only as a witness. Yet, *he* was the instigator. He not only started the ball rolling, he also deliberately kept it rolling. As much as the murderer, *he* would have been responsible for my death, but like Mindy and Keefer, he wouldn't have suffered any consequences.

Like Mindy, he's really not a villain. He's a confused, bitter, old man looking to finally get even with the White man who in his mind, has been oppressing him all his life. In every mob, in every riot, there's always someone like him. Sometimes it's a demagogue with a microphone. More often, it's a little person on the sidelines who's clever enough to know which buttons to press. No one ever remembers him afterwards.

We discuss the instigator last because it's the common denominator between group anger and personal anger, our subject heretofore. Unless you've experienced it personally, it's easy to dismiss a rioting mob as a foreign experience, something irrelevant to your personal existence. If you have experienced it personally, you'll never forget it. I can compare it only to an experience I had thirty yards off a Mediterranean beach.

I'm a strong swimmer. I have life saving certificates. I've never been scared of the water. The water looked inviting. Though the beach was deserted, it didn't feel unsafe. I was only in the water up to my chest. I didn't know about the undertow. By the time I sensed it, I was helpless to fight it. I was pulled out to where the waves were breaking on some exposed rocks.

I never felt so insignificant in my entire life. I was like a cork bobbing in the water. I would be first pulled by the undertow, then thrashed by the waves. It was all I could do to gasp a breath of air before I was submerged again. To this day I don't know how or why I survived. As I lay on shore bleeding profusely, I cried like a baby. I couldn't stop for many minutes.

In a sense, the anger of the mob is the ultimate anger. The madding crowd is a gross exaggeration of the rage that we all carry inside of us, but only occasionally experience. If we understand the anger of the group, we better understand the anger of the individuals who comprise it, including ourselves.

I didn't cry that June night in Harlem. I should have.

> *"When civil dudgeon first grew high,*
> *And men fell out, they knew not why;*

> *When hard words, jealousies and fears,*
> *Set folks together by the ears,*
> *And made them fight, like mad or drunk,*
> *For dame Religion as for punk;*
> —Samuel Butler (1612-1680)

Notes

---

1 *Exodus* XXXII:22, 25.

2 The most famous use of the word "mobile" is in the familiar Italian aria from *Rigoletto*, "La Donna e Mobile" (women are fickle) sung prominently by Luciano Pavoratti, among many others.

 While the English word "mobile" usually refers to movement, its alternate meaning is "volatile in mood," consistent with a mob.

3 It is fascinating to note that while "*a* mob" refers to a disorganized spontaneous amalgam, "*the* mob" refers to organized crime, a secretive, structured, hierarchal group which is the veritable antipode of "a mob." I know of no other word whose meaning is diametrically altered when changed from an indefinite article to a definite article.

4 Joining a mob has been compared to having a drink. As reformed alcoholics explain: "At first you have a drink. Then the drink has a drink. Before long the drink has you."

 Before long the mob has you.

5 In Victorian England, Syphilis was called "the French Disease." Simultaneously, in France it was named "the Spanish Disease."

6 Stanley Kubrick's 1960 movie *Spartacus* visually illustrated both the attitude and the result. Four decades later Best Picture and popular hit *Gladiator* illustrated the same era as *Spartacus* but with an audience-pleasing, anachronistically democratic perspective.

7 Lord Richard Attenborough's eponymous film about Gandhi is an illuminating counterpoint to *Spartacus*. Revealingly the three movies about mobs, *Spartacus*, *Gandhi* and *Gladiator*, each separated by two decades, were each critical and box-office winners. The three movies were nominated for, and received,

dozens of Academy Awards, including two Best Pictures and two Best Actors. They created the careers of actors as disparate as Sir Peter Ustinov, Sir Ben Kingsley and Russell Crowe.

8 Movies in which the hero dies, usually courageously and/or sacrificially, are many and diverse. They include: *Spartacus, From Hell, Easy Rider, Butch Cassidy and the Sundance Kid, Gandhi, Pay It Forward, The Sixth Sense, McCabe and Mrs. Miller, Silkwood, Thelma and Louise, Jack, Life is Beautiful, The Cowboys, The Shootist, The Alamo, The Charge of the Light Brigade, They Died With Their Boots On, Hart's War, Saving Private Ryan, Gladiator* and *Titanic.* This list contains movies of all genres, calibers, and eras, and could be interminably expanded.

9 The only movies in which the villain survives, albeit with some comeuppance are the serial horror flicks in which the villain is, in some senses, really the hero, and, in all senses, the audience attraction, and thus both the raison d'etre and the sine qua non for the film. Examples include: *Halloween, Nightmare On Elm Street, Friday the 13th*, and, on a higher plane, the Hannibal Lecter films, *Silence of the Lambs, Hannibal* and *Red Dragon.*

10 Avery Brundage, President of the International Olympic Committee at the Munich Olympiad, was notoriously insensitive. Characteristically, he always demanded that he be addressed, and treated, as "His Excellency". Not only did he insist on the Olympics restarting immediately, seemingly without consideration for those murdered, but he then also inexplicably connected the massacre with the issue of excluding Rhodesia. (*The New York Times*, Richard Sandomir, September 2, 2002.)

11 Though born in Israel, my teacher considered himself American and was referring to the U.S. being cheated out of a gold medal in one of the more notorious of the innumerable Olympic scandals. In the 1972 basketball finals the U.S. was ahead of Russia by one point with three seconds left. Russia inbounded the ball and missed. The U.S. won. No. The referees inexplicably gave the Russians another chance. They inbounded again and missed again. The U.S. had won a second time. No. The referees gave the Russians a third chance, and they finally scored. The

U.S. team was understandably so outraged they unanimously refused their silver medals. As Frank Gifford, who broadcast the game, said: "It was absolutely, blatantly, cheating and stealing."

12 On occasion, contests offer as their first prize not the opportunity to win a car, but the opportunity to destroy it. Radio stations frequently use this as their gimmick especially if they are at that moment bashing the car's country of origin.

13 The *Lethal Weapon* series is so popular it created or advanced the careers of Mel Gibson, Danny Glover, Joe Pesci, Chris Rock, Rene Russo, Jet Li and Gary Busey. The first two films, directed by Richard Donner, were critically acclaimed as well.

14 *Sports Illustrated*, June 24, 2002.

15 *Sports Illustrated*, June 9, 2002.

16 *Ibid.*

17 *The New York Times*, Margaret Talbot, June 2, 2002.

18 The fact that mass hysteria occurs primarily in girls has nothing to do with the origin of the term "hysteria," a runaway uterus. ("Hysteria" is Greek for "uterus".) It has to do with the fact that girls are both more likely to talk to each other about their health, and to seek medical attention. Under the "right" circumstances, e.g. "infected" food in a prison, men of any age can be equally susceptible to rumors, and the resultant mass hysteria.

19 According to the Palestinian Human Rights Monitoring Group, as many Palestinians were murdered by other Palestinians, ostensibly for being collaborators, as there were Palestinians killed by Israeli gunfire during the hostilities. It was only the former group's victims that were tortured, mutilated and then put on public display. (*The New York Times*, August 18, 2002.)

20 Of the many unfortunate memories of the Vietnam War, perhaps the ugliest was the phenomenon of soldiers killing their own officers. At times they did it because they thought they could save their own lives; at times they did it out of revenge, or hatred; at times they did it because they had been driven mad. Cinematic depictions of this harrowing experience can be seen in *Platoon* and *Apocalypse Now*.

21 Revealingly, in Jim Brown's abbreviated, unsuccessful movie career

he always played an angry character. Whether as the lead, or in a supporting role, whether hero, or villain, he was always sullen. In movies as different as *The Dirty Dozen* or *100 Rifles* the one consistency was the scowl on his face. Jim Brown portrayed rage convincingly.

22 John Hinkley's imagined "love" of Jodie Foster is pathognomonic of stalkers. Given the opportunity, he would have shot Foster instead of Reagan, the same as Mark David Chapman shot his idol, John Lennon. In 1949 Philadelphia Phillies first baseman Eddie Waitkus was shot in the chest by a teenage girl who was so "in love" with him that she had a shrine for him in her bedroom. (This scene appears in the Bernard Malamud novel, and Robert Redford film, *The Natural.*) Similarly the young actress Rebecca Schaffer was murdered by a "fan" who had traveled across the country to meet the great love of his life. The stalker's self-professed love is always but an impulse away from murder.

23 Lincoln's assassin, John Wilkes Booth, has been the subject of movies, plays, even musicals. Lincoln's successor, Andrew Johnson, has not.

24 Andrew Johnson, Lincoln's Vice President who succeeded him in the presidency, was himself impeached by a Congress angry with the unprecedented anarchy of the times. Johnson's trial was ironically one of the subjects of John F. Kennedy's famous *Profiles In Courage.*

25 *New York Post*, Michelle Malkin, April 28, 2002.

26 *Ibid.*

27 *The New York Times*, Henry Fountain, September 17, 2002.

28 Corresponding to the boredom etiology, cardiologists observe that most extra, or irregular, heartbeats, (medically referred to as P.V.C.s, Premature Ventricular Contractions) occur only when the heart is at rest. When the body is excited and the heart is beating rapidly, the extra beats usually disappear. (If they don't, it is a far more serious cause for concern.)

29 The New York *Daily News*, David Hinckley, August 4, 2002.

30 *Masters of Death: The SS-Einsatzgruppen and the Invention of the Holocaust* (2002), Richard Rhodes, Knopf.

31 *Ibid.*

32 *The New York Times,* Paul Krugman, April 23, 2002.

33 In view of the many etiological similarities between a riot and the Nazi nightmare, can Hitler's reign be considered as such? On the surface, a comparison of this sort is nonsensical. Riots last hours usually, at most days. The Nazis lasted years. The Nazis were methodical, meticulously planned and hierarchically organized, all in contrast to a mob.

When history is viewed from a distant perspective however, in terms of centuries and millennia, rather than years or even decades, it is possible that future journalists will view the Nazi debacle as something akin to a riot, an aberrational barbaric explosion of feral rage. It would speak well for our civilization, and our species, if such turns out to be the case.

EPILOGUE

Don't Go Away Angry

A Conclusion

"(God) never holds on to his anger." [1]

The most important event of my life occurred before I was born.

My parents were Holocaust survivors. They lost their parents, their siblings, their friends, their spouses and their children. Though they remarried and started a new family, they never stopped being affected by their experience. Neither did I.

One of my earliest childhood memories involved our neighbor, Mr. Shultz. If Mr. Shultz had a first name, no one ever learned it. At best, he could be called a curmudgeon. In reality, he was a misanthrope. He had no use for children. He had no use for adults either.

Mr. Shultz had a dog. No one ever learned its name, since Mr. Shultz never spoke to it, or anyone else. Mr. Shultz was scary. So was his dog. The dog wasn't particularly big. Neither was Mr. Shultz, but they were both constantly growling. Everyone gave them wide berth. Rumor had it that the dog once bit someone so badly that he was taken to the hospital. Mr. Shultz didn't try to stop the attack. No one ever verified the rumor. No one ever tested it either.

I remember as a child opening the door of our apartment and seeing Mr. Shultz and his dog by the elevator. The dog turned to me and growled. My mother immediately closed the door. She explained to me: "He's angry and he has a dog." She looked through the peephole until the coast was clear. Only then could we leave.

Although Mr. Shultz could never be found without his dog, his dog could sometimes be found without him. He would leave his door open and his dog would wander the hall. We all knew to stay inside our apartments until the dog reentered his. In retrospect, the entire situation seems outrageous. At the time however, it seemed perfectly natural to me and my friends. We knew to avoid the third rail on the subway. We knew to avoid the mound of rocks near the river where the rats lived. We knew to avoid Mr. Shultz and his dog. We knew that our parents were intimidated by authority and anger. So were we.

Years later, in my therapy, I learned to analyze my own dreams. I realized that when Mr. Shultz and his dog appeared in a dream, they represented someone angry at me. I was amazed to discover how important the theme of anger was to me. It felt like my dirty, little secret.

Then I found that my secret wasn't unique. My earliest patient shared his intense fear of his father's temper. Then another patient brought anger up, and another, and another. The subject would come up repeatedly in group. I came to learn that not only wasn't my secret unique, in fact, it was universal. Anger was everyone's dirty little secret.

When I started to write on the subject, the response was startling. Everyone was interested in it. It wasn't only friends and patients, as with previous topics. It was everyone. Total strangers, including renowned authors, and celebrities, would beg to see the chapters I had completed. When the chapters were returned, (*if* they were returned), there were commonly notes in the margins. Some were to me; most weren't.

The purpose of this book is by now obvious. It is not to promote anger. It is not to suppress it. It is only to understand it. The more we understand it, the more we can begin to control it. The less we understand of it, the more it continues to control us.

As mentioned in the introduction, my uncle had written his book for his two sons. I have written this book for my three daughters. They are twice removed from the Holocaust. Although their father was scarred by it, hopefully the scars are smaller than their grandparents'. How scarred are they?

My daughter had a classmate who lived in the top floor of a brownstone. As I was bringing her home from a playdate, we were suddenly accosted by a dog on a lower floor. The dog scurried out his open door and confronted us. It didn't try to bite, but it growled threateningly, preventing us from advancing. I quickly moved my daughter behind me. We waited for the standoff to be resolved. Within a minute, a lady came out and smilingly reprimanded the dog: "Horace! You're being a bad boy!" She didn't punish the dog. Neither did she apologize to us, though she did smilingly explain: "He thinks he owns the floor."

After we left the building, I stopped to calm my daughter. She wasn't crying, but she did have QLL, Quivering Lower Lip, which is one step removed. The angry dog had scared her. It didn't seem fair, she said. We had been walking down a public corridor. I agreed with her. It wasn't fair.

Several months later, my daughter had another playdate there. She expressed concern about Horace. Her classmate's mother reassured her she would ask that Horace be kept inside. When I went to pick her up, I had to take the baby with me. I noted with relief, on my way up, that Horace's door was closed. I informed my daughter of that fact. She seemed relieved as well. When we went downstairs however, we were unpleasantly surprised by Horace's growl. Apparently, his door was now open again. My daughter was upset. The baby started crying. Horace, if anything, was bolder. Being cooped up didn't agree with him. He approached even closer than last time forcing us backwards. Now my daughter started crying, as well.

I don't know if it was my baby crying in my arms, my daughter crying behind me, or my memory of Mr. Shultz's dog that triggered it, but I lashed out at Horace. I kicked at him. He snapped at me. As he came at me a second time, I caught him solid with my instep and punted him ten yards down the hall. He landed on his back, slid a few more yards before he stopped, scampered to his feet and fled whimpering into his apartment.

This time his owner came out immediately. This time she wasn't smiling. "What happened?," she demanded to know. My baby was still crying, but my daughter had stopped. She was now giggling. Carrying the former and holding the latter's hand, I brushed past the lady. "I asked you what happened!," she repeated. I replied smilingly, "He thinks he owns the floor."

There were several repercussions to this incident. Horace's owner complained to my fellow class parent who dutifully expressed her apologies. To me, she expressed only the regret that she didn't see Horace fly. I have returned to the brownstone to pick up my daughter. I have bumped into Horace again. He remembers me. Every time he sees me he runs back into his apartment. His owner glares. I smile.

My daughter to this day delights in telling the story. Each time she retells it Horace flies higher and slides farther. (She has a future fishing). One day she told the story to my mother. My mother was upset. She told me privately that I never should have done it. She said that I don't understand the kind of trouble that can ensue. I was 41 years old when she told me that I don't understand. She's right. There are so many things that she understands that I never will. Anger however, isn't one of them.

When I was my daughter's age, I used to wait at a bus stop with my friend Nettie. Nettie's parents were also

Holocaust survivors. They were even more fearful than mine. Nettie's father, for example, always stayed at the bus stop with her. He was the only parent there.

One day David, a bully two years older than us, started hitting her. She ran to her father and told him what happened. He asked her what had she done to provoke David. She swore that she was blameless. I corroborated it. Her father immediately took action. He told Nettie to avoid David.

Thirty years later, Nettie had another confrontation with another David. This time she was married to him. Her husband was verbally abusing her daily and physically abusing her weekly. He was withholding money from her, making her beg. He was having an affair with their neighbor, which the entire neighborhood knew about.

Nettie wanted to get divorced. Her father forbade it. He said she didn't understand the kind of trouble that could ensue. He suggested that she try to avoid David. In my presence he compared David to a Kapo, a prison guard at a concentration camp. I asked him why he would want his daughter to remain in a concentration camp. He told us we didn't understand what it meant to make a Kapo angry. Kapos must be appeased at all costs. Her father's obstinacy cost Nettie her life savings and several years of her life.

Many years later my mother asked me if I heard that Nettie was getting divorced. I feigned ignorance. I didn't know if Nettie would want my parents privy to the information that I possessed. I didn't want to repeat what Nettie's father had said about Kapos. The Holocaust is still a very raw subject for my parents. Most of all I was afraid that my mother might have agreed with Nettie's father. If she did, I didn't want to know.

Perhaps as a result, as we readied to leave that night, I was feeling uncomfortable. As I kissed my mother goodbye, my daughters went to get the elevator. Suddenly I heard shouting. "What are you doing out here?" My mother immediately ran outside and pulled the girls back inside. She quickly locked the door. As she peered through the peephole, she explained: "She's angry, and she has a cane."

All I could think of was Mr. Shultz. First I was frightened. Then I was furious. I wanted to go out there and beat this lady with her own cane. I pulled my mother aside. She protested: "Isaac, don't! You don't understand!"

I opened the door. I saw an angry, possibly demented, lady glaring at me holding not a cane, but a cudgel. She stared at me. I stared at her. Neither of us said anything. As with Horace, it was a standoff.

Just then, the girls walked out the open door, passed me and the lady, and returned to get the elevator, as if nothing had happened. They ignored the lady and her cudgel. She looked at them. She looked at me. Without a word, she returned to her apartment.

I no longer felt uncomfortable. I felt on top of the world. I couldn't have been prouder of my daughters and the way in which they didn't resemble me.

For the moment, I felt totally devoid of anger. For the moment, no more dirty, little secret. That little I could understand.

"Anger dwells only in the bosom of fools."
-Albert Einstein (1879-1955)

Notes

---

[1] *Micah* VII:18 (This reading is from the afternoon service on the Day of Atonement.)

INDEX

ABOUT THE AUTHOR

Isaac Steven Herschkopf graduated Phi Beta Kappa from the City University of New York and N.Y.U. School of Medicine. His valedictory addresses at both his university and medical school graduations were broadcast widely. In medical school he was President of his class, Captain of the championship basketball team and Editor-in-Chief of the yearbook. He completed his psychiatric residency at Mt. Sinai Hospital in N.Y. in three years. In addition to a private practice in psychiatry, he heads an executive consulting firm, is President of an international business corporation and the Yaron Foundation.

He has been on the teaching faculty of the N.Y.U. School of Medicine for 25 years. He has lectured at Harvard, Columbia, Cornell, Madison Square Garden, Carnegie Hall and internationally. He has been frequently quoted in *The New York Times*, *The Wall Street Journal*, *Time*, *Newsweek*, *Sports Illustrated*, *The New Yorker*, and many other publications. He has been frequently interviewed on television and radio, nationally and internationally.

He has been elected repeatedly to the Board of Governors of the N.Y.U. School of Medicine Alumni Association. He was elected Chairman of the School of Medicine's Sesquicentennial and in 1997 President of its alumni. In 2002 he received The Samuel Leidesdorf Award. In 2003 he received the AOA Honor Society Great Teachers Award.

He has delivered Grand Rounds to departments of Medicine, Surgery, Pediatrics, Medical Ethics and Orthopedic Surgery on topics including Eating Disorders, Anxiety Disorders, Personality Disorders, Factitious Disorders and Psycho-Somatic Illnesses. He has both supervised and lectured medical students, Residents and Postgraduate Physicians. He is an Attending Physician at Bellevue Hospital and the N.Y.U. Medical Center.

He has been elected to the American Psychiatric Association, American Society for Adolescent Psychiatry, American Group Psychotherapy Association, and the N.Y. Academy of Sciences among others. He has lectured on psychiatric aspects of spirituality, sexuality, capital punishment, drug addiction, stalkers, music and the cinema. He has consulted on movie scripts and productions. He has been awarded a platinum record for his work with rock and heavy metal groups. He has written seven novels and four non-fiction books.

Dr. Herschkopf lives with his wife and three daughters in New York City and Southampton. His elder daughters currently attend Harvard and Yale.